*With God's Blessings
And my Best Wishes*

To: _____

Date: _____

Place: _____

Occasion: _____

_____
Name and Signature

RODOLFO I. DUMAPIAS

What readers say about
Kingdom Beyond Diplomacy:
Journey to the End of the Age

The author and his wife were part of the modern-day diaspora as they served in China, Malaysia, Germany, Romania, South Korea, Bahrain, and Mexico. He vividly describes their incredible experiences of trials and triumphs from the personal realm to the public arena. With the repeated encouragement of God's Word, they chose God's ways over the world's ways. Miraculous interventions were encountered as a result. The author's urgent plea is for the reader to take the spiritual journey and begin preparing to face the inevitable end of the age. –
    Dr. T.V. Thomas, Chairman of Global Diaspora Network; Director, Centre for Evangelism and World Mission (Canada)

Kingdom Beyond Diplomacy *is an important reminder of the central and indispensable nature of the Gospel to transform people at any level of society. It is a marvelous blend of biblical principles and practical insight forged in the reality of life and expressed from the vantage point of a God-centered diplomat. Having experienced both career success and personal tragedy, Ambassador Dumapias underscores the truth of a kingdom beyond and provides the reader with a way forward in an increasingly uncertain world.* –
    Charles Cook, Ph.D., Professor of Global Studies and Mission Ambrose University, Calgary, Alberta, Canada

By profession and practice of his Christian beliefs, my friend and brother, Rodolfo Dumapias, is a living testimony of 2 Corinthians 5:20, "We are therefore Christ's ambassadors, as though God were making his appeal through us...Be reconciled to God." This book is an account of how he has lived out God's kingdom reality in multiple contexts and in many countries. I have personally witnessed how he winsomely combined Christian character in his diplomatic functions in a Christ-like manner, honoring Mark 10:45, "For even the Son of Man did not come to be served, but to serve." —
    Dr. Enoch Wan, former President of Evangelical Missiological Society, Director of the Doctor of International Studies, Western Seminary, Portland, Oregon, USA

Thrilling, witty, and entertaining – but a true life story! A diplomatic reconnaissance! You will discover what to look for and what to do to overcome today's alarming global headlines and persistent deception. Ambassador Dumapias, through his testimony, demonstrates that in all circumstances, the Almighty rescues, directs, changes, and strengthens those who call on His name in the midst of perilous times. –
Dr. Vergil Schmidt
Consultant, International Board of Advisors, GDN

This book powerfully packages international issues and behind-the-scenes diplomatic challenges, with spiritual growth. Weaving philosophical principles in his personal experiences with national leaders, the Ambassador reveals patterns of truth that often evade today's secular post-modern culture. An encouraging work that delivers hope and new sources of wisdom amidst impossible circumstances. –
Brian Veneklase
Author, Shattering Stained-Glass Jesus.

KINGDOM BEYOND DIPLOMACY

Journey to the End of the Age

RODOLFO I. DUMAPIAS

Foreword by Dr. Sadiri Joy Tira

Kingdom Beyond Diplomacy:
Journey to the End of the Age

Published by

Cover Design by:

Anthony D. Paular

Copyright © 2015 Rodolfo I. Dumapias

All rights reserved. Printed in the U.S.A.

ISBN-10: 0692538763
ISBN-13: 978-0692538760

Unless otherwise specified, all Scripture quotations are taken from:

The Full Life Study Bible, New International Version
General Editor: Donald C. Stamps
Associate Editor: J. Wesley Adams
Zondervan Publishing House
Grand Rapids, Michigan 49530, U.S.A.
Copyright © 1991 by Life Publishers International
All rights reserved

This book or parts thereof may not be reproduced in any form, stored in a retrieval system, or transmitted in any form by any means—electronic, mechanical, photocopy, recording, or otherwise—without written permission of the publisher, except as provided by United States of America copyright law.

DEDICATION

To my daughter Myra Sheila and grandson Daniel Rudolf, that they may greatly serve the Lord. Written in memory of my wife, Evangeline Zaragoza Vitug, who died in March 2014, and my sister Rebecca, who died in February 2013, that more souls may receive eternal life through the grace of Jesus Christ.

CONTENTS

Foreword   xi
Acknowledgment   xiii

Prelude   1
Part One: Journey to the Kingdom   5
  1. The Last Days   7
  2. Treasure Beneath the Fire   12
  3. The Silent Side of the Revolution   29
  4. Dying and Rebirth   44
  5. Experiencing the Almighty   50
  6. Serving God and Man   56
  7. The God Factor .   64
  8. Outreach to the Diaspora   71
  9. Into the Deep Water – Masuk   79
Part Two: Faith and God's Sovereignty   87
  10. The Unification Challenge   89
  11. God's Continuing Protection   102
  12. Sheikh Khalifa and the Philippine School   106
  13. The Sikatuna Award   119
  14. Shadow of an Invisible Force   127
  15. Faith is a Choice .   136
  16. The Heart of a Prince   141
  17. The Kingdom of Heaven and You   147
Part Three: End of the Age   161
  18. Signs of the End   163
  19. End Time Technology   173
  20. Diplomacy: Rise of the Antichrist   182
Part Four: The Kingdom and Immortality   189
  21. Truth Behind the Lies   191
  22. The Highest Kingdom   203
  23. Jesus Reigns in the New Millennium   217

Bibliography   229
Addendum: Iran's Nuclear Program – An Omen? 233

RODOLFO I. DUMAPIAS

FOREWORD

I was first exposed to diplomacy when my older sister, the late Mercedes Aurora Briones Tira, served as Information Attache of the Philippine Embassy in Bucharest, Romania in the late 1970's. I recall her stories of the three years she lived under the dictatorial rule of Romanian President Nicolae Ceausescu. As early as that time, the reign of fear pervaded in the political and spiritual life of Romanians. Believers of Jesus Christ were outwardly tolerated but were closely monitored, warned, and subjected to propaganda and persecution. While many cowered and few Christians stood firm in their faith, my sister faithfully shared the love of Christ to those in need even at the height of the Cold War. As a young believer then, I have often wondered if the affection of Jesus she and others shared would have lasting impact. In this book, *Kingdom Beyond Diplomacy,* an answer to my quest comes clear. Yes, the Almighty honors the work of His ambassadors who share His love with the forsaken, and protects those who call on His name.

I first met Ambassador Dumapias in 2000 when I made a courtesy call at the Philippine Embassy in Manama, Bahrain. I gave him a copy of *Jesus,* a film on the life of Christ according to St. Luke. He was delighted to receive the video copy and said he would share it with foreign workers and anyone who wishes to know the Nazarene. Hence, my partnership with the author grew.

In 2004, I requested him to contribute a chapter for the seminal book on diaspora and Christian mission, *SCATTERED: The Filipino Global Presence,* edited by Luis Pantoja, Jr., Sadiri Joy Tira, and Enoch Wan (Manila: LifeChange, 2004). His article, "My Journey as a Christian Ambassador," added a diplomat's perspective on the modern-day diaspora phenomenon.

Then, in 2006, the author and his wife, Eva, welcomed me to the Philippine Embassy in Mexico City as he and his Bible study group co-hosted with me the seminar, *Outreach to Latin America (OLA).* He and I later traveled to Panama City where he advocated for two Filipino seafarers who were accused of a serious crime on the high seas. I joined him as he visited them in a national penitentiary, and watched him pray over them as they renewed their faith in Jesus Christ with tearful eyes. Without compromising his duties as a representative of his government, he revealed his calling as Christ's ambassador, assuring them of God's love, mercy, forgiveness, and compassion. The occasion gave me the opportunity to share the life of Jesus with the detainees before Ambassador Dumapias and I left to meet with another Christian leader, former Guatemalan President, Dr. Jorge Serrano, and his wife Magda. I learned later from TV broadcast that the Panamanian court released the two prisoners shortly after our visit.

In his book, the ambassador addresses the quests of today's global society. What do all these frightening headlines on the Middle East, financial meltdown, and natural disasters mean? Where is the world headed to? How can I protect my family? Is there a sure way out of these chaos? In the search for answers, he directs the readers to look above human power as he testifies on the reality of the Kingdom of God. Upholding his faith in the true Messiah, he invites his readers to persevere in times of trials and challenges as he demonstrates humility, sacrifice, integrity, and love—even in seemingly hopeless situations. Beyond man's reach and endurance, the Lord's power, love, and judgment persist.

Kingdom is a rare book, indeed, as few diplomats have the courage to testify about their faith and higher calling. Thus, I humbly but strongly commend this volume, as I believe it will be a source of inspiration and encouragement to private sector and government leaders around the world, and to every *ambassador* of the Kingdom.

Finally, I encourage everyone to pray for persons in authority, especially the diplomats and other officials who have responded to a higher calling. Paul set an example with these words: *Therefore, I exhort first of all that supplications, prayers, intercessions, and giving of thanks be made for all men, for kings and all who are in authority, that we may lead a quiet and peaceful life in all godliness and reverence.* (1 Timothy 2:1-2 NKJV)

Sadiri Joy Tira, D. Min., D. Miss.
Senior Associate for Diasporas
The Lausanne Committee for World Evangelization, www.lausanne.org
Diaspora Missiology Specialist
Jaffray Centre for Global Initiatives, Ambrose University, Canada

ACKNOWLEDGMENT

I wish to thank my brothers and sisters and their respective families for their support and encouragement: Rebecca and Paul Paular, Florencio and Rufy, Ely and Eugene Obillo, Fe, Lorna, Virgil and Wella, Jesse and Josephine, and Jessilyn and Paul Carver. Many thanks also to my in-laws and their families: Lethie Vitug Oteyza, Dr. Catalino "Munding" Vitug, Nora V. and Rudy Chua, and Merlee Vitug; and sister-in-law Elena Brioso, for their invaluable assistance.

I thank the following for their encouragement and detailed guidance to help me refine my writing skill: Brenda Blanchard, Co-President of the Christian Writers Group of Greater San Antonio, Texas; Dr.Chuck Bagby, Dr. Philip Williams and Brian Veneklase.

I also thank the following for their advice and inspiration: Mother Theresa; Bishop Efraim Tendero, Secretary General and CEO of the World Evangelical Alliance; Dr. David Yonggi Cho, President of the Yoido Christian Church (Seoul, Korea); the late Bishop Fred Magbanua, Chairman of the Council of Christian Bishops of the Philippines and President of Jesus Our Life Ministry; Bishop Bro. Eddie Villanueva, Presidential candidate, Chairman of the Philippines for Jesus Movement and Jesus is Lord Ministry; Bishop Leo Alconga, Philippine Bible Society; Pastor Jaren Lapasaran, Jesus Our Hope Fellowship; Rev. Dr. Joyce Abugan, President of Philippine Baptist Theological Seminary; former President of Guatemala Pastor Dr. Jorge Serrano and his wife Magda; Magsaysay Awardee Rev. Dr. Kim Bum-il of Canaan Agricultural School; Rev. Dr. Joy Tira, Senior Associate for Diasporas of the Lausanne World Evangelization Conference; the late Rev. Dr. Luis Pantoja, former Senior Pastor of Greenhills Christian Church, Makati, Metro-Manila; Pastor Mark Sosmena, former Secretary to IBA, Global Diaspora Network; Rev. Pastor Dr. Vergel Schmidt; missionaries Rev. Pastor Angel and Sis. Elma Ignacio; Rev. Dr. Koshy Eapen; Pastor Fred Cudiamat; Pastor Gil Bantugan; Pastor Ellie Bautista; Pastor Boni Villanueva; Pastor "Ignar" Ignacio Reyes; Pastor Celso Camat; Pastor Pete Gamez; Pastor Douglas Thompson, and other PEOPLE OF GOD.

Rodolfo I. Dumapias

RODOLFO I. DUMAPIAS

PRELUDE

"Is this the one who is going to die?" The nurse muttered as the orderly wheeled the patient into the ICU. The word had gone around in the Intensive Care Unit of Salmanya Hospital that the woman who was rushed for CT scan and then to the operating room had all the signs leading to death.

The nurse knew that whenever a blood vessel bursts in the brain stem, the patient loses consciousness and sinks into a coma. In most cases, the patient never wakes up. Had the bleeding been on the cerebrum, commonly known as the right and left lobes of the brain, the threat to life would be less fatal and the patient would have a better chance of recovery. But a hemorrhage in the cerebellum affects all nerves including those directing motor movements, thoughts, and sensory functions. Most threatening is the damage to the function of breathing. The nurse knew that most patients with brain stem infarction die within forty-eight hours.

Earlier in the morning at the Emergency Room, I sat by my wife's bedside as she uttered her last words, "Whatever happens, don't leave me alone."

I had the most frustrating experience in my life because I knew Eva was losing consciousness, yet I could not do anything to stop it. Her speech gradually became slower and softer, then slurred as she repeatedly said, "…don't leave me." Then, she did not talk anymore. Her grip on my hand loosened. She did not move anymore.

I sank deep to the lowest point of personal sorrow, shocked at how unexpectedly quick Death comes to make a claim.

As the nurse and the orderly transferred Eva to a bed in ICU, I remained speechless, groping to comprehend the unfolding events.

The silence in the room seemed to have deadened my senses until a doctor approached me and began to talk in whisper. In a halting faint voice, he explained, "She is in a coma. We don't know whether she would wake up. If she survives, she will have permanent physical disability and serious mental incapacity."

Then he concluded, "We have done everything. At this point, healing of your wife is in the hands of God."

Trauma in our Time

The above-described trauma happened in the fall of 2002, in the Kingdom of Bahrain. But in the spring of 2008, my wife and I chose to share those moments because the world was faced with global events that were also impending yet devastating, and seemed impossible to surmount. Though we were thousands of miles away from the Middle East, those moments remained fresh in our memories. So I began to write this book while taking care of Eva as she sat on a wheelchair.

As grim as the prospects Eva and I faced in 2002, today's headlines about the conflicts in the Middle East, deepening global financial crisis, and rising intensity of natural disasters are causing anxiety to millions of people. Though they fear the impact these phenomena would have on their lives, they dread there is nothing they can do to escape the inevitable. As I looked then to the doctors for Eva's healing, most people today look to the human authorities—world leaders, multinational bodies, economists, and diplomats—for the solutions to these global problems.

Look Beyond Diplomacy

But can these wielders of sovereign powers with their titles, wealth, and force provide relief as they search for world peace and safety in the halls of diplomatic forums? What lies behind the threatening events? Shouldn't the world look outside the mortal box, beyond human diplomacy, to find the *truth* and enduring *salvation?*

The doctor at ICU released a profound wisdom when he admitted human limitations and recognized that beyond a certain point, healing was "in the hands of God."

It was not political power, military might, wealth, or personal charisma that delivered Eva from death. It was the Spirit of the Highest Authority to whom I prayed, the Sovereign above all human sovereigns, that denied Death its victory. That is the truth.

A Glimpse into the Highest Kingdom

Despite its title, *Kingdom Beyond Diplomacy* is not a book on the foreign affairs of any country. Rather, it is a spiritual journey beyond the glitters of statecraft, political power, palace ceremonies, and protocol. It is a revisit to a world many claim they know but have either forsaken, misunderstood, or taken it for granted. Many ignore this kingdom, but it waits for them as the home they have searched for all along. This book offers a peek into the realm that extends beyond national borders and whose power exceeds the combined forces in the interplay between human sovereigns. It is a journey to truth, a glimpse into the kingdom of God.

The need to revisit the kingdom is urgent as signs in our time unfold fulfilling the prophecies on the end of the age. God is about to render His judgment on today's world and release His wrath on those who trample His laws.

Experiencing the Reality of God

Though I did not have a formal theological education, I came to know God and His kingdom from reading the Scripture and actual experiences. Eva and I lived through, felt, and witnessed the reality of the Creator. When she had the stroke, I was then the Philippine Ambassador to the Kingdom of Bahrain. In my most desperate moment, such an overwhelming power reached down to envelop me with so much love and comfort. The assurance of protection He gave was personal, yet more intimate than any human embrace could offer. Now, I know that as God asserts His sovereignty over the world, He wraps with love those who turn to Him for salvation.

My Prayer

Having gone through a spiritual journey, I offer my testimony as a prayer for believers to find encouragement and fulfillment as they assume God's plan in their lives. I also pray that this book will serve as refreshment to faith of other believers whose spiritual integrity may have been disturbed by the overwhelming flood of deception in our time. And I hope these narratives would inspire those who yet don't know Christ to accept the invitation and come into the kingdom that awaits them beyond diplomacy.

Take the Spiritual Journey

Before the prophesied end of this age, shouldn't you revisit the kingdom you may have misunderstood or taken for granted? If you have not received Jesus Christ as Lord and Savior, shouldn't you find out more about the promise you have rejected?

Even if at first you do not believe, even if it is only for curiosity or just to humor the author, you may wish to read on.

Your choice now can change the course of your life.

PART ONE

JOURNEY TO THE KINGDOM

*The Lord your God, who is going before you,
will fight for you, as he did for you in Egypt, before your very
eyes, and in the desert. There you saw how
the Lord your God carried you, as a father carried his son,
all the way you went until you reached this place.*

*In spite of this, you did not trust in the Lord
your God, who went ahead of you on your journey,
in fire by night and in a cloud by day,
to search out places for you to camp
and to show you the way you should go.*

Deuteronomy 1:30-33

CHAPTER ONE

THE LAST DAYS

> *At one time, we too were foolish, disobedient, deceived and enslaved by all kinds of passions and pleasures. We lived in malice and envy, being hated and hating one another. But when the kindness and love of God our Savior appeared, He saved us, not because of righteous things we had done, but because of His mercy.*
> **Titus 3:3-5**

Violence, blood, death, gunfire, smell of rotting flesh, and wailing of the living—these sights, sound and senses shocked us and recurred in our nightmares when we lived through martial law and People's Power revolution in the Philippines in the 1970's. In the midst of turmoil we cried out, "God save us!" But we allowed our senses to be overwhelmed by the roar of tanks, the sight of raging fires, and the angry faces of the mob. Not having the Creator in our lives, we listened more to the noise of chaos than to His voice.

Some years later, in 1989, we saw and felt more of the same human tempest in the Romanian revolution. But the outcome was different. The silent hand that brought down a communist dictatorship also took hold of Eva and me, and in the swirl of the revolution, led us on the road to a world that forever changed our lives.

Last Days of the Old Life

When I began my work as a diplomat at the Philippine Embassy in Bucharest, Romania, Eva and I felt we had everything needed in life. We were financially secured, surrounded by friends, young, and confident, and I had a respectable career. We attended either Catholic mass or Methodist service, whichever fitted our schedule. We displayed Santo Nino statuettes of various sizes and color at home, and hanged a rosary from the rear view mirror of our car. We were "good Christians" and did not need to change our lifestyle, we thought.

To me, the assignment offered another exciting challenge even as I faced immersion in Romania's political landscape founded on atheistic communism and dialectic materialism. After all, communism in theory and practice was a major subject of my studies at the University of California, Los Angeles. I subscribed to *Izvestia* and *Peking Review* and began learning to read Russian to upgrade my research. Having been a member of the team that opened the Philippine Embassy in Peking a few years earlier, I expected to gain in the Bucharest assignment more expertise in the historical evolution of an ideology that removes God from the life of men and society.

"An atheistic political backdrop, how can anything spiritual grow in such a world?" a fellow academician once wondered aloud. The issue did not matter to me, and the question did not even cross my mind as I prepared to go to Bucharest.

The Journey for Change Began

My steps to revolutionary Romania began in revolutionary Manila. The year 1973 was a time of tension and uncertainty when communist rebels and separatist Muslims threatened the rule of Philippine President Ferdinand E. Marcos. I was then an assistant professor of Political Science at Far Eastern University and Lyceum of the Philippines, and an occasional lecturer and thesis adviser at the National Defense College of the Philippines. As the President declared martial law, the academe became a hotbed of pro-and-con debates and student activism. Boycott of classes and student demonstrations led to marches on the streets of Manila. Traffic jams, riot police, tear gas, Molotov cocktails, pillboxes, and water cannons became common sights and sounds to the city folks, many struggling to eke out just enough for their family sustenance for that day. Deep into the night, rattles of gunfire continued to break the silence of tropical air, and death occurred on the roads leading to Malacanang Palace, the seat of political power. Rebellion was in the air. Many of the student leaders came from my Political Science classes and served as officers of the "poli-sci" club of which I was the adviser. University authorities monitored me and my name reportedly appeared in the government security watch list.

Painfully for an academician, I threw away many of my books on revolution before investigators could use them against me. I moved my wife and baby daughter to another address, just in case.

A Paradigm Shift: Career as a Diplomat

The political events that ensued compelled me to make a pivotal decision.

Years earlier, after my graduate studies at the University of Southern California, I made the decision to come home from the United States as a way to counter the "brain drain." While many college graduates left their homeland to look for a greener pasture in the West, I decided instead to return to the country of my youth. I resolved to use my skills to benefit my people. I planned to serve in the government.

But before I landed on Philippine shores, I already witnessed corruption. Some customs officers who boarded to inspect the passengers of *S.S. President Wilson* extorted dollars from innocent Filipino "old-timers" who traveled home to spend their last days in their ancestral land. Nevertheless, I remained optimistic and sought an advisory position in the Senate Foreign Relations Committee. I was denied as the position had already been given to a lawyer. After personally meeting a number of officials and sensing their lack of resolve to reverse the widespread poverty in the country, I questioned whether I should really pursue a government position. So, I decided to teach in the universities instead. I had intended to just remain and get old in the academe.

However, my thoughts began to change when President Marcos

declared martial law and suspended the writ of habeas corpus. When he later banned travel for abroad, I felt the only way to keep my future options open was to leave the country. Diplomatic service offered a way out.

So, I seriously took the advice of my father, then a Philippine consul in Bangkok. I agreed to take the Foreign Service Officers Examination scheduled in 1973. Thus, while students and police clashed as anti-Marcos demonstrations jammed the streets of the capital, I sat down to take the FSO written tests, considered the toughest civil service examination in the country. More than 1,700 professionals and college graduates qualified for screening but only several hundreds were allowed to take the written tests conducted simultaneously in Manila, Washington DC, Bangkok and London. Only a few were left to undergo psychological, protocol, and conference tests as well as personal background check. In the end, fifteen of us passed.

It was a strange irony, indeed, that martial law led me to become a career diplomat[1] although I had earlier avoided joining the government. While I did not intend to stay long in the government, I convinced myself that from the inside, I could help bring about change.

Foreign Secretary Carlos P. Romulo

I received my appointment as Foreign Service Officer Class IV, signed by President Marcos. My name was dropped from the security watch list. I took my oath of office in December 1974 to serve in the Department of Foreign Affairs, headed at the time by Secretary Carlos P. Romulo, the world-famous first Asian to serve as President of the United Nations General Assembly. I was designated a director in the Office of Political Affairs. Its head,

---

[1] In the diplomatic service, "career diplomat" is a term to distinguish the successful FSO examinee from others who are also appointed to diplomatic or consular positions.

Ambassador Armando Manalo, who drafted most of the speeches of the Secretary, must have sensed some potential in me after Sec. Romulo accepted the draft I was asked to make and used it for a major policy speech, with minor revisions.

I will never forget the morning Ambassador Manalo brought me to the Secretary and said to him, "This is the new officer I was telling you about."

The Honorable Secretary Romulo, himself a Pulitzer Prize winner and a diplomat *par excellence*, motioned me to come closer. Then he said to me, "We will develop you."

I was already humbled as I stood in the presence of such an extraordinary intellect, and for him to speak to me those words, I felt more than honored. With those words, my role in the Department began to be defined. I started drafting more speeches in addition to my duties as Director for American Affairs.[2]

Nevertheless, the Department's Personnel Section suddenly assigned me to Peking, China. Then, in less than a year, I was transferred to Kuala Lumpur, Malaysia where I stayed for nine years. I then served in the Home Office in Manila for two years; Hamburg, Germany for two years; Bucharest for two years; and then Seoul, South Korea for six years. After serving again in Manila, I was posted to Bahrain, and finally to Mexico, before I retired.

In Bucharest, Romania I began to die, and a new seed in my soul began to grow.

---

[2] Foreign Secretary Romulo was world-famous for his eloquence, wit, and humor as a public speaker. He did not need a speech writer. As a subordinate tasked to draft the speech, my role was to piece together facts, policy, and viewpoints in a framework and presentation that proximate his style and language. The final version reflected his exclusive genius.

CHAPTER TWO

TREASURE BENEATH THE FIRE

> *The kingdom of heaven is like treasure hidden in a field. When a man found it, he hid it again, and then in his joy went and sold all he had and bought that field.*
> Matthew 13:44

Romanian people were friendly and hospitable. However, they lived under a political and economic system founded on an ideology and administrative structure that suppressed individual initiative. Like most people behind the Iron Curtain, their enthusiasm for hard work and excellence was supplanted by a series of unsuccessful, centrally programmed, socio-economic Five-Year Plans devised by a regime strapped in socialist-communist doctrines.

Ripe for Revolution

"A country ripe for revolution," a diplomat described the socio-political landscape of the idyllic Dacian nation when I arrived in spring 1989 as Minister Counselor and Consul General of the Philippine Embassy in Bucharest. A few months later, after Ambassador Ernesto Querubin retired, I headed the mission as the *Charge d'Affaires, a.i.*[3]

---

[3] Governments designate the next ranking officer to take charge of their embassy in the absence of an accredited ambassador. The Charge, known also as CDA, is "acting ambassador" in his functions. He is recognized as the chief envoy of his

Scarcity, Bribery, and Toilet Paper

Diplomats and other foreigners did not escape the effects of scarcity and bureaucratic technicalities. Even in the Diplomatic Store[4] where supply of commodities was supposed to be assured, some shelves barely contained any merchandise as some basic food items including rice, milk, eggs, and meat were oftentimes absent. The Romanian people had it worse. Throughout the city, local citizens had to line up for almost everything, especially bread, meat, and fuel. While vegetables were abundant in the open flea market (thanks to enterprising families who grew these in their backyards), some other basic items such as clothes, shoes, and toiletries remained beyond the budget of most working people.

Shortage of gasoline had even brought trying times, if not amusing moments, to me and my family. At one time, after traveling several hours from Hungary, we stopped in a small Romanian town for gasoline only to find out that the station had already closed for the night. To avoid the risk of running out of gas in some isolated dark road in Transylvania—the dreaded "Dracula Territory" according to Western myths—we decided to wait until the station opened again. We fell asleep in the car. We woke up in the morning, startled at the gaping eyes penetrating through all the windows as children from a nearby school surrounded the car. They were obviously entertained watching foreign folks snore loud in a chorus, with mouth wide open.

"Extreme situation breeds extreme measures" became the motto we followed. Values, indeed, were turned upside down where cigarettes labeled "Hazardous to your health" had saved lives, and

---

country until the regular ambassador returns or a new chief of mission is accredited. Among the diplomatic corps in a subject capital, the CDAs are next only to the ambassadors of the other countries in the protocol precedence. The initials "a.i." (ad interim) indicate the designation is temporary.

[4] Owned and operated by the host government, the Diplomatic Store was intended to be the duty-free grocery outlet for diplomats and other foreigners residing in the country.

where toilet paper was a valued commodity among dignified diplomats. "Tonight we'll have fish!" exclaimed our Romanian hostess to express her excitement for an evening's event. So we dressed up for a special dinner—over a can of sardines.

To cut through the red tape, we learned to give bribes. A carton of Marlboro cigarette—not any other brand—given in secret to the right person brought out from the Diplomatic Store storage the scarce food and other basic necessities for survival. To overcome the shortages, we learned to hoard almost everything, especially frozen meat. Following the examples of senior diplomats, we travelled to far-away Vienna and Budapest to buy groceries only to have in the end an oversupply of toiletries and hygienic items.

Although we remained compassionate and generous to our Romanian friends, it was in the aforesaid areas of our character where we began to drift away from the ideal norm. By giving bribes, we encouraged corruption among the local Romanians, and our hearts grew calloused to irregularities so that eventually we also became corrupt. By hoarding, we subconsciously confirmed deep fear of the future and exaggerated suspicion that some people sought to get our precious supplies. Without realizing it, we became self-centered, arrogant, and overly self-protective.

Without a moral compass to guide us on the truth, we drifted farther and farther away from whatever little faith we had in God.

A Christmas Vacation?

On the 16th of December, Eva and I and our private staff, Bobby Difonturom, left Bucharest for a long drive to Germany. We planned to spend Christmas in Hamburg, my previous post, where my car could have much needed repair while we visit friends and relatives. We were also to bring back to Bucharest food, medicine, and household supplies for the embassy staff. On the following day, we passed the city of Arad and crossed into Hungary.

By the time we reached Hamburg, some incidents regarding

violence in Timisoara, Romania on the 17th and 18th of December were on TV news. On German television, we also saw images that we had not seen in Romania: East and West Berliners tearing down the Berlin Wall with sledge hammers. Sensing the worsening conditions in Romania, I decided to return to Bucharest as soon as possible. But my options narrowed down rapidly. Telephone connection to Bucharest was cut off. Railway and commercial airline operations had been suspended. All entry points by land into Romania had been closed except to holders of diplomatic visa who were allowed entry into the country in any situation. Thus, I decided to return by car.

No time remained for full repair of the car. So, when the repair shop opened, I checked out my car, quickly bought food and provisions to bring back to Bucharest, and loaded these into the car. On the morning of December 22, we proceeded for Romania.

Freezing on the Alps

To avoid the cities in Romania where there may be hostilities, I decided to enter the country via Yugoslavia, at the Drobeta-Turnu Severin border crossing. On the map, the Salzburg-Zagrev-Belgrade-Drobeta route over the Austrian Alps was a shorter distance than the lowland Vienna-Budapest-Arad approach.

Winter in Europe was bitterly cold as in previous years, and the temperature on the Alps went down to about 20 degrees below zero. The sky grew dark when we reached more than ten thousand feet elevation, and the falling snow made the evening more gloomy and cold.

Then we felt the first sign of trouble. The car that did not get full service in Hamburg now overheated and stopped. After a few minutes, I added water and we moved again but did not get far. It stalled again and again until we ran out of water. We got so desperate for water we collected snow and melted it. But when finally we had enough water, the engine would no longer start.

Chill Creeps in

No engine, no heater. No cars passing by. No houses in sight. Only the graying white of the snow on the ground and a single light bulb of a distant lamp post gave contrast to the total darkness all around. After a few minutes, the heat inside the car began to dissipate. We knew that unless we were rescued soon, we would eventually freeze to death. I began to feel the chill, so I whispered, "God, save us." I was too proud to let anyone know I was praying. But as I waited for a headlight to appear on the highway, the steady rhythmic thud of snow on the car roof was luring me to sleep. I dozed off.

Who Called?

"Rudy, wake up!" I sensed someone called me. It was not the voice of Eva or Bobby. Then, I noticed that the snowfall had stopped. Beyond the icing on the window, I could see clearly the highway and the shimmering reflection of a street light. Then I noticed what looked like a tall parking meter just a few yards from the car. Perched on a four-foot metal pole was a box, about one-foot by one-foot by one-foot. Carefully, I opened the car door and stepped outside. The snow was knee-deep. As I walked closer to the "meter," I noticed an embossed drawing of a telephone on its side. It turned out to be a hotline for emergency, one of the several installations placed along selected sections of the highway. I was able to call for a rescue.

On Top of the World

After about twenty minutes, a tow truck arrived. The mechanic attached thick chains to our car, then turned on the pulley which lifted up my personal, second-hand, four-year old Mercedes Benz 250 to the hump of the tow truck, and set our vehicle about six feet above the surface of the highway. The three of us stayed in the car, excited to finally get to safety and fascinated to be riding so high above the road. Past midnight, in the crispy dawn mist of 24 December 1989, while people in the lowlands were warm asleep after singing Christmas carols, we were cruising over the Alps by Bischophofen, Austria, literally "sitting on top of the world!"

Voice of God?

The faint voice saved us, and its timing was perfect. But I never went beyond asking my wife and Bobby who could have awakened me. I simply dismissed it as my imagination, or a product of my sub-conscious mind. In fact, I felt proud, *"I was that good."* But I asked myself: granted it was my imagination, how could have I programmed the wake-up call since I was not even aware I drifted to sleep? And if it was my sub-conscious that awakened me, then how could it rise to the conscious level enough to wake me up? And how can one explain the precise timing of the "voice"? It was as if "someone" wanted to lead us out of danger, that it was already safe to go out of the car to take effective action as help could be accessed just a few meters away from us. There was no way I could have known about the emergency hotline. Coincidence? ESP?

Nevertheless, I increasingly became curious. Were we saved because I called on God?

The Guns in Winter

At the winter resort of Bischophofen, we had warm food, warm shower, and warm bed in an inn near the local auto repair shop. Repair would take two weeks, the mechanic told us. The local folks were so hospitable and helpful. On the following day, they brought us to a nearby place where we were able to rent a small diesel-fueled, front-wheel drive Japanese car. We transferred all the food and household supplies from the old car to the small car. I prepared a white towel on which I wrote in bold letters the diplomatic plate number of the Mercedes car; the towel was to be secured to the rented car when we enter Romania. On the morning of 25 December, Christmas Day, we resumed our journey to our battle-torn destination.

After an overnight drive through Zagreb, we rested in Belgrade where Philippine Ambassador to Yugoslavia, H.E. Jose and Mrs. Fernandez, received us. At the chancery, our long-time friends, Yugoslav diplomat Minister Counselor Mirko Jelic and his wife

Olivera, visited us. They suggested, for our safety, we should travel together with the Yugoslav Red Cross convoy that was to leave for Bucharest on the following day.

Joining a Red Cross Convoy

After several hours of delay due to a flat tire in Novi Sad, a Yugoslav village, we reached the border of Romania at Drobeta-Turnu Severin. The Yugoslav Red Cross convoy was already at the border and was about to start its journey to Bucharest. I requested if we could join them, and the head of the convoy said, "*Da*." The Romanian immigration officer advised us to avoid the cities and to stop whenever signaled to do so by any roadblock or checkpoint. I tied the white towel to the front of the rented car in order to identify us as foreign diplomats. We joined the Yugoslav Red Cross convoy, confident we were safe as our car trailed behind the second vehicle in the line of five covered trucks.

Indeed, as we drove through Turnu Severin, there were roadblocks, bonfires, and sporadic gunfire. The air smelled of gunpowder and burning flesh. A scorched sedan occupied a large part of a crossroad, its front tires punctured, and its seats, dashboard, and paint totally charred. The Red Cross convoy carefully avoided the pieces of broken glass scattered around the burned car as we drove deeper into the city. The streets were practically empty except some armored vehicles and uniformed troops remained on guard at some intersections. Some men and women in white uniforms with Red Cross armbands carried a bloodied person on a stretcher. Then some soldiers waved for us to pass through as the Red Cross convoy approached the outer edge of the city. We passed some rifle-carrying civilians piling up old tires and wood to add fuel to their roadblocks as the convoy gradually picked up speed toward the countryside.

Longing for Summer

As we drove further away from the city, the atmosphere seemed to offer a special scent of serenity—no more deafening gunfire, no more burning buildings, no more shrieks of wailing women, and no more dog barks. It was at the same roadside where I saw in summer a squirrel climbing swiftly on a tree while another one picked up a walnut that fell on the ground. I thought with envy that while men were killing each other in the city, these little creatures lived at peace in their sanctuary with no reason to fight or work, having the initiative to amass sufficient provisions to last through winter. *They seem wiser than men*, I thought.

How strange, I pondered, *that the conditions we became familiar with were fading rapidly.* Barely a year earlier, Eva and I drove from Hamburg to East Berlin to personally hand over our daughter's forgotten contact lenses during an International School-Hamburg student field trip. The drive through East German farmlands to get to West Berlin was eerie, as though we were transported back many years when we saw decades-old farm implements. Going through Check Point Charlie into East Berlin, seeing the Brandenburg Gate from the other side of the Berlin Wall, and watching the goose-steps of East German soldiers in their knee-high boots were unforgettable. I also remembered the guard houses on high stilts along the Hungarian border with Austria; when we drove in August through Budapest to Vienna, they were manned by soldiers armed with AK-47. On our return two days later, the soldiers were gone. With a slight nostalgia but not regret, I surmised those inherent features of the Cold War would no longer come back. I felt privileged to have personally witnessed the end of the bipolar world and the beginning of a new geopolitical system.

And as I faithfully followed and kept pace with the Red Cross trucks in front of us, I forgot for a moment that the country was going through its most tumultuous period in its recent history. The graying shades of winter made me long for the summer visits to the beaches of Constantia by the Black Sea. I recalled the springtime picnics in scenic Brazov where my family and embassy staff devoured our fare in the middle of lush gardens, surrounded by flowers and manicured lawns abounding in full color. I even smiled when I remembered how we got lost one time in Bulgaria. I asked, "Is this the way to Bucharest?" And the farmer shook his head. So we went the other way. I did not know then that a nod was "no" and a shake "yes."

It grew late on that cold December afternoon, and the low grey clouds made the horizon look even darker. From the country road, we could see beyond the trees and fields the skyline of Craiova. We could hear occasional outburst of automatic guns and we knew fighting still raged in that city. Meanwhile, flurries of snow began to fall.

A Militia Roadblock

I wanted to get to Bucharest as soon as possible. *Before the weather gets worse,* I thought. So, I pulled out of the Red Cross convoy, passed the second and then the first truck, and speeded so fast I could see the convoy trucks becoming smaller and smaller in the rear view mirror.

The brief moments that followed became the longest seconds in my life. On the highway about a hundred yards in front of us, I saw the silhouette of people with rifles. A civilian militia with a bonfire as roadblock!

"Stop!" I remembered the immigration officer's advice earlier at the border.

I immediately stepped on the brakes. But at 100 kilometers per hour on a provincial road and with a thin layer of snow building up on the pavement, the tires failed to grip the road surface. The car skidded as the momentum forced the weight forward. It swerved left and right, lost its balance until it fell on its side with a loud noise, and rested on a canal.

Last Moments?

I have never experienced dying before, but in seconds, I saw what could be the last moments of our lives. In an instant, I longed for the carefree days of my youth in Asingan and Los Angeles High School, the comfort of my mother's embrace, the assuring faces of my father and siblings, and the smiles of little boys and girls as their helpful mothers brought them to the Filipino Cultural (Summer) School at the Filipino Christian Church in Los Angeles. Eva told me later she also thought of her family and classmates in Asingan, our hometown in Pangasinan, Philippines.

The car settled on its right side, its left wheels up in the air. In order for us to get out, I would have to push up the driver's side door. But there was no more time to get out of the car and run. The militia of about twenty men and women carrying rifles were shouting and coming fast towards us. They could just easily shoot and kill us still fastened with our seatbelts and lying defenseless.

I looked at my wife. She remained strapped, slouched on the passenger seat, shocked. We looked at each other without a word; we knew what that moment meant. I whispered, "I love you." I quickly glanced at Bobby who was slumped behind Eva's seat and said to him, "I am sorry."

The armed civilians in grey winter coats reached the car and looked at us through the windshield.

"This is it. Good-bye, world." I whispered.

Not a Movie

At that precise moment, the first of the Red Cross trucks arrived and stopped. After a few quick words in Romanian, the militia and the Red Cross men surrounded our car. They were big and husky. They lifted up our small rented Japanese car and put it right side up back on the highway.

That's right. They did not kill us as it happens in the movies. They laughed and patted each other on the shoulder, obviously proud for having done a good deed.

We could not believe what had just happened. We were still alive. Not one of us was bleeding. And the civilian militia was friendly.

We got out of the car and repeatedly said, "Thank you. *Multumesc. Spazebo. Grazie. Danke schon.*" We opened the trunk and from the provisions bought in Germany, we took out whatever we could reach and gave them to the Red Cross men and the militia.

Eva even opened the precious can of Danish cookies we reserved for our snack during the trip and offered its contents for the local freedom fighters to take a few, for taste. But one woman grabbed the whole can and ran away with it. The others ran after her.

Well, they were not hostile indeed. Just hungry.

Hand of God?

As we rejoined and resumed the journey with the Red Cross convoy, some questions filled my thoughts. The impact of the car as we slammed into the depression was so forceful, but no one was injured, not even a bruise. The car showed no permanent damage, just superficial scratches. What softened the impact even as it made much noise? Was it the hand of God?

And suppose the Red Cross men did not stop to help, what would the militia have done? Would the militia still understand the white towel and recognize us as diplomatic personnel entitled to courtesy and assistance? In times of chaos, hunger, and vengeance due to suffering and loss of loved ones and property, how many of the village folks would understand and still honor diplomatic courtesy? With the breakdown of law and order, it would have been tempting for desperate people in a remote field to just finish us off and take our food supplies. Instead, they helped us.

And before reaching the Drobeta-Turnu Severin crossing, we had a flat tire at Novi Sad. If we were not delayed for few hours, we would not have traveled with the Red Cross. Was the timing a coincidence? We had no knowledge when the Yugoslav Red Cross convoy would arrive at the border, nor did *they* know when *we* would cross into Romania. But when we reached the immigration checkpoint at Turnu Severin, the trucks were about to start their journey and so we simply joined the convoy. If the timing was coincidental, it seemed intentional, a predetermined rendezvous. Was the flat tire planned by a higher power?

Stranded in Snowstorm

It was already nightfall when we and the Red Cross convoy

reached the junction with Piteste Highway, the four-lane artery leading to Bucharest. From that point of the highway, in a clear weather, we would reach the capital in three hours. But that day was different.

The snow flurries that began in the afternoon had grown to a snowstorm. An unusually heavy snowfall and strong wind raged through the night making it impossible to go on. By morning, the blizzard had stopped. Snow covered everything around us as far as our eyes could see. The trees, distant cottages, hills, railroad tracks, and telephone lines—all were immaculate white. For a moment, the beauty and serenity made me forget about the fighting. I came back to reality when I turned to see hundreds of stranded vehicles, including the Red Cross convoy, lined up on the winding stretch of Piteste highway, trapped in knee-high snow that covered the whole landscape. I installed the tire chains. With bare hands, Bobby and I cleared the snow that blocked our way. But the car could not get far, not until the afternoon. After the highway was cleared, we then proceeded on our journey home.

Battle in Our Neighborhood

When we reached Bucharest, tanks, militia, and uniformed men roamed the streets. Broken glass, ammunition shells, rocks, chunks of cement, splinters of wood, and all kinds of debris littered the streets as I carefully maneuvered the car to our home at Stirbei Voda Avenue.

Bobby opened the gate, and I drove into the driveway. We were tired and hungry. However, I became curious about the numerous pock-holes on the front wall of the house. I also noticed the broken branches and leaves scattered on the porch and the front yard. The tree by the fence whose trunk used to stand straight was now bent and many of its branches limp. A small basement window was pried half-way open, its glass broken, with bullet holes around it. The front yard looked mushy and muddy, unlike the pristine smooth snow-covered ground at the side of the house. Fortunately, not one of the main windows on the façade of the building was broken.

As I walked toward the back of the house, I wondered why the garage door was partly open as Bobby closed it before we left. Drops of blood patterned the muddy floor. Then, at the corner of my eyes, I saw something that sickened me. In the backyard, one of the stray dogs that used to come for food laid motionless, bloodied, and dead.

Suspicious that some terrible things must have happened at home during our absence, I talked with our neighbor, Mrs. Colina, a heavy-set Romanian lady in her fifties. She confirmed our fears.

Colina's account made sense. Stirbei Voda was the main avenue the country's leader, President Nicolae Ceausescu, used in going from his residence to the Central Committee building. He and his wife, Elena, used to pass in front of our house in their limousine with their white furry dogs looking out the car window. Stirbei Voda was also a major road walked by the marchers from the provinces whenever called to rally at the Central Committee grounds.[5]

Fighting at Stirbei Voda

Two blocks from our house, on the other side of Stirbei Voda, was the Radio-Television Romania Building where concerts and other performing arts were held and aired live nationwide on radio and television. Although used mainly for cultural events, its strategic importance was nonetheless obvious. Whoever controlled the building could use it to influence the opinion of the people and mobilize the public for political ends.

Colina's English was sketchy, but I understood that in the first encounter, on the 21st of December, the people who defied Ceausescu at the Central Committee plaza ran in all directions as the

---

[5] At Stirbei Voda, in an anti-communist post-revolution rally, the marchers flashed the *laban* (fight) hand signal of the Philippine People's Power revolution as they passed in front of our house and saw the Philippine flag. *Filipino experience in political change was indeed shared with the world*, I thought.

Securitate responded with teargas and gunfire. Part of the crowd flowed into our street, and some came into our front yard and climbed the trees, while others hid in our front porch to escape the pursuing forces.

Later, the Army declared its refusal to side with the President, leaving Ceausescu with only the *Securitate* loyalists as his base of support. The Army sided with the people, gave arms and ammunitions to civilian volunteers, and formed an alliance with the militia. The Army was further emboldened with the formation of the National Salvation Front, a caretaker government composed of leaders opposed to Ceausescu, many of whom were former members of the Communist Party. The shift of loyalty by the Army had ominous implications to the security of our house.

Our Home in a Crossfire

Before the revolution, Army personnel already occupied the building on our right while *Securitate* operatives used the building on our left. As can be imagined, the possibility for our house to be in the crossfire between two armed groups at war with each other proved exciting, to say the least.

Stirbei Voda Avenue became an actual battlefield. In the succeeding days and nights following the turmoil at the Central Committee plaza, some fighting waged on our street as the Army deployed tanks and troops to secure the radio-television headquarters. On the night we were stranded in a snowstorm at Pieste-Bucharest highway, a very intense fighting occurred again in our neighborhood, according to Colina. As the adversaries exchanged gunfire in front of the house, one *Securitate* operative entered our property and tried to seek cover.

"We hear gunfire in front of your house," Colina continued, "then the *Securitate* man…he run to the back of the house, kick the dog…he is barking loud, then no more barking. But he (*Securitate*) go inside the garage; he not run away. And the Army…they catch him."

As the snow melted the following day, I recovered from the front yard and porch at least seventy-five shells and slugs.

A Higher Power with a Purpose?

I have often wondered why a series of delays occurred during our return journey from Hamburg to Bucharest. I wanted to get back home—and to my office—as quickly as possible. Had I spent additional days to complete the car repair in Hamburg, we probably would have avoided delays and could have arrived home days earlier. But even when we proceeded with the journey in a new car, still we encountered delays beyond our control.

Events happened as if a higher authority allowed my foolhardy decisions, impatience, and arrogance to lead to their logical outcomes. However, in every mishap we encountered, such an invisible higher power seemed to have rescued us—for a purpose. The breakdown of the car on the Alps became an occasion for me to hear the call apparently of His Spirit. The call awakened me not only from my weariness and stress, but from my spiritual slumber and blindness. Although we suffered a motor accident near Craiova, the event became an occasion in which we experienced the power and loving protection of the Lord Almighty, and witnessed first-hand the innate kindness of the Romanian people despite the years of repression under communist rule. Then the snowstorm prevented us from reaching Stirbei Voda until the fighting was over. Had we arrived in Bucharest earlier, we would have reached Stirbei Voda when fighting around our house was most intense. There was no guarantee that security condition in the capital and our neighborhood would have allowed us to safely proceed to the comfort of our home.

I also wondered why God allowed us to go in the first place for a vacation leave. Had I not left, I would have been in the middle of action to get a fresh eyewitness report to Manila. I probably would have been bold enough to get close to the rally at the Central Committee building. On the other hand, in view of the actual events that transpired, I would have been among those who had to run for cover when the *Securitate* opened fire at the crowd. Thus, I probably would have ended up staying at home just the same, waiting for the telephone lines to open, comparing notes just as before with my diplomat friends from Asian and Western embassies on updates. Although the reports I could have sent may be closely similar to what my government could have gotten from TV news, I regretted not playing my role simply because I could not get home early enough.

It was uncanny, but every misfortune we experienced led to a "shocker"—call it moral lesson, revelation, or message—that greatly changed our outlook on the Creator and our standing before Him.

Life: The Treasured Gift

In principle, the Lord wants everyone to encounter the truth. Having created us with ability to discern, choose, and make decisions, He did not control my actions but allowed me to see the consequences of my errors. In winter 1989, He showed me that hidden beneath the misfortunes stood His love, care, and deliverance, waiting to be recognized. He left it to me—a man—to acknowledge the reality of His grace and salvation that He offered despite of my imperfections, that I may receive them.

The traumas we experienced became living lessons on the fragility and importance of life. Whatever we were born with and had made of ourselves, and all our plans, hopes and dreams for our family, can all be dashed away in an instant. The value of life was no longer confined to theory. The principle became personal, tangible, and eternally true.

The Hamburg-Bucharest journey also reinforced the mercy, love, protection, and grace God showed Eva and me earlier in the year. In summer, while driving home from Belgrade, tired and sleepy yet over-speeding at two in the morning, we hit a deer that suddenly ran in front of us. The impact was so strong the deer was thrown twenty meters away and forced us to slow down until we eventually stopped at the side of Piteste-Bucharest highway. When we resumed driving, we saw the Dacha car that overtook us had rammed into an improperly parked truck about two hundred yards from our impact with the deer. The Dacha was totally demolished, and its passenger killed. As we saw the Gypsy woman lying bloodied and lifeless on the pavement and partly covered with newspaper, we quivered, for it could have been us had there not been a deer that stopped us. Shocked, I felt compassion, regret, and guilt thinking I may have led someone to a tragic end.

Recalling that summer event, I then realized that in Christmas 1989, we were given a second chance to life—a gift we treasured above all gifts—by the grace and mercy of a higher power.

A Spring of New Outlook

As spring began, the grass sprouted and garden plants in our front and back yards bloomed with colors again. Green leaves budded on the poplar trees to replace those that fell in autumn. Meanwhile, Eva and I became increasingly aware we were crossing over into a new season of our lives.

The events of that winter stirred our soul. The door of our hearts opened to seek His divine realm, the kingdom of Heaven.

> *Here I am! I stand at the door and knock.*
> *If anyone hears my voice and opens the door, I will*
> *come in and eat with him, and he with me.*
> **Revelation 3:20**

CHAPTER THREE

SILENT SIDE OF THE REVOLUTION

> *For God is the King of all the earth; sing to Him a psalm of praise. God reigns over the nations; God is seated on His holy throne. The nobles of the nations assemble as the people of the God of Abraham, for the kings of the earth belong to God. He is greatly exalted.*
> **Psalms 47:7-9**

Beyond the physical dimensions of violence and death, the upheaval in winter 1989 revealed a manifestation that was subtle in its voice, yet most profound in its impact. Though hinted in the Scriptures, it was a silent message that many failed to hear.

Twilight of the Demigods

An invitation to attend the XIVth Congress of the Romanian Communist Party in November, 1989 brought all foreign ambassadors and *charges d'affaires* in Bucharest to the National Assembly Building.

The ambassadorial car carried me to the line of other diplomatic vehicles on the road leading to the legislative building. It was one of those rare sights in the country to have more than fifty foreign cars—Mercedes, Volvos, Toyotas, Cadillac, Bentleys—all in line, converging in one place, each carrying the chief envoy of countries identifiable by the national flag flown on the hood of the vehicles. Police had cordoned off the strategic intersections leading to the venue of the meeting to assure unhindered flow of traffic. The Romanian government dignitaries, most of whom were top Communist Party leaders, were also arriving in their locally produced Dacha sedans. Some special foreign guests were each driven in highly secured state vehicles accompanied by plainclothes security and intelligence operatives.

As my chauffeur patiently followed the long winding line of flag-decked diplomatic cars leading to the ceremonial state building, I could sense the power of the man who ruled the country for the last twenty-two years. Giant portraits of President Ceausescu and Elena loomed atop government buildings. School children in their uniform stood on both sides of the road waving Romanian flag, and huge billboards proclaiming "Long Live President Nicolae and Elena Ceausescu" could be seen everywhere.

Inside the legislative building, the plenary session proceeded with the representatives from various levels and geographical units of the Communist Party seated at the Assembly Hall. The diplomatic corps was seated at the balcony where we watched the delegates responded with standing ovation and resounding applause to every sentence of Ceausescu from the start to the finish of his speech.

The Romanian Congress of the Communist Party concluded its plenary session with the re-election of Ceausescu for another 5-year term as General Secretary of the Communist Party, at age 71. Since the State apparatus was totally subordinated to the Party, Ceausescu also remained in his position as Head of State. The "personality cult" he established continued to secure his control over the Party and the State, using the para-military *Securitate* to destroy any opposition. Ceausescu had been the head of the CPR since 1965 and the President of Romania since 1967.

The Huge Ceausescu Palace

President Ceausescu must have been impressed with North Korea's urbanization scheme. Like Emperor Nero of Rome who burned his capital city centuries ago in order to rebuild it in fulfillment of a poetic inspiration, Ceausescu ordered the razing of one-fifth of Bucharest, a beautiful city formerly known as the "Paris of the East." Ceausescu removed forever some 7,000 historical buildings, churches, eighteenth-century-built houses, and a monastery and replaced them with his vision of new complexes as a monument to his reign. While many Romanians starved, the country's wealth went into the construction of new government offices, workers' apartments, canals, and roads with fountains.

But the most ambitious of his projects was the colossal Palace of the People (or "Ceausescu Palace," as diplomats called it then) which Romanian officials claimed to be the "second largest building in the world, next in volume only to the Pentagon Building in Virginia and comparable to the Empire State Building in New York." It had hundreds of chandeliers of various sizes and design, gold-plated faucets, marble floor, and thick carpets. The huge plaza in front of the palace was as broad as, if not wider than, Tien An Mein Square in Peking. The palace was designed so that President Ceausescu could stand at the ceremonial balcony and would be seen by all the troops gathered at the huge plaza. He would be seen also by the marching workers and children lined up on the fountain-filled avenues that extended from the plaza.

As Nero played the violin to suppress his guilt while Rome burned, Ceausescu told the Party Congress that the eroding power of regimes in other Soviet bloc republics would not happen in Romania because of its robust economy and successful five-year plans.

No Remorse

At the end of the Party Congress, each Head of Diplomatic Mission and spouse were ushered from the balcony to a reception hall. We were individually presented to Chairman Ceausescu and Elena to extend congratulations to the "great leader."

As I talked with and shook the hand of Romanian President Ceausescu, I wondered whether behind his deep hazel eyes there was remorse for sacrificing the basic needs of his people. Such sacrifice led to hunger and death to thousands of his countrymen. Nonetheless, it was my duty to extend greetings to him from

Philippine President, Her Excellency Corazon C. Aquino. He did not say much except to utter thanks in Romanian, *"Multumesc."*

But revealed in his speech during the assembly, and confirmed by officials with whom I conversed, the President was proud of his accomplishment of completing the payment that year of Romania's foreign debts in record time. It was a commendable feat, indeed. But because scarce resources were used to pay off foreign debts, most Romanians tightened their belts while others no longer had belt. In many cases, there was no more stomach.

The Spark and the Fall

God's judgment fell on Ceausescu through an unexpected incident.

On December 17, evangelical Protestant Pastor Laszlo Tokes, a Romanian-born ethnic Hungarian, was being banished from Timisoara. The attempt to enforce the order led to violence as his congregation surrounded his house to prevent the police from physically removing him. The next day, a "people's power"[6] situation developed as students joined the swelling number of church members. But on the basis of a decision by the Executive Political Committee and as the Acting Head of Government while Nicolae was abroad at the time, Elena Ceausescu ordered the use of real bullets.[7] The police opened fire at the crowd, killing hundreds.

---

[6] The term "people's power" was coined during the Philippine uprising against President Marcos, referring to popular resistance employing the physical presence of people to block the movements of tanks, armored vehicles, police, anti-riot squads, etc.

[7] "The Development of the Lazslo Tokes Case," http://www.procesulcomunismului.com/marturii/fonduri/nemioc/anticomrev/docs/03htm, accessed December 5, 2013.

What began as an eviction issue became a general protest spreading like wildfire throughout the city.

Thereafter, events moved quickly. By the time President Ceausescu returned on December 20 from a state visit to Iran, rumblings already spread to the major cities. The people killed as reported in Western broadcast numbered in the thousands, some reports even claiming 60,000 killed with bodies found floating in the Dumbovita River. On December 21, a mass rally was assembled in Bucharest, in front of the Central Committee Building, supposedly to show support for Ceausescu. But as he was speaking from a balcony, one demonstrator booed him, and others followed with shouts of "Timisoara!"

The surprised and scared look on Ceausescu's face was carried live on national television. The brief vulnerable image seen by millions in the country and those at the Central Committee plaza destroyed the mask of invincibility of the "great leader." Emboldened, the thousands of young people who were brought to Bucharest to support the dictator instead turned against him. The Army and the *Securitate* dispersed the crowd with warning shots and tear gas.

On the following day, thousands again gathered at the Central Committee Square, but this time the Army refused to support Ceausescu and instead sided with the people. Overcoming tear gas, water cannons, and *Securitate* forces, the demonstrators stormed the Central Committee Building.

The rest is history. Only seconds ahead of the pursuing rioters, Nicolae and Elena Ceausescu fled for their lives on board a helicopter. But the pilot reportedly landed the craft on orders of the Army. Unable to leave the country, the Ceausescus were captured and turned over to the Army, tried by a "kangaroo court," sentenced to death, and were executed on Christmas day, 25 December 1989.

The Silent Wave

The issue on Pastor Laszlo Tokes as the trigger of the revolution was only the tip of the iceberg, for below the surface there was a larger historical force sweeping across Romania. The Romanian authorities did not mention much about their reason for wanting to transfer Pastor Laszlo except to say it was in line with the "systematization" policy, an urbanization program. Ceausescu aimed at creating cities in the countryside, thus requiring relocation of millions of people from small villages to the new centers. Laszlo openly criticized the program from the pulpit.

Bible Studies and Prayers

But the regime's deeper concern was the spread of the Bible studies in private homes, a situation the *Securitate* did not have effective system to monitor. These meetings constantly changed venue and time, and the appetite of the Romanian people for the Gospel of Jesus Christ was insatiable. Secret meetings were spreading like wildfire. The transfer of Pastor Laszlo was supposed to set an example in order to arrest the trend.

To the *Securitate*, which was patterned after Hitler's Gestapo, Honecker's Stasi, and Russia's KGB, the Bible studies could double as a meeting of people opposed to the president. Even if the meetings were essentially free from political subversion, worship of anything other than "the great leader" was enough reason for the secret police to be concerned. At the outset, the communist doctrine called for the eventual demise of religion which, according to Karl Marx and Friedrich Engels in *Communist Manifesto*, is "opiate of the people."[8] In Romania and elsewhere behind the Iron Curtain,

---

[8] Religion, according to the pamphlet *Communist Manifesto (London, 1848)*, is an unnecessary activity that has no place in dialectical materialism which determines the course of history. Communist ideology says religion was not founded on material reality, and it was no more than a concoction devised by the ruling class to oppress and control the masses.

The manifesto says that human society had evolved from one economic system to another through a continuing class struggle. Seen through Friedrich Hegel's concept of the interplay between thesis and antithesis that results to a

religion was tolerated with the expectation that it will eventually disappear when the ruling class is finally destroyed and the world consequently evolves into the ultimate "classless society."

In principle, the government allowed freedom of religion but worship had to be done in the open. When we arrived in Romania in spring 1989, I noticed the government allowed the Catholic Cathedral in Bucharest and the churches of the Orthodox religion to continue receiving their respective worshippers. But the bishop and heads of these churches were required to make reports to the Communist Party regularly as a way for the authorities to monitor the activities of the believers. In fact, the Bishop of Oradea of the Hungarian Reformed Church was compelled to cooperate with the communist government for the transfer of Pastor Laszlo.[9]

Having Bible study at homes, however, presented more problems to Ceausescu and the *Securitate*. The Bible studies were also suspected to be a part of the network that smuggled disgruntled

---

synthesis, the slavery system (slave vs. master) evolved to feudalism (peasant vs. landlord) which itself evolved to the industrial revolution (proletariat vs. bourgeoisie) and to the present capitalism (worker vs. capitalist). In the final stage of the world economic system, the manifesto predicted the middle class will be reduced to the ranks of the working class resulting to only two classes left in the class struggle, workers vs. capitalists. The Marxists believed a revolution of the masses will occur and result in the demise of the ruling capitalist elite. With only the working class left, there will be no more antithesis and thus no more class struggle. One class left equals no class, a "classless" society. The means of production, distribution, etc. belong to everyone, "from each according to his ability, to each according to his needs." In theory, all the so-called "instruments of oppression" such as the nation-state and religion will also disappear. A borderless world emerges.

Historical reality, however, differs from the theory. Socialism as an intermediate transition to communism had failed. After their successful revolution, the new leaders themselves became the new oligarchs, new elites, fulfilling Robert Michels' warning on the "iron law of oligarchy" (Robert Michels, *Political Parties,* 1911). The communist parties behind the Iron Curtain had been discredited following the collapse of the Soviet Union.

[9] Op.cit., "The Development of the Lazslo Tokes Case."

citizens such as the famous Olympic gymnast, Nadia Comaneci, out of Romania.

A Grandmother's Remark

"He is prophesied in the Bible," an old woman blurted out by impulse during our visit at their apartment days before the revolution broke out. Fear reflected in her eyes and voice, so her daughter, who was a friend of my wife, explained that the grandmother had been attending Bible study. Apparently, many attendees of the Bible studies believed that President Ceausescu had violated God's laws and was an antichrist, a forerunner of "the beast" prophesied in Revelation, Chapter 13, of the Bible.

The grandmother's honesty revealed more than what a foreign diplomat was supposed to know. From her short outburst, I saw the deeply human, spiritual dimension of the revolution.

Praying for God's Intervention

The grandmother's remarks confirmed that Bible studies were already widespread, especially in major cities, and mostly held in neighborhoods where even grandmothers could attend. It was also clear that many Romanians grew increasingly disillusioned over the communist system and resentful of President Ceausescu and his wife Elena. Her remarks revealed that many Romanians had turned to prayers and implored divine intervention to save the people from the repressive regime.

I noticed the sudden change in the grandmother's face to a picture of confidence and joy when she talked about the "higher authority." It seemed that the Bible studies presented to the people an alternative focus to which they could direct their hopes, trust, and confidence—above and beyond President Ceausescu. The Bible studies did not teach rebellion against the government, but they gave answers to whether the leaders used their authority in line with the will of Almighty God.

By forcing the transfer of Pastor Laszlo Tokes, the government intended to shoot several birds with one stone. First, it would make the Hungarian ethnic group in Romania a scapegoat for the country's economic ills. Second, it would discourage the further spread of the Gospel of Jesus Christ. And third, it would underscore the importance of the systematization program of the government.

But it was already too late for the communist dictatorship to arrest the silent force spreading among the populace. Students and Bible believers from various ethnic backgrounds joined in resisting the police to defend the bilingual pastor who spoke both Romanian and Hungarian. Widespread discontent grew against the regime, and many had turned to God for deliverance.

Biblical Connection

Even after the revolution, the grandmother's remarks still lingered in my thoughts. Her confident look when she talked of a higher power led me to search for the connection between the political events and what the Romanians read in the Bible. I was curious. Could the words in the Bible assume reality in the life of the suffering Romanians? Was Ceausescu's downfall a reflection of God's power in answer to their prayers? If so, how does one attain this level of faith?

In pondering over these questions, I also considered the events that shook our old outlook when Eva and I took the journey from Hamburg to Bucharest. From a series of dangers, we were saved—perhaps because I called on God. However, it seemed clear that the Romanian people were delivered from more harm after they prayed for God's intervention. So, I asked silently: *Could God, who I had taken for granted, be real and care for us?*

In a copy of the Bible I found tucked inside an unpacked piece of luggage, I ran across a story.

The Ruler Who Mocked God

King Sennacherib was the ruler of Assyria (705-681 BC), the most powerful nation on earth at the time. With one hundred eighty-five thousand men, he laid siege against Jerusalem. Convinced of his invincibility, Sennacherib called the defender King Hezekiah to surrender as even the God of Abraham could not defend Jerusalem.[10] Hezekiah gathered his people and, in sackcloth, humbled himself before God and prayed. With the same humility as the Romanian people felt when they prayed in the late 1980's, Hezekiah implored the Almighty to open His eyes and ears to his people's predicament. He pleaded, '*Now, O Lord our God, deliver us from his hand, so that all kingdoms on earth may know that You alone, O Lord, are God*' (2 Kings 19:19).

Through the prophet Isaiah, the Lord conveyed to Hezekiah, '*I have heard your prayer*' (v.20). And God assured, '*I will defend this city and save it, for my sake and for the sake of David my servant*' (v.34).

Then, at night, an angel of the Lord went out into the camp of the Assyrians and killed all the 185,000 soldiers (v.35). The strongest army in the world at the time was annihilated. Overnight. And the defenders of Jerusalem did not have to shoot a single arrow. It was the Lord's battle, and God took a direct hand in assuming the task Hezekiah and his soldiers could not have successfully accomplished.

Judgment and Compassion

Sennacherib escaped and returned to Nineveh. But he could not escape the eyes of God. One day, while worshipping in the temple of his idol god, two of his sons sneaked behind the Assyrian leader and cut him down with their swords, killing him. The assassins ran away and another son became the new king of Assyria (v.37).

The scriptures show God renders judgment on the arrogant and mockers of His divinity as He reveals compassion to those who believe in Him. The communists ignored the existence of a higher power. Instead, they openly defied Him and challenged His sovereignty as they opposed the work of those bringing His word to

---

[10] 2 Kings 18:13-19:37; 2 Chronicles 32:1-21

people who hungered for salvation.

Having ignored the fate of Sennacherib as a warning, President Ceausescu and his wife Elena chose a path destined to a tragic end. They were unceremoniously killed by their own soldiers who turned against them, and were buried in unmarked graves in a small cemetery somewhere in southwestern Bucharest.

Sovereign Above Sovereigns

The Romanian television repeatedly showed a 15-minute video of the final moments of Nicolae and Elena. It showed doctors checking their blood pressure before they were subjected to a trial in which they were accused of many crimes. They argued back as they held tightly to their coats and bags that reportedly contained jewelry. Though no video existed on the actual execution, the soldiers reportedly shot husband and wife like escaping chicken trapped against a high concrete wall.

I have lived through the People's Power revolution in the Philippines a few years earlier. And I witnessed the impact on personal lives resulting from the death of Premier Chou En-lai in Communist China during my posting in Peking. To me, the image of the Romanian dictator and his wife lying on the snow-covered ground proved a grim reminder of the fragility of political power.

Like most people, I knew from the start my need of Him who is our Lord and Savior, but my knowledge remained on the intellectual level. Deep inside, I was not ready to step beyond the old lifestyle where values were defined by worldly measures such as power, wealth, popularity, and political correctness. Being in the government, the name of the game was "pleasing the boss" as an employee pursues rapid promotion and good postings. And when congressmen, senators, cabinet secretaries, and other high officials visited our post, like some civil servants, I also overspent to please and impress the guests with the intention of asking their favors someday.

Although unwilling to admit it, I was like many others who often relied on their own plans and abilities without God in the equation. On matters beyond my personal control, I placed my hopes more on what was tangible—the President of the Republic, politicians, and my superiors in the Foreign Department. Others relied on their CEOs, managers, wealthy clients, commanders, and their bank accounts, stocks, investments, and material possessions. Like many others, I also suffered spiritual myopia. God to me was reserved for Sundays, Christmas, Holy Week, after-life, and when I needed something more.

What Eva and I witnessed in the Romanian revolution woke us up to the truth that human sovereigns themselves face limitations no matter how sincere they may wish to serve their fellow men. Some in power fall into temptations and in the end become living examples of Machiavelli's theorem, "Power corrupts, and absolute power corrupts absolutely." Although the scriptures say God established the authorities that exist,[11] the Sennacherib story warns judgment will come to those who abuse the authority given them.

Looking back at our experiences in 1989, the Romanian revolution not only shook our old values but it also began to change my perspective on the authorities I served. Not that I loved my government less, but a higher authority who I had taken for granted all these years had become real in my life.

It is better to take refuge in the Lord than to trust in man, says Psalm 118:8. And Psalm 146:3-4 teaches: *Do not put your trust in princes, in mortal men who cannot save. When their spirit departs, they return to the ground. On that very day, their plans come to nothing.*

When I read the aforesaid passages, I felt reassured of protection from a power higher than the human sovereign I served.

---

[11] Romans 13:1

The End Had Begun

The human drama that transpired in Eastern Europe carried a message many failed to hear. Historians marked the events as the melting of the Cold War while the world focused on their political dimensions, not on their prophetic sounds. Covered beneath the noise, violence, and emotions of those days, a subtle voice implored the world to heed the signs of the times.

The prophesied End of the Age[12] had begun. At first, the monumental upheaval in Eastern Europe did not make sense to me until I read the Scripture. The Bible contains prophecies about the conditions of the world at the closing of the age, with events centered on a nation called "Israel." I found it amazing that those passages were written when the aforesaid nation was scattered and the land ruled by foreign powers. Yet, after some two thousand years, Israel was reborn as a nation-state in 1948 and the "dry bones"[13] came back to life. Eschatology scholars believed Israel's rebirth and the return of Jacob's descendants to their land signaled the beginning of the last days. The collapsed Soviet Union was among the domino chips lined up until the last piece falls to mark the final moment of the End of the Age.

Gospel to All Nations

One such prophecy is contained in Matthew 24:14 regarding the End of the Age: *And this gospel of the kingdom will be preached in the whole world as a testimony to all nations, and then the end will come.*

The aforementioned prophecy is not a passive prediction. On the contrary, it carries the power and force of the Lord's command for

---

[12] Some writers use the term "End Time" although it does not appear in the Bible. In this book, "end time" is synonymous to the biblical term "end of the age" which appears in Matthew 13:39, 40; 24:3, 28:20; and Hebrews 9:26. This book agrees that the "end time" period starts from the rebirth of Israel as a nation-state in 1948 and ends at the Second Coming of Jesus Christ. See also Footnote 112, p. 195 regarding the terminology.

[13] Ezekiel 37:4

the preaching of the Good News as a prelude to His judgment on the people of the earth.

I will shake all nations. (Haggai 2:7)

The other such prophecy indicating the fall of the Soviet bloc as an omen of the end time is contained in Haggai 2:7: '*I will shake all nations, and the desired of all nations will come, and I will fill this house with glory,*' says the Lord Almighty.

The aforesaid verse reveals the destruction of things not founded on the kingdom of God while those made for His glory shall remain. On earth, God shakes the institutions made for the edification of mortal man; they shall be shaken and destroyed to clear the way for divine restoration as the new dispensation begins. The atheistic communist regimes that opposed His deity and prevented their own people from receiving the Word of God were shaken and torn down. The passages, *the desired of all nations* and *fill the house with glory,* promise the fulfillment of *thy kingdom come on earth as it is in heaven*[14] which shall be fully realized in the reign of Jesus on earth following the end of the present age.

The events in Eastern Europe cannot be oversimplified by historians as exclusively the work of man. Bringing down regimes engrained for decades in Stalinist-style administrative structure was unthinkable. And overcoming a network of the Communist Party that controlled over every aspect of the state apparatus, economy, politics, police, and military was next to impossible. Repudiating an ideology and economic system that had been the core of the societies' political culture had to start with a change of heart and mind, which could not have come from man alone. I believe these series of changes in several nations within a short period of time as in a symphony transpired with the intervention of a higher power.

In 1989, the collapsing socialist economy and public outcry against political monopoly of the Communist Party led to mounting demand for systemic change in each of the Warsaw Pact countries. Rumblings against the communist system built up earlier in the year

---

[14] Mathew 6:10

in the Baltic States and then spread to the rest of the Union of Soviet Socialist Republics. In Bulgaria, long-time dictator Todor Zikhov resigned in November. In Czechoslovakia, the generally peaceful Velvet Revolution led by Vaclav Havel forced the Communist Party to relinquish power allowing the process of constitutional reforms to begin. In East Germany, rapid increase of illegal departure to the West and widespread demonstrations to open the borders led to the ouster of strongman Erich Honecker by the Politburo. By December, the East German Politburo itself and the Central Committee of the party resigned. The Berlin Wall was opened and both East and West Berliners took part in chiseling and hammering out the bricks of the physical divide. In 1990, Hungary became the first republic behind the Iron Curtain to institute political reforms.

By 1991, the last of the communist regimes fell as Albania's dictator died, and the federal system of Yugoslavia crumbled. Eventually, throughout the entire Soviet bloc, the one-party system as power base of the Marxist-Leninist communist regimes was abandoned and replaced with multi-party system. Even in Russia, the Communist Party was banned in 1991 and the various republics in the USSR declared their independence from Moscow.

Looking back at the events in Romania and Eastern Europe, I found it ironic that in the midst of chaos and noise in an atheistic political backdrop, the very foundation of my material, worldly values began to break. My spiritual window to truth creaked open.

> *The closing call of the Iron Curtain echoed from the silenced banging of sledge hammers that tore down the last brick of the Berlin Wall.*
> **Author**

CHAPTER FOUR

DYING AND REBIRTH

> *Do not conform any longer to*
> *the pattern of this world, but*
> *be transformed by the renewing of your mind.*
> **Romans 12:2**

In the summer of 1990, I arrived in Seoul, South Korea to assume my post as Minister Counselor and Consul General at the Philippine Embassy. Eva and I marveled at the number of Christian churches in the city. At night, one could look in any direction and see hundreds of lighted crosses on top of buildings.

Undersecretary of Foreign Affairs, Gen. Manuel Yan (the former Chief of Staff of the Armed Forces of the Philippines), who earned the respect and admiration of the Filipino people for his integrity, humility, and sincerity, effected my transfer from Bucharest to Seoul. Eva and I became friends with him and his wife before he retired, but I have wondered whether he knew his kindness was to have a great impact on our lives.

Why My Spiritual Journey

In previous years, every time we visited the US, my sister Rebecca, the eldest of nine children and who became "born again," always prayed over Eva and me and gave us tracts and a copy of the Bible. Then, in Seoul, staff members of the embassy, Nenet Partosan and John Reandino, often hosted Bible study at their respective homes. The study sessions revived, reinforced, and added to what I had learned long ago from Rebecca and Sunday school teacher, Mrs. Josephine Elegado Neri-Mason of the Filipino Christian Church in Los Angeles, California.

Although Eva and I desired to know more about the kingdom of God, we viewed the Lord from a distance. We *knew about Him*, but we really did not *know Him* as a child would know his parents, brothers, and sisters.

Goliath of a Threat

Then, in the spring of 1991, a high-ranking official in the Department of Foreign Affairs in Manila hurried to transfer me to Bangladesh only a few months after my arrival in Seoul, and shortly after I took over as acting Chief of Mission.[15]

In diplomatic circles, such rapid sequence of transfers suggests a negative impression on my competence and would thus impede the normal pace of my professional advancement. His motives, whether personal or professional, were not my primary concern. I worried more about the ease by which he could manipulate the paperwork to get his ways.

The high-ranking official was a Goliath to me. He belonged to a well-known political family, claimed personal connections with top politicians, and was the second-ranking official in the Department of Foreign Affairs, in charge of administration. All my appeals addressed to the Secretary of Foreign Affairs, The Honorable Raul Manglapus, landed first in the hands of this powerful official. To him I was just a thin matchstick he could easily break. Furthermore, my proposed replacement, also very disturbed by the events, was being rushed to leave his post in Washington, DC for a transfer to Seoul, obviously to consummate my transfer. Like most

---

[15] More details of the high official's attempt to remove me from Seoul are in Rodolfo I. Dumapias, "My Journey as Christian Ambassador," in *Scattered: The Filipino Global Presence,* edited by Luis J. Pantoja, Sadiri Joy Tira, and Enoch Wan, (Manila, Philippines: Life Change Publishing) 2004, pp. 313-326.

government employees faced with bureaucratic problems, I sought the help of politicians. Still, this did not stop the ongoing process of transfer.

Our Journey to the Kingdom Began

Desperate and feeling helpless, I remembered how the Lord delivered us from death in Romania. I also remembered the confident look on the face of the Romanian grandmother when she talked about God. With those recollections, I knew then to whom I should turn.

I sought the Lord, and He answered me; He delivered me from all my fears, my heart echoed Psalms 34:4.

So, Eva and I decided to seek divine help and turned to the Lord. I remembered my sister Rebecca's earlier efforts for us to accept Jesus into our lives. In those times, we did not understand what she meant. But this time, we were ready.

In a long-distance call in the summer of 1991, Rebecca prayed over us, she in Los Angeles and us in Seoul. On the phone, Eva and I prayed for God's forgiveness of our sins, and thanked Him for sacrificing His son who died on the cross in order to save us. We declared our faith in Jesus Christ as our personal Savior and Lord of our lives. With that prayer, Eva and I were reborn in spirit. We have embarked on our spiritual journey.

The famous passage, John 3:16, sums up the promise to those who enter the kingdom, *For God so loved the world that he gave his one and only Son, that whoever believes in him shall not perish but have eternal life.*

Journey and Transformation

After the phone call, Eva and I experienced peace of mind like never before. At first, we were unaware of the changes in us, but later our taste of music, movies, and literature favored those that inspired love of God and fellowmen. Our choice of TV shows changed so that violence, dirty jokes, and pornography were no longer enjoyable. Eventually, I burned all my *Playboy*, *Penthouse*, and other adult magazines and pornographic videos collected years earlier when I thought it "cool" to do so. Meanwhile, Eva gave away to a nun all the religious statuettes and images displayed at home. We attended Bible study regardless where it was held. Singing Gospel songs and reading the Bible became enjoyable. Had anyone told us a year before that we would be doing these things, we would have laughed and dismissed it as a joke.

We joined the Filipino Christian Fellowship (FCF) that met in the basement of a two-storey house at Haebanchon, a modest district in Seoul. People used to ask us why, as high officials of the embassy, we mingled with maids, workers, and musicians. We answered, "Because we see Jesus in their midst."

The passage in 2 Corinthians 5:17 became real in our life. *If anyone is in Christ, he is a new creation; the old has gone, the new has come!*

Promotion

I used to sulk whenever I was left out of the promotion list. But since I embarked on my spiritual journey, it did not matter anymore for I believed my future rested in the hands of my Savior. Also, I used to resent smart remarks to ridicule me. But after I received Jesus in my life, even when they made jokes about "Praise-the-Lord Dumapias," I let the remarks go out the other ear.

After some years, I eventually caught up with those promoted ahead of me. As Special Assistant for Intelligence to the Secretary of Foreign Affairs, I attended meetings with the President in Malacanang Palace, and of the National Security Council, on highly confidential, Top Secret matters. I represented my country in UN meetings in Vienna, and regional conferences in Peking and Tokyo, on multinational crimes. Being the head of the Department of Foreign Affairs' Office of Intelligence and Security, I worked with law enforcement agencies and the National Intelligence Coordinating Agency in combatting intrusion into Philippine territory, terrorism, illegal immigration, drug smuggling, human trafficking, and passport anomalies. Before I left for my assignment in the Middle East, I served as Asia-Pacific Regional Co-Chairman (with Australia) of the Anti-Money Laundering Coordinating Council.

Pride and Arrogance

Before the Lord began to re-create me, I thought my future rested exclusively in my hands. Being part of the government, I falsely assumed that "people need us more than we need them." And being an official in the prime department of the government—the Foreign Affairs Department—I boosted my pride thinking I belonged to the elite of the society, the *crème de la crème*. I was becoming the kind of official I used to despise. With the guidance of the Holy Spirit, I saw my error and guarded against pride and arrogance.

Materialist Faith

Pride also blinded me from seeing how shallow my faith was. Before our experiences in Romania, I thought I knew enough about God. I was sincere in my worship practice, but I did not have Jesus in my heart. The focus of my worship was not Him but on the rites of worship. In my college years, I read the Bible cover to cover, but only for the purpose of winning arguments with my Sunday school teacher. Although I had knowledge about Jesus, the need to submit to His lordship did not enter my mind. To Eva and me, church attendance was enough to take us to heaven. Sunday morning was for God, afternoon was for the shopping mall. I was spiritually blind and did not know what I did not know.

At first, I misunderstood why the Lord allowed our 6-year-old car to break down when we lacked the money for repair. But later, after undergoing hardships, I began to understand His purpose of teaching me about the futility of misplaced faith.

For several months in winter, Eva and I traveled by public transportation. We learned to get by without the comfort of a private car when we visited Filipino workers in remote corners of the city and in the countryside to conduct Bible study. We walked to the subway station with the pastor and an elder from the FCF carrying the guitar, keyboard, and a bag of Gospel songs. We clung to a strap on board a crowded train, traveled for an hour, then disembarked and ran after a provincial bus to travel for another hour. We again disembarked only to walk in the dark of night over snow about a kilometer more to reach an isolated factory with one light bulb to guide us of its location, in the countryside near the border with communist North Korea.

In the end, the drive to share the gospel became stronger than my desire to drive the material vehicle with a shallow faith.

Ungrateful

Then the Lord showed me another kingdom principle: our abilities, capabilities, and accomplishments are gifts from God. The credit for any of these gifts belongs to God, not to us. The thanks and praises belong to Him alone.

Many in the managerial and executive levels in public and private sectors, after having acquired the knowledge, connection, social position, legal authority, wealth, and skill to overcome problems, had forgotten that their capabilities were gifts from God. I, too, never thanked Him but took the credit for myself.

But Romans 1:21 warns: *For although they knew God, they neither glorified him as God nor gave thanks to him, but their thinking became futile and their foolish hearts were darkened.*

The Lord showed me He can deny or take the gifts away from us in an instant and give them back at any time. I remember when my car broke down, I borrowed a car in order to avoid the inconvenience in the middle of winter. But the borrowed car got damaged in an accident at a time when I had no resources for its repair, much less for the repair of my own car. Then, after I spoke in a church, a Korean pastor whom I met for the first time gave a check "for whatever you wish to use it." The amount was *exactly* the same figure quoted by the repair shop to fix both cars.

CHAPTER FIVE

EXPERIENCING THE ALMIGHTY

> *Jesus said: "I am the vine, you are the branches.*
> *If a man remains in me and I in him, he will bear much*
> *fruit; apart from me you can do nothing.*
> *If anyone does not remain in me, he is like a branch*
> *that is thrown away and withers; such branches are*
> *picked up, thrown into the fire and burned.*
> *If you remain in me and my words remain in you, ask*
> *whatever you wish, and it will be given you."*
> John 15:5-7

Foundation of Relationship

One early evening as Eva was alone, reading the book by Benny Hinn, *Good Morning Holy Spirit,* (Thomas Nelson Inc., 1990), she became aware of the unusual brightness in our apartment at Hillside Village. She looked outside through the living room window, but the sun had already set and darkness had descended on the Hangang River and the city below. Realizing that no lights were turned on inside the apartment, she became alarmed. But she calmed down as she sensed an encompassing power of love, comfort, and assurance.

Emmanuel, God with Us!

To Eva and me, the brightness was an unusual manifestation of the Holy Spirit's reality that is sometimes sensed by those eagerly seeking God's presence. Supernaturally, the foundation for a relationship with Jesus is laid as one loves and obeys the Lord. In John 14:21, Jesus said, *'He who loves me will be loved by my Father, and I too will love him and show myself to him.'*

Eva's experience was a sign that we became a part of a divine mystery. Jesus assured: *'The Spirit of Truth...lives with you and will be in you...On that day, you will realize that I am in my Father, and you are in me, and I am in you* (v.17 and 20). By giving Himself to redeem us, and as we accept His Lordship, Jesus becomes a part of us through the Holy Spirit, and us of Him.

The Lord further assured, *'And I will do whatever you ask in my name, so that the Son may bring glory to the Father'* (v.13).

Grace and Faith

Jesus gave His life on the cross because of His love for all humanity, although as sinners we deserve to be condemned. He paid the price for man's sins and took the punishment that should have been ours. Because of His sacrifice, salvation is made available and offered as a gift; we do not need to work for it. It is given free, as His grace, to those who open their hearts and receive Him as Lord and Savior. The following passage sums up the principle of salvation: *For it is by grace you have been saved, through faith—and this not from yourselves, it is the gift from God—not by works, so that no one can boast* (Ephesians 2:8-9).

The essence of man's relationship with God, in response to His grace, is expressed through our faith in Jesus Christ. It is not the sacrifices we offer, nor the symbolic materials we buy and pray to, but our obedience to His will that He prefers to see in our hearts. *To obey is better than sacrifice,* Samuel 15:22 reminds us.

Constant interplay of God's grace and man's faith helps believers develop awareness of His reality and presence in our lives. Through His word and the guidance and intercession of the Holy Spirit, we learn to align our spirit with His will. With greater awareness of His responses to our prayers, we build up our confidence in such a relationship and increase our faith in Him. On the basis of actual experiences, Eva and I began to *know Him* beyond our knowledge *about Him.*

The Holy Spirit Speaks

As narrated at the beginning of the previous chapter, a high-ranking, powerful man who represented a Goliath to me ordered to take me out of Korea, a move that could impair my career. From one of his official trips to the US, he and his wife made an overnight stopover in Seoul on their return to Manila. As the CDA of the mission, I made sure their short stay was proper and pleasant. But that night, I received hurting words from him. It was a tense and painful moment for Eva and me, so we decided to take a bold step. We prepared to go to their hotel, talk to him and his wife regarding personal matters, and clarify in person why I disagreed with him on policy regarding the Korean Peninsula and the internal administration of the embassy.

Hurting and in tears, Eva was in front of the mirror dressing up in our room upstairs. Then she sensed the Holy Spirit say, *"I know how you feel. If only I could embrace you. But do not go. Let me do it in my own way, in my own time."*

Eva was startled. The words came directly to her heart and mind, not from a sound. Immediately, she concluded the Lord had spoken to her.

Waiting downstairs, I saw her pale and trembling as she slowly walked down the steps. She told me what she "heard." So, we decided not to push through with the plan.

Goliath Down!

After about a week, the unexpected happened. Through an unlikely connection, a Korean businessman named Peter Kim, we met the only daughter of Secretary of Foreign Affairs Raul Manglapus who, together with her husband, made a brief visit to Seoul. We became good friends with Ben and Tina Manglapus-Maynigo who gave us contact numbers of the Secretary for emergency situations.

Thus, I re-sent copies of all my earlier letters, but this time directly to the Secretary—to his bedroom. After a few days, he declared null and void whatever was done by the powerful man. He voided, *ab initio,* my transfer from Seoul and the assignment of my replacement. Secretary Manglapus also prohibited any *acting* head of the foreign office from issuing transfer or promotion of diplomatic officers during the absence of *the* Foreign Secretary.

Our spirit shouted, *Hallelujah!* The truth prevailed. The attempt to take me out of Seoul was aborted and the threat to my career removed. As the master of events, God touched obedient hearts and directed them to unfold His will.

Years later, the powerful official asked me to pray for the recovery of his wife who suffered a stroke. Yes, we prayed.

We learned from this experience to wait on the Lord and to allow Him to do it in His own time, in His own way. Psalm 37:5-7 describes the reward for trusting and waiting on the Lord:

> *Commit your way to the Lord; trust in Him and He will do this: He will make your righteousness shine like the dawn, the justice of your cause like the noonday sun. Be still before the Lord and wait patiently for Him.*

God's Purpose in Eva's Dream

God sometimes conveys His will through dreams.

I was sound asleep one night when Eva frantically shook my whole body and asked, "Papa, are you leaving me?"

Half-asleep and with eyes still closed, I answered, "No. Go back to sleep." And I went back to sleep.

Then she woke me up again, crying and saying, "Then I don't want to be a widow."

"No. Go back to sleep," I said. I tried to catch my sleep.

"You will die soon. God said so," she said.

That got my attention. So I opened my eyes.

"God said, 'I will take your husband. He will glorify me. He will glorify me,'" she said between sobs.

"It's only a dream," I assured her.

Then she slept soundly. But this time, it was I who could not sleep.

"I will glorify Him? But how?" I asked myself in a whisper. "Am I to resign soon from my job and become a priest? Or a pastor? If I stay at my job, how can I glorify God? I do not have any training or formal education in church work or religion, so how would I know what to do to glorify God?"

I spent hours thinking of all the possible meaning of her dream and flipped back the time to see if our past experiences offered any clue. Then I saw the hand of God behind my transfer from Bucharest to Seoul, and the reason why my "Goliath" was downed. I concluded—to Korea I was brought, and in Korea I was to remain. In my present capacity, I was to serve Him—for His glory!

"But am I qualified?" I blurted out aloud. I startled Eva, and she woke up.

She said, **"No!"**

That shut me up. We went back to sleep.

"We will develop you."

Like many people who are called for His purpose, I groped in the dark and felt unprepared for the task. Unlike a soldier who is trained before going to battle, I had no preparation—no training, strategy, skill, formal education in theology, nor experience—for waging a campaign to glorify the Lord. I had nothing to offer except my young faith and trust in Him who brought down my own Goliath of a threat.

"We will develop you," Statesman Carlos P. Romulo told me years ago. But these words could have been said this time by the Almighty God, the Creator of the universe, for the Bible promises change through the works of the Holy Spirit. And He is faithful to complete transforming me *until the day of Jesus Christ.*[16]

When I arrived in Seoul several months earlier, I had no inkling my old self would soon die. Chief of Mission to Korea, Ambassador Tomas Padilla, was later recalled to the Foreign Office in Manila to assume a high and powerful position second only to the Foreign Secretary. Being the Minister Counselor, I was designated the acting Chief of Mission, or Charge d'affaires, a.i., even as I kept my functions as Consul General. It was in this capacity that I faced the Goliath of a threat. After receiving Jesus as my Lord and Savior, I began to change. Through trials, manifestations of God's presence in our lives, dreams, and a crisis in my career, I transformed into a new person—"*a new creation.*"

> *Then a teacher of the law came to Him and said,*
> *"Teacher, I will follow you wherever you go."*
> *Jesus replied, "Foxes have holes and birds of the air have nests, but the Son of Man has no place to lay His head."*
> *Another disciple said to Him,*
> *"Lord, first let me go and bury my father."*
> *But Jesus told him,*
> *"Follow me, and let the dead bury their own dead."*
> **Matthew 8:19-22**

---

[16] Philippians 1:6

CHAPTER SIX

SERVING GOD AND MAN

> *And we know that in all things God works for the good of those who love him, who have been called according to his purpose. For those God foreknew he also predestined to be conformed to the likeness of his Son, that he might be the first born among many brothers. And those he predestined he also called; those he called, he also justified, those he justified, he also glorified.*
> **Romans 8:28-30**

Can a Government Official be a Servant of God?

As Eva and I went deeper in our relationship with Jesus, I dealt with a haunting question a thousand times. My outlook changed since I became a follower of Christ. Someone cautioned me against speaking on the pulpit because of "separation of church and state." Can I still serve as a government official and be a servant of God at the same time?

The Central Issue

The term "servant of God" traditionally referred to priests, pastors, nuns, missionaries, and others employed as functionaries of a formal church or a ministry. Nowadays, however, the term also refers to untitled functionaries such as the leaders of house churches that are rapidly multiplying in many countries. Since anyone sent to perform a task by a master is a servant, anyone who believes in Jesus Christ and does the will of the Father is a servant of god.

Can believers of God, Jesus Christ, and the Bible freely live their faith, that is—speak, behave, decide, write, and relate with people consistent with their beliefs—and still function within the parameters required of them as servants of the State? Some people question: Isn't it incompatible for believers to live their faith while serving in the government?

The question penetrates to the very core of Christians' existence: as true believers of *the* God of the Bible, they think and feel in ways that reflect their hopes, beliefs, outlook, and moral values based on the Word of God. Simply by being true to their faith, they radiate the image of Jesus Christ without the slightest intention to proselytize or offend anyone. So, even without the title of Reverend, Pastor, Evangelist, or Missionary, they become reflections—*ambassadors*—of Christ.

Described in the Bible as "salt of the earth" and "light of the world,"[17] believers indeed emit certain effects on others. As light rolls back darkness by its presence, believers inspire curiosity on the secrets of their patience, forgiveness, and other virtues. And as salt gives flavor and preserves the food simply by being salty, true believers display ways that resist moral decay and corruption. While some non-believers are attracted to adopt the inner strength of the believers, others feel uncomfortable and self-conscious in the presence of believers. To non-believers, followers of Christ present an alternative lifestyle that somehow challenges their own. In many cases, by remaining true to their faith, believers bring about change to others even without intending to provoke change.

Critics of Christians want to prevent them from evangelizing in their place of work. However, viewing the issue within the framework of "proselytizing" or "evangelizing" when these terms are interpreted in their broadest sense, is a slight of hand. Such views immediately make the Christian guilty simply by being around, whatever he does. Believers can be brought to court in some Western countries for expressing moral views rooted to their faith. By simply referring to some Bible passages in response to social

---

[17] Matthew 5:13-16

issues, Christians can be accused of being offensive, judgmental, prejudice, politically incorrect, bigots, and abrasive to the self-esteem and lifestyle of some individuals in the society.[18] Because believers practice integrity in living out their faith, some critics misunderstand and wrongly accuse Christians as "haters". In essence, the critics are really asking Christians to either repress their real nature, or change their beliefs, or simply disappear.

A *Non Sequitur*?

Each time I wrestled with the issue of "separation of church and state," I questioned why it leaves out the central factor—God. Historically, the phrase stems from the issue of political control between the papacy and the throne of England; it was a secular controversy and not a spiritual matter. From the perspective of the Bible, everything, including the nation-state and the church (which is distinguished from the Church, with capital "c," referring to the believers as "body of Christ"), is intended to radiate His glory. But governments and the formal churches are operated by mortal men, subject to fallibility outside of God's domain. Although leaders of these institutions are meant to express God's principles, some step beyond the limits of God's will. Since the believer lives according to his faith founded on the word of God, he does not pursue the dictates of institutions whenever they operate outside of God's will, whether such institution is the government or the formal church. A servant of God is guided by God's will—not man's.

"Separation of church and state" remains a Western concept and its definition is still debated. Constitutionalists caution against encroachment by the church in government affairs and, vice-versa, by the state in religious affairs. In the U.S., controversy arises whenever the Federal government attempts to impose laws

---

[18] For example, rebuked by advocates of same-sex marriage is Romans 1:25-27: *They exchanged the truth of God for a lie...Because of this, God gave them over to shameful lusts. Even their women exchanged natural relations for unnatural ones. In the same way the men also abandoned natural relations with women and were inflamed with lust for one another. Men committed indecent acts with other men, and received in themselves the due penalty for their perversion.*

overriding Church principles. Ironically, the separation principle is a non-issue as President Barack Obama woos Iran and other countries where state religion calls the shots in state affairs. In essence, the separation principle refers to a person's loyalty to either of two man-made institutions—the church or the state—not to man's relationship with his deity.

The Legal, Cultural, and Political Environments

In living a life as a servant of God, a believer needs to be aware of the nature of the legal, cultural, and political parameters in which he exercises his faith. The guarantee of basic human rights such as religious freedom and freedom of expression exists in the national constitution of most countries. But the actual practice of these principles vary from one country to another as these rights are interpreted through legislation, statutes, jurisprudence, and the practical exercise of police power by the State. Traditionally, the church, family, and schools served as the main institutions for the formation of the society's culture. But technological innovation in mass communication now qualifies multimedia as a major channel in the formation of a community's values and moral norms.

For example, America has a constitution that is premised on biblical principles, but apostasy among the present generation has sprouted and open display of Christian worship in government facilities is now prohibited.[19] While assigned in Europe, I also noticed low attendance in the churches. And in a number of countries, a history of persecution of Christians exists.

In the Middle East, strict restrictions on religions other than Islam are imposed although some countries such as Bahrain allow certain freedoms to foreigner Christians in the practice of their faith. In Muslim countries, Christians are not allowed to proselytize to the Muslims, or criticize Islam and Mohamed. The Bible is prohibited

---

[19] Read Brad O'Leary, *America's War on Christianity,* (Washington D.C.: World Net Daily Books, Inc.), 2010.

and *Mutawas* (religious police) are around to enforce the rules.

In contrast, the legal, social, and cultural framework in most of Asia, Latin America, and Africa south of the Sahara offers a freer atmosphere for a believer to live his faith even as he serves in the government. Even in stringent and less affluent conditions, the spiritual need of man for a divine link is never subdued. As in Romania of the 1980's, man's spiritual hunger becomes greater and God's word reaches him with greater impact.

The Answer

In a restrictive country, a faithful believer must exercise caution, wisdom, wit, courage, imagination, and boldness to go around environmental challenges. For example, Christian foreign workers in some Islamic countries in the Middle East follow a thin line of living their faith while carefully evading arrest for violation of local laws against possession of the Bible, public worship of non-Islam religion, proselytizing other foreigners, etc. They bury their Bibles in the sand, sing Gospel songs without sound, conduct Bible study in "safe" venues such as homes of diplomats who enjoy immunity, and rent buses that roam the city non-stop as they hold on board church anniversary and other faith-based events. One's faith is tested in a restrictive environment.

'We must obey God rather than men,' declared Peter and the other apostles when told not to preach about Jesus.[20] Peter's answer has inspired millions to live their faith in any situation.

A follower of Christ, whether in the government or private sector, regardless of rank and position, elected or appointed, should not fear to speak, behave, and relate with his co-employees and others in ways consistent with his faith. In appropriate situation and context, a believer should live his beliefs to the extent that his official functions are not neglected, violated, or impeded. The

---

[20] Acts 5:29

Scripture makes it clear that when presented with opposing agendas, a believer must choose God's law above man's law.

The Philippine Case

The Philippines is among the countries where a believer, public servant or not, can fully practice his faith.

Government personnel are directed to serve along principles parallel with Christian values. Republic Act No. 6713, approved in 1989, otherwise known as "Code of Conduct and Ethical Standards for Public Officials and Employees," does not endorse any religion but it also does not prohibit government people from practicing their religious beliefs. In fact, many of its provisions coincide with biblical principles. For example, Sec. 4 (c) calls for officials and employees to "remain true to the people at all times," "act with justness and sincerity," and refrain from going against "good morals." Item (e) requires officials and employees to extend "prompt, courteous, and adequate service to the public" and to "develop an understanding and appreciation of the socioeconomic conditions prevailing in the country, especially in the depressed rural and urban areas."

In brief, the Code of Conduct prods government officials and employees to serve the public with justice, sincerity, love, humility, kindness, understanding, and sympathy—the same ethics ingrained in the heart of true followers of Christ. Ecclesiastes 12:13-14 reminds:

> *Fear God and keep His commandments, for this is the whole duty of man. For God will bring every deed into judgment, including hidden thing, whether it is good or evil.*

Thus, instead of conflict, compatibility prevails between the Code and Christian precepts. Christian values reinforce and justify a civil servant's loyal observance of the laws.

Love: Basic Ingredient of Service

The Word of God underscores Love as the foundation for service regardless whether one works for the government or private sector, or is self-employed. In 1 Corinthians 13:2-3, it is written:

> *If I have the gift of prophecy and can fathom all mysteries and all knowledge, and if I have the faith that can move mountains, but have not love, I am nothing. If I give all I possess to the poor and surrender my body to the flames, but have not love, I gain nothing.*

To the followers of Christ, God's greatest gift—*love*—is the source and fuel for service. Love is the essence of Jesus' washing the feet of His disciples: the more one serves, the greater becomes his love; the greater his love, the more he finds joy in serving.[21]

With love and fear of God in his heart, a government official will remain faithful to the trust given him and shall perform his mandate with honesty and diligence. Without these two ingredients as spiritual seeds in his spirit, a government employee may belittle, misunderstand, or totally ignore the predicament of those he is supposed to serve. And the God factor remains the basis by which officials should regard each other with fairness, truth, and justice regardless of rank or position. Without God's laws as the foundation for moral values, corruption grows like yeast until it destroys the man, the government, and the society.

Christian Presidents

A number of Heads of State remained faithful to Christian principles even as they performed their official duties. The list includes Philippine leaders President Corazon Aquino and President Fidel V. Ramos, as well as President Jorge Serrano of Guatemala, now retired and currently runs a Christian radio program and charity ministries in Panama.[22] Also, a number of leaders in Africa south of the Sahara remained Christians such as Uganda's President Yoweri Museveni, South African President Jacob Zuma, Kenyan

---

[21] John 13:2-17 teaches the link between love, service, and humility.

[22] I was privileged to have met and spent some time with President Serrano and his wife Magdalena, during my brief visit to Panama in 2005.

President Uhuru Kenyatta, and Zambian President Michael Sata.[23]

In Cabinet meetings during the administration of President Ramos, an ecumenical prayer began each session. As a matter of tradition, Philippine Presidents observe the annual Day of National Prayer with the presence of representatives of other Heads of State. And every President consulted with the Catholic, Muslim, *Iglesia ni Cristo*, Methodist, and Evangelical leaders on social, political, and economic issues.

I believe a correlation exists between prayers and the well-being of the community. For example, during my ambassadorship in Bahrain, the president of the Filipino Community Association, Alex Ginete, included a prayer before each meeting and social activity, and the association was able to pay all its outstanding debts. In that period, a number of community members became recipients of awards granted by the Philippine government and business groups.

Bible Study with Officials

The political system and culture of the Philippines allow unrestricted practice of one's faith, whether Christian, Muslim, or otherwise. During my service in the government, many offices including the Bureau of Customs, Bureau of Internal Revenue, Office of the President, Manila City Hall, Philippine National Police, and the military allowed Bible study for their personnel in government premises.

The Department of Foreign Affairs allocated a Catholic chapel, a prayer room for the Muslims, and a Bible study room for the Protestant Christians. The three religious groups held a morality enhancement and value formation program at the DFA auditorium in line with an executive order, featuring prayers by a Catholic priest, a Muslim imam, and a Protestant pastor.

---

[23] For more information on Christian leaders in Africa, see Terence O. Ranger (Editor), *Evangelical Christianity and Democracy in Africa,* Oxford University Press, 2008.

CHAPTER SEVEN

THE GOD FACTOR

> *Come to me,*
> *all you who are weary and burdened,*
> *and I will give you rest.*
> *Take my yoke upon you and learn from me,*
> *for I am gentle and humble in heart,*
> *and you will find rest for your souls.*
> **Matthew 11:28-29**

Human factor remains the over-riding *raison d'etre* and the central subject requiring sensitivities and care in public service. Although I viewed my functions from the secular legal context, my duties became occasions to express the love and compassion that come from God.

Workers in Distress

At first, I did not realize that some people who came to the embassy needed more than the routine consular, assistance to nationals (ATN), and labor services.

Worker: "I want to kill my wife, then myself."

When Lito (not his real name) came to see me at my office, he appeared distraught and emotionally drained. He later confided why he wanted so much to go home. He sacrificed and sent most of his wages to his wife for the sustenance of their three children. But he found out she was unfaithful and had misspent the money. He felt so hurt and vowed to end all that he had worked for. He wanted to go home and kill her and then himself.

He came for passport renewal and a letter to the Korean Immigration Office. However, after hearing his story, I knew he needed more than consular service. So I read with him Bible passages on love, the value of life, forgiveness, and trust in Jesus Christ. We went on a deep whisper prayer. He later accepted Jesus as his Lord and Savior.

Then the lament and hatred written on his face gave way to an unashamed sob as he suddenly cried in front of me. Shaking his bowed head, he repeatedly said, "I'm sorry, Betty. I love you. I will never hurt you." He then turned to me, still with tears on his eyes, and promised not to kill his wife and himself. I gave him a Bible as he left my office. From what I heard later, Bro. Lito returned home to Pangasinan and reconciled with his wife.

From that day on, as the Consul General, whenever distressed Filipinos came to my office, I listened carefully to their stories and tried to place myself in their situation. In most cases, they needed more than a routine consular service; they needed someone to listen to their problems, understand their situation, and sympathize with them.

The Raped, Blinded, Beaten, and Homeless

Compassionate attitude reflected in friendlier, efficient, and faster embassy services especially in the areas serving the overseas Filipino workers (OFWs).[24] The embassy later initiated measures to more effectively meet the needs of our compatriots.

---

[24] A modern day phenomenon, many in the Third World countries go to developed nations to fill labor requirements in the host economy. Since the 1960's, droves of Filipinos went abroad under labor contract while others traveled as tourists to find work. OFW refers to both contract and undocumented foreign workers. For a detailed study on the trend, see Graziano Batistella and Maruja M.B. Asis (Editors), *Unauthorized Migration in Southeast Asia,* Scalabrini Migration Center, Quezon City, Philippines, 2003.

At the time, more than 30,000 Filipinos were in South Korea. Most of them entered the country as tourists but later became "undocumented foreign workers"[25] after they found employment and overstayed in violation of their immigration status. Their illegal status made them susceptible to labor abuses.

Many undocumented workers came to the embassy after they became victims of rape, physical maltreatment, and unpaid wages. Others came already suffering from industrial accidents with damaged eyes, severed fingers, and crushed foot. Without any insurance coverage, the victims were dismissed from their jobs. Still others showed symptoms of mental breakdown and serious emotional stress. One compatriot was picked up by the police as he walked alone on the freeway, arguing with himself. Another was brought to the embassy by his employer since no one could make him stop laughing at everything and crying uncontrollably. A large number of OFWs were abandoned by their recruiters, thus leaving them without a job and a place to stay.[26]

Embassy Basement: Shelter for Foreign Workers

The embassy opened its doors to accommodate the increasing number of Filipinos with labor and immigration problems.

At the time, the embassy in Seoul did not have a Labor Attaché. The Consular Office handled labor issues in addition to its ATN duties. Consul Jerryl Santos and his team prepared the basement of the embassy to accommodate the Filipino workers who needed shelter. Monetary donations, canned goods, sacks of rice, cooking utensils, a portable stove, and clothing were voluntarily given by the embassy staff, the Filipino community, and the Catholic and Evangelical churches. The American military base at Yongsan

---

[25] Used in official documents, the term refers to those whose immigration status had lapsed but remained abroad to seek employment or other reasons.

[26] In many cases, both recruiting agencies and sponsors at the destination countries, after receiving fees, failed to fulfill their promise of jobs, yet could not provide accommodation for OFWs abroad.

donated more than forty army cots (folding canvas bed), and Lotte Hotel donated fifty sets of blankets and pillows with cases.

The number of workers we accommodated ranged from twenty to a hundred at any one time as some of them received help in going home to the Philippines while others found alternative shelter or employment. Meanwhile, many more workers came to the embassy needing a place to stay. The embassy drew up rules separating a women's section from the men's and prohibiting gambling, drinking, drugs, fighting, stealing, and sexual immorality. The occupants were encouraged to choose from among them a "mayor" while others volunteered as cook, dishwasher, and cleaner to serve on alternate basis. By the time the Labor Attaché set up the Labor Center, the embassy had already served a several thousands of foreign workers.

A few years later, South Korea declared amnesty and introduced laws to extend legal immigration status to foreign workers, thereby granting them protection from accidents and other benefits. But before the introduction of the new laws, Korean Lotte Welfare Foundation, which was founded in August 1994 and headed by former South Korean President Lho Shinyong, extended financial assistance to the victims of accidents and labor injustice. The Christian Korean Global Mission Fellowship, some business establishments, and non-government organizations (NGOs) coordinated with the embassy to identify deserving recipients of their charity projects.

Letters to Immigration

The case of each worker was documented, studied, and reported to Manila even as the embassy recommended to Philippine authorities the filing of legal cases against illegal recruiters and violators of foreign workers' rights.

Meanwhile, the Consular Section wrote letters of appeal to the Korean immigration authorities for the reduction of, or exemption from, penalty of each individual who overstayed. The Korean government responded positively with kindness and understanding. The embassy also requested meetings with the host Ministry of

Foreign Affairs, Labor Ministry, and Police authorities for the protection, lenient treatment, and assistance to the growing number of Filipinos who became victims of unfair labor practices. The Embassy issued to OFWs identification cards; the local police honored it in times of accident, death, and other emergencies. When the Korean government proclaimed amnesty and conducted raids in several factories, we visited the detained workers, prayed with them, and brought clothes and toiletries to those caught unprepared.

Cooperation (not Separation) of Church and State

In response to the request of the workers sheltered at the basement, the embassy opened its doors to religious groups—Catholic, Protestant, Evangelical, and Muslim—that wanted to hold worship service for their respective believers.

Catholic Mass and Bible Study

The Catholic Church, represented by Fr. Ray Sabio from Inchon, and Fr. Eugene Docoy, Fr. Decena and Sis. Mary Anne Terenal from Good Shepherd Church at Chayandong, conducted mass on Sundays at the basement. Evangelical churches, represented by Rev. Pastor Dr. Tereso Casino, Pastor Enrique Supsup, Pastor Samuel Natividad, Pastor Jesse Arce, Pastor Paula Koh, Pastor Tony San Buenaventura, and Pastor Serlina Rufin conducted Bible studies and prayers while they brought Bibles and more provisions for the Filipino workers. No imam came to talk about Islam to the stranded workers.

Consular Service, Prayers, and the Word

I saw the impact of God's words to those who, like Lito, felt disillusioned and overwhelmed with personal problems.

Having experienced the comforting power of God in desperate situations, I shared with them the promises of God as we read from the Bible. In all cases, the worker wished to join me in prayer. In each case, the compatriot expressed relief from sorrow, pain, fear, and anger. Whenever I visited the compatriots in detention facilities to arrange for their release, prayer always preceded successful negotiations. To the hundreds of workers who were rounded up and scheduled for deportation, prayer *en masse* brought a big relief as newly arrived Ambassador Francisco Benedicto and I successfully convinced the police to remove the deportees' handcuffs before they were brought to the airport.

Church, Community, and Embassy Joint Campaign

Common objectives of the embassy, churches, and the Filipino community inspired their joint efforts to address the increasing incidents of murder, gambling, theft, drinking, drug abuse, and immoral cohabitation among the foreign workers. Their series of meetings held at the embassy brought closer camaraderie between our staff personnel and the public as the meetings led to greater coordination for improving the conditions of the workers. Together, the embassy, churches, and community produced the series, *Open Letter to Our Kababayans* (Countrymen), and distributed these to various congregations and worksites. The churches also brought to the attention of the embassy actual cases of abuse on the Filipino workers. And the Filipino Community Association of Korea, whose members were mostly American citizens serving either at Yongsan military base or in nuclear and engineering projects, provided material support as the needs arose.

The framework for embassy-church-community joint efforts was in place and further utilized when Ambassador Benedicto arrived and the Philippine government finally opened its Overseas Labor Office (POLO), attached to the embassy in Seoul. Operated under newly-arrived Labor Attaché Arturo "Jun" Sodusta, POLO had immediately a functioning access to the Filipino foreign workers in South Korea. The embassy-issued identification card for Filipinos in Korea was distributed as rumors of impending war with North Korea spread. The churches and community associations later served as contact centers for reaching and mobilizing the OFWs.

Mother Theresa and More Men of God

Events unfolded pulling me deeper into ministry activities even as I continued to serve as a public servant.

Many years earlier in Bucharest, Eva and I had a rare conversation with world-famous Mother Theresa who was then the guest of Indian top envoy to Romania, H.E. Ambassador Julio Ribeiro, and his wife. Together with my own guests, Philippine Philharmonic Conductor Redentor Romero and Korean concert pianist Miss Minja Shin, we were so much enlightened with the advice of Mother Theresa.

She said, "We should spend more time listening to God and knowing His will rather than rushing to do our own things." Such wisdom served as a guidepost when Eva and I went deeper into the ministry of Jesus Christ. Thus, when I was later made chairman of an evangelical ministers group in Korea, I listened more to the pastors rather than talk. Even as I went on to study the Bible and read additional literature during my free time from the office, I took the opportunity to meditate and pray for God's will and guidance. I spent hours talking on the phone with Rev. Dr. Tereso "Terry" Casino as I listened to his advice on church work, pastoral functions, and the kingdom of God.

As the Lord brought me further in my spiritual journey, He led me to meet and personally learn from various men and women of God who influenced my outlook, attitude, priorities, and plans.

A cousin of mine who I had not seen since my professorial days in Manila exclaimed, "I never expected you'd become like this." Neither did I expect I'd be serving God like this.

CHAPTER EIGHT

OUTREACH TO THE DIASPORA

> *Have I not commanded you?*
> *Be strong and courageous. Do not be terrified,*
> *for the Lord your God will be with you*
> *wherever you go.*
> **Joshua 1:9**

As the Lord sent Joshua and the Israelis to cross the Jordan River on the journey to the Promised Land, He assured them of His commitment and support toward the success of their mission. He strengthened their resolve with the promise of His presence in every step of their way to their divine destination. He told them: *'No one will be able to stand up against you all the days of your life. As I was with Moses, so will I be with you. I will never leave you nor forsake you'* (Joshua 1:5).

The Chief Commander and the Lieutenants

Expressed in our present day language, God was telling them, "I sent you, so I will help you. Be brave. I am by your side." The mighty El Shaddai's message is unshakable. Believers serve as His lieutenants. But as the Commander-in-Chief, it is His battle.

Indeed, as Joshua and the Israelites proceeded in their divine destiny, God caused the Jordan River waters to part, like what He did with the Red Sea to allow Moses and his people to cross on dry ground in their long march to the Promised Land. And the Lord also caused the walls of Jericho to fall and expose the city to its downfall. He guided Joshua to victory over the city of Ai and against the

Amorites, Canaanites, Hittites, Jebusites, and other tribes.[27]

Joshua's successful march into the Promised Land underscores an important principle of the kingdom of God. Divine presence, support, and protection accompany those who are called according to God's purpose. Although the promise was said to Joshua thousands of years ago, God's words reverberate in our time and continue to fulfill His promise. God's promises become real, alive, and relevant today as they were then. One does not have to be a Moses, Abraham, Samson, or Jacob to receive the heritage available in the kingdom of God. One simply obeys and does God's will to receive His promise. God assures His lieutenants:

> *I took you from the ends of the earth,*
> *from its farthest corners I called you.*
> *I said, 'You are my servant';*
> *I have chosen you and have not rejected you.*
> *So do not fear, for I am with you;*
> *do not be dismayed, for I am your God.*
> *I will strengthen you and help you;*
> *I will uphold you with my righteous right hand.*
> (Isaiah 41:9-10)

Husband and Wife Team

Eva had another unusual experience. On our window sill which overlooked the Hangang River and the city, two doves were resting and chirping. Soon their bird talk was drowned by a clear sound coming from an unknown source: "Elijah! Elisha! Elijah! Elisha!" Eva was startled, scared and puzzled. At that time, she did not know these names.

What she experienced prompted me to study closely the Old Testament passages regarding prophets Elijah and Elisha.[28] After consulting with pastors and meditating on relevant passages in the

---

[27] For the fulfillment of God's promise on the conquest of Canaan (part of it now known as Israel), see Joshua 3:9-24.

[28] 1Kings 19:21 and 2Kings 2:15

Bible, we concluded that God meant for husband and wife to move as partners. The husband was to take the leading role of Elijah, and the wife the supporting role of Elisha, in the service to the Lord. And even when pastors uttered words of prophecy, they referred to Eva and me as a team—"two wild horses pulling the same chariot"—that was given a different kind of preparation. A pastor's prophecy declared we were not to envy others whose preparations were less rocky, for we were being bred in line with the task purposed for us by the Lord.

Preaching and Outreach

In a basement of a two-story house at Haebangchon, a humble district of Seoul, during a Sunday service of the Filipino Christian Fellowship (FCF), I first spoke in front of a congregation. I testified on the love, justice, and power of the Lord Jesus Christ. I cited as an example the unexpected and seemingly impossible outcome of the Goliath threat. I thought it was going to be the first and last time I would speak before a church audience. I did not know that my presentation before fifteen people—including my wife, our daughter Myra, and maid seated with factory workers, musicians, and house maids—would be the first step in my journey to serve God in a church ministry.

As *the Consul General*, I wanted to have first-hand knowledge of the life condition of the factory workers. Whenever I could join in an outreach, the host workers announced in advance that the consul general would come with the pastor to give an update on immigration matters and consular services available to undocumented foreign workers.

Being a public servant, I had a series of diplomatic dinners, meetings, and receptions to attend. But I was glad I used my free evenings to go with the pastor in his ministry visits. With him, Eva and I walked the snowy fields and narrow alleys the workers treaded on. We shivered at the bite of winter wind they felt, and smelled the stench of open countryside pit toilet they endured. We were with the workers in their living quarters at the factory, in apartments in the cities, in mud huts in the countryside, and in makeshift shelters on the roof of worksite buildings in isolated fields. But we were also with them when we read passages in the Bible, sang Gospel songs and Filipino folk songs as we partook of the aromatic Filipino dishes they prepared. Through them, we met other Filipinos from nearby factories. We gave tracts containing scriptural passages, donated Bibles to the new attendees, shared the latest immigration news, and updated the workers on developments in the Philippines.

What I saw equipped me with greater insight into the root of the social problems the foreign workers faced. I gained knowledge of their background, aspirations, family obligations, social life, and even gossips circulating among them. Life was lonely, tough, and boring. Their situation was critical because it could lead them to be either assets to their family and motherland, or scourges bringing shame and burden to their name, nation, and host country.

I also saw their situation from the spiritual angle. Under constant pressure, stress, and loneliness, the foreign workers faced temptations of the flesh, money, gambling, drinking, and drugs. Behind the forced half-smile, camaraderie, group singing, and exchange of jokes as hallmarks of "Pinoy"[29] social life, deep in the heart of the foreign workers lurked sadness, anxiety, and spiritual thirst seeking to be quenched. A silent spiritual panic within led some workers to call the churches for regular Bible study at their living quarters or factory.

Jesus' Principle of Leadership

The outreach experience was an eye-opener for me and Eva. By going out of our comfortable warm home in those winter months, we learned more principles of the kingdom. By washing His disciples' feet, Jesus served them; yet, he remained as their teacher and master. (John 13:2-17) His message was this: by serving one another, the bond of love between the teacher and the taught, the leader and the led, as well as among the "servants," grows stronger even to the point of sacrificing one's comfort and *life*. The greater

---

[29] Colloquial for "Filipino."

the sacrifice, the greater love becomes; the greater love is, the greater is the sacrifice one is willing to give. And to this day, millions follow Jesus because of the love He made real by giving His life on the cross.

Preparing a Servant of God

The Lord knows our weaknesses and strengths, and whether we are ready to tackle the task He has for us.

Up to that time, Eva remained behind the scene. Since we became born again, her spiritual life was limited to prayers, reading the Bible and Christian books, and tagging along wherever I went for Bible study. Though she was friendly with everyone, she was generally bashful.

In early November 1994, Eva "heard" the Holy Spirit telling her to testify about the miracles God had done in her family. Being a shy housewife, she was nervous to stand in front of an audience.

The Holy Spirit added, *"If you testify, I will give your family more miracles."* So, Eva volunteered to testify during a Sunday worship service of the FCF. Since it was a small group and she personally knew the listeners as friends, she fearlessly stood in front of the congregation of about forty factory workers, musicians, and housemaids. Eva's testimony went easy. She had complied. Mission accomplished. She thought.

But on the following day, the Holy Spirit told her to testify at the coming anniversary celebration of the FCF. Her performance on the day before was just a rehearsal to prepare her for this bigger event. So, this time, she really had more butterflies in her stomach. When I told her the gathering would be at Capitol Hotel, Itaewon (at the heart of Seoul), with some three hundred people from various churches, the more her stomach turned. The butterflies multiplied as I mentioned that the audience would include special guests including Philippine Ambassador Francisco and Tina Benedicto, the El Salvador Ambassador and his wife, and Philippine Congressman and Mrs. Simeon Valdez.

"Go to the Mission House; they are now preparing the program. Tell the senior pastor that you are giving a testimony," added the Holy Spirit. With cold feet and sweaty hands, she had to obey. When we got to the FCF mission house, the founding pastor, Rev. "Solomon" Ocampo, was indeed finalizing the program. Eva was scheduled to speak.

At the anniversary, she spoke with cautioned confidence. She told about her brother, Dr. Munding, who had a serious heart problem, but after some prayers, he no longer needed operation and his illness became controllable with medication. She also related about her niece, Gwen, who failed twice the nursing board exam although she was class valedictorian in Indiana; but after some prayers, she passed it with flying colors. As Eva spoke, I was nervous; but she talked without notes. She became a new Eva.

Angelic Visitation?

In the summer of 1994, my housing contract was to end and I faced the problem of having to look for an affordable housing in one of the most expensive cities in the world. For several months, I looked at several places, but even small apartments required more than my living quarters allowance. In every step, I asked God for guidance, but still I have not found a place. Under pressure to move out soon, and in the absence of a better option, I decided to take a place much too small although it costs more than my housing allowance.

One morning, a few hours before I was to make a deposit for the small apartment, I received a phone call at the office. The caller said: "You do not know me and I have not met you, but someone told me that you are looking for a place to rent." I almost put down the phone.

But he added: "I know how much is your housing allowance, and I know that there are only three of you – yourself, your wife, and your maid. And your daughter is studying in the US and visits you now and then. Why don't you take a look at my place?"

How did he know? I wondered. I have not told anyone about my budget and about my family, yet he mentioned the exact amount of my monthly living quarters allowance. And he was correct about our daughter.

Then he explained, "Someone who came to my lab told me." That someone was not from the embassy. He was a Korean, the caller clarified.

But how was it possible? How would a Korean know?

When I asked again, he said: "Strange, but when I called his number, I could not connect. I called several times, but it seems the phone number never existed."

Never existed! That boggled my mind. I almost gave up hoping for God's help when I did not see His provision. Frustration was completely reversed as help came through an untraceable source. Yet, the answer to my family's need simply dropped on my lap.

Had I been impatient and knocking on the wrong door? I thought He did not hear me, but all the time He knew my needs. The apartment was the perfect answer. It was affordable, usable for entertaining by a diplomat of my rank, and within walking distance from the embassy. And the landlord allowed us to move in without advance deposit.

In all things God works for the good of those who love Him, who are called according to His purpose (Romans 8:28). The preceding verse echoed in my thoughts. For those He called, He protects, provides for their needs, and guides them not only to fulfill His plan but for them to have sufficiency.

To me, there was no other explanation except a divine intervention. When all my efforts failed, God moved in such a way that there could be no other conclusion: He sent an angel to touch the new landlord.

God's Assurance of Support

I believe His move was meant to assure Eva and me to proceed with confidence as He positioned us to go deeper into the ministry. He intervened for several reasons:

First, to demonstrate His presence even if we think He does not hear us;

Second, to assure us He is aware of our personal problems and cares about our predicament; and

Third, to assure that, as we take action in obedience of His will, He can take direct action to fill the gap in matters beyond our ability to achieve or endure.

The aforesaid experiences taught us another principle on faith and God's faithfulness. We must have faith before we see His ways; but the more we see His ways, the greater becomes our faith.

And we saw more of His ways when He brought us to Masuk.

> *"Come, follow me," Jesus said,*
> *"and I will make you fishers of men."*
> *At once they left their nets*
> *and followed him.*
> **Mark 1:17-18**

CHAPTER NINE

INTO THE DEEP WATER – MASUK

> *When he had finished speaking, he said to Simon, "Put out into the deep water, and let down the nets for a catch." Simon answered, "Master, we've worked hard all night and haven't caught anything. But because you say so, I will let down the nets." When they had done so, they caught such a large number of fish that their nets began to break.*
> **Luke 5:4-6**

A Place to Hide

Masuk was about two to three hours from Seoul by bus and more than an hour drive by car halfway to the border with communist North Korea. Located some distance from the town proper were furniture factories straddled on a cluster of hills in a mountain range, hidden from the highway by an elevated terrain. The factories were located far from bus and train stops but accessible by private vehicles through a narrow winding road.

Although foreign workers stayed in Masuk because of available jobs, a number of them chose to remain because they had reason to hide. The terrain and vegetation surrounding it provided immediate cover to those evading immigration arrests. But some worked there to hide from their spouses, creditors, gossips, or police as some reportedly have been accused of murder, drug pushing, embezzlement, and identity theft.

A Call from the Deep

The FCF and other evangelical churches had no Bible study in Masuk although they held several studies elsewhere. So, in response to a call from a worker expressing difficulty in going to church, Eva and I decided to open a Bible study in Masuk in the summer of 1994. From the start, we faced our own River Jordan obstructing our goal of bringing the Gospel to the workers.

A Korean Catholic priest helped us in gathering the workers in his church's social hall. However, in response to my announcement that we would start a Bible study in Masuk, some workers questioned the competence of pastors and the sanity of born again people. Thus, I explained that it is Jesus Christ that is the focus of the study regardless of one's religion; the persons leading and attending the study are not the issue. Then other workers questioned my motive as an "army general" as they suspected I was a military spy in search of people hiding from the law. This mistake was also corrected. As consul *general*, I explained, my purpose was to help them in their immigration and consular issues, in addition to bringing the Gospel to those who want to come closer to God. Still, some workers did not want to miss their regular Saturday night beer sessions, and they made fun of anyone wanting to attend the Bible study.

Bible Study Begins

The Lord orchestrated every step of our way to Masuk. In the first meeting, four workers attended. But after a few sessions, more workers joined. We met every Saturday night at the factory where Rosie Abalos and Gina Loyola worked, with the permission of their manager. Eva led the praise singing supported by our private staff Lita Mina, while Cerich Ponteres (Music major graduate from University of Santo Tomas, Manila) accompanied us on his keyboard. I shared the Gospel. Bert Lozano, an accomplished guitarist and a musician by trade, later joined us. We gave Tagalog (official Filipino language) translation of the Holy Bible as fellowship with the workers lasted until dawn. We drove back to

Seoul at four in the morning. Though untrained neophytes, we moved with enthusiasm to share the love of Jesus.

Apparently inspired by the Holy Spirit, a number of the workers took the extra mile to welcome the other attendees. On their own initiative, Sis. Rosie, Sis. Gina, Sis. Precy, Sis. Ofie, Sis. Mary, and Sis. Daniela regularly prepared Filipino dishes. After the Bible study, the attendees scooped food into their paper plates and looked for a comfortable spot anywhere in the furniture worksite to sit and enjoy a late dinner. While they were having their meal, I briefed them on immigration and consular matters. The workers spent the rest of the evening strumming the guitar and singing Gospel songs. Their favorite melody, *Why Me Lord,* a song of reconciliation with God written by Kris Kristofferson, later became the signature song of the Masuk group.

After a few weeks, the number of attendees grew to thirty workers, sometimes to eighty during special occasions such as birthdays. Some workers even offered to host the Bible study either in their dormitory, work site, or apartment, and so we held the meetings in different places. Even in those cold winter nights, many walked long distances over piles of snow and slippery pathways on hilly terrain to get to us. At the worksite, we huddled around the empty metal drum with burning pieces of wood as heater. They came to get the latest on consular and immigration news. Some came because their friends were with us, while others came for the home-cooked Filipino food. A few came to avoid beer drinking and gambling sessions. To a number of them, the study provided a way out of illegal, expensive, and immoral routines. But the Lord had plans for each of the foreign workers who came to hear the word of God.

Through the sessions, I noticed a consistent pattern. Without any training on church work, I was not eloquent and my explanation of the Scriptures was neither clear nor uplifting. But somehow, the workers received the message of the Good News with clarity and impact greater than what my simple explanation could inspire. Many of the workers were hungry for spiritual food, but the Holy Spirit prepared their hearts so that by the time they heard the word, their soul became fertile soil ready to receive and nourish the spiritual seed.

I learned that when we obey God and share His word, the message carries power and creates an impact on the audience. His word does not return void, and its power does not come from our presentation. In Isaiah 55:10-11, the Lord says:

> *As the rain and the snow come down from heaven, and do not return to it without watering the earth and making it bud and flourish ... so is my word that goes out from my mouth: It will not return to me empty, but will accomplish what I desire and achieve the purpose for which I sent it.*

The kingdom principle is explained in apostle Paul's words: *I planted the seed, Apollos watered it, but God made it grow. So neither he who plants nor he who waters is anything, but only God who makes things grow* (1Corinthians 3:6-7).

From Broken Dreams to Fresh Hopes

To many of the workers, the Bible study was a first-time experience. Most of them had never read nor owned a Bible before. But the Bible study changed their lives. The following stories are samples of real-life tales of painful childhood, broken dreams, and the birth of fresh hopes:

1. Manong Ben "lived by the sword." Coming from a tenant farmer family and abandoned by his wife, he was left to raise his daughter alone. He was among the hired goons of a political warlord in the Ilocos region where politics in the 1980's was the bloodiest in the country. A massacre blamed on the *saka-saka* (barefooted) gang led to his imprisonment. In jail, he received Jesus Christ, and the unexpected happened. Somehow, after ten years in detention, he and the others accused were released. Years later, he became a factory worker in Korea. In Masuk, he was responsible in bringing a number of workers to the Bible study. He found a worthy reason for life.

2. Bro. Mac grew up bitter about life. He hated his mother for forcing his hand into a pot of boiling water. His father died when he and his sister were very young. His mother, unable to face the hurt and responsibilities, turned to alcohol. He then had to drop from school after only third grade as he and his sister were given to work for a family. He could not forgive his mother for taking all the wages he and his sister earned only to spend the money on beer, cigarettes, and gambling. In Masuk, he used to escape through a window to avoid our Bible study so he could join his friends in drinking sessions. But God touched his heart. One Saturday night, he skipped the "happy hour" drinking session, initiated arranging the chairs for the study, and joined us in the session. After he accepted Jesus Christ, he became a completely new person. He gave up drinking and forgave his mother. When he returned to the Philippines, he and his mother had a loving, emotional reconciliation.
3. Sis. Precy longed for her father's love. Her father was always away, and before she could receive the wristwatch he promised her, he failed to come home. Even as an adult, she collected wristwatches as if each last piece could have been the present from her father. In the Lord Almighty, she found the Father who is always present, available, caring, and loving. She and her partner, Tony, became eager workers in preparing and serving food for the attendees.
4. Bro. Rodel belittled the born again Christians. He laughed and made fun at pastors and Bible study the first time we met the workers in Masuk. His wife Josie had been praying for years for him to be saved. One Saturday night, he accompanied his wife to our Bible study at Sis. Rosie's place. He did not come in the study area but stayed at the hallway. While we were singing praise songs, the Holy Spirit touched him. He started crying without knowing why. Then he came in and joined us. I prayed over him as he accepted Jesus Christ as his Lord and Savior. Bro. Rodel became a new person; even when provoked at work, he turned the other cheek. He gave up drinking and became a more loving husband. He and Josie were rewarded with a baby after many years of trying to conceive. And he later

brought more workers to join us and served as president of the congregation when the Bible study grew into a church.
5. Bro. Romel, Bro. Philip, Bro. Ramir, Bro. James, and Bro. Daniel were close friends from Indang, Cavite. Having attended Bible study before they came to Korea, they testified that the study sessions at Masuk redirected them to the Word of God and saved them from being pulled by other workers into drinking, gambling, and fights. They encouraged many others to attend the study.
6. Any doubt as to certain workers' sexual orientation was apparently dispelled as some of them rediscovered their true gender through the Bible studies. As the consul general, I officiated marriage between a confirmed gay male (from another church) and a woman. He later fathered children and lived happily with a wonderful wife.

Workers and Prayers

A great number of workers claimed that prayers helped them overcome the stress, hurt, and shame caused by their masters and co-workers. Some said they developed the practice of praying for their families back home, and their prayers led to some remarkable blessings. Many claimed that praying for protection saved them from the immigration agents and police whenever the authorities conducted surprise raids on the factories. Sis. Rosie told stories of workers quickly rushing to the hills to hide, but the pursuing police and immigration agents did not see them though they were only a meter away behind tall grass. Perhaps, the pursuers were touched with compassion and they pretended not to see them. In either case, their escape from arrest was a blessing.

Bible Study Becomes a Church

The Bible study grew so large by winter 1994 even though the sessions were held around a metal drum filled with burning wood, its black smoke making our nostrils black. In January 1995, a Korean prayer mountain in nearby Sudong village offered its place for the Bible study group to start regular Sunday worship service. It was headed by its president Senior Pastor Rev. Lee Tae Hee and managed by Pastor Chun Young-bum, a graduate from the Philippine Baptist Theological Seminary (PBTS) in Baguio. The Sudong Prayer Mountain allowed our group the free use of the chapel, musical instruments, canteen, and rooms, and they offered free pick up of workers to and from the church. After collective prayers and meetings with pastors of FCF in Seoul, the Bible study group agreed to form itself into an FCF branch church.

On the morning of 25 February, the panoramic landscape of hills and trees at Sudong Prayer Mountain was still covered with snow. Several chartered buses arrived at the scenic site bringing about a thousand foreign workers to attend the inauguration of the Filipino Christian Fellowship-Masuk. Our special guests were Philippine Senator Blas Ople and Ambassador Francisco Benedicto. During the inauguration program, before an audience of OFWs, Korean believers, and expatriate workers of various nationalities, Sen. Ople promised the foreign workers' churches in Korea will be recognized by the Philippine Senate as a voice of Filipino overseas workers.

When the Masuk Bible study became a church, I served as its pastor. About a month later, as a result of prayers and meetings, the Masuk congregation decided to separate from the FCF-Seoul church of Manila-based Pastor Solomon Ocampo.[30] We also changed our church's name to Filipino Evangelical Christian Fellowship (FECF-Masuk) to distinguish it from FCF-Seoul.

Before my posting in Seoul ended in July 1996, I asked the help of Pastor Jaren Lapasaran (Jesus Our Hope, Cubao, Quezon City); he sent Pastor Paul Pambid to take charge of the church. A year later, Pastor Charlie Pablo from Jesus Our Life Ministry of Bishop Fred Magbanua, served as the next pastor for the FECF-Masuk.

---

[30] Divergent views on "spiritual covering" led to the drift. The mother church claimed it provides spiritual protection over FCF-Masuk, while the Masuk church claimed it receives protection directly from the Holy Spirit.

EMFK

Recognizing the widespread spiritual hunger of thousands of foreign workers in South Korea, the evangelical pastors and I held a series of meetings and formed the Evangelical Ministers Fellowship in Korea (EMFK). An association of pastors and elders, EMFK aimed to reach foreign workers regardless of country of origin. I was elected Chairman and Rev. Dr. Pastor Tereso Casino of Touch International Christian Church as Vice-Chairman. EMFK was inaugurated in October of 1994.[31]

A number of Korean churches with foreign workers in their congregation joined the EMFK, including the Yoido Full Gospel Church of Rev. Pastor Paul (David) Yonggi Cho. EMFK received the advice of Dr. Ho-Jin Jun of Asian Christian Theological School and Rev. Yung-Joon Kim of Somang Presbyterian Church, and the support of Lotte Welfare Foundation and the Global Mission Fellowship of Korea. EMFK published its periodical, *Vision*.

EMFK-organized programs, such as Christmas celebrations, catered to foreign workers from the Philippines, Indonesia, Nigeria, Ghana, Nepal, Burma, and People's Republic of China. Korean companies, Christian ministries, charity, and some NGOs donated unused wardrobes and gifts to the foreign workers in these programs. The organization linked the Filipino evangelical ministries with the Korean body of Christ. EMFK also served as a forum for the foreign workers for mutual assistance on immigration movements, job opportunities, and financial aid in cases of hospitalization, accidents, and death. It became an active partner of the embassy in serving the Filipino foreign workers.

---

[31] The other founding members who headed the various committees were Pastor Sammy Natividad and Pastor Jesse Arce of Soebuk Foreigners Church, Pastor Enrique Supsup of Philippine Body of Christ Church, Pastor Tony San Buenaventura and Pastor Rey Castro of the FCF, Sis. Serlina Rufin of Freedom in Christ Church, Pastor Paula Koh of Grace Full Gospel Church, and Pastor Helen Byum representing Rev. Paul (David) Yonggi Cho of Yoido Full Gospel Church.

PART TWO

FAITH AND GOD'S SOVEREIGNTY

And what more shall I say?
I do not have time to tell about Gideon, Barak, Samson,
Jephthah, David, Samuel and the prophets,
who through faith conquered kingdoms,
administered justice, and gained what was promised;
who shut mouths of lions, quenched the fury of the flames, and
escape the edge of the sword;
whose weakness was turned to strength;
and who became powerful in battle
and routed foreign armies.

Hebrews 11:32-34

CHAPTER TEN

UNIFICATION CHURCH CHALLENGE

> *Then Saul, who was also called Paul, filled with the Holy Spirit, looked straight at Elymas and said: 'You are a child of the devil and an enemy of everything that is right! You are full of all kinds of deceit and trickery. Will you never stop perverting the right ways of the Lord? Now the hand of the Lord is against you. You are going to be blind, and for a time you will be unable to see the light of the sun.'*
> Acts 13:9-11

A sinister cloud cast a dark shadow as events led to an ominous challenge threatening my life, the safety of my family and the embassy, and placed in jeopardy hundreds of my compatriots.

Little Signs of a Big Problem

In Manila, the Unification Church (official name Holy Spirit Association for the Unification of World Christianity)[32] held a mass wedding ceremony at the Philippine International Conference Center (PICC).

---

[32] The Unification Church remained a controversial entity primarily because of its doctrines, emphasis on business, and mass wedding program. See *Unification Church: Christian or Cult?*
www.rapidnet.com/~jbeard/bdm/cults/unificat.html

Events moved fast after the mass wedding as the "brides" were enplaned to consummate their "marriage" in Korea. An earlier article, "My Journey as Christian Ambassador," describes the fate of the women:

> "Several hundred Filipinas were 'wed' to Korean men whom they were seeing for the first time, and in some cases the 'groom' was not even present. Shortly thereafter, about 280 Filipina 'brides' were boarded on the plane bound for Seoul where they were later brought to a Unification reception center. They were then brought to various Unification churches for 'training' before they were distributed to their respective 'husbands.'"[33]

Two Tell-Tale Signs

Two seemingly unrelated events in summer 1995 later joined and revealed a developing major social storm.

I received a call from the Department of Foreign Affairs, Manila, requiring me to check on the background of a church sponsoring the travel of about 300 applicants for passport. I made research from open sources and consulted with Korean pastors regarding the Unification Church. Because of the Church's controversial background, I advised the Foreign Office to exercise "extreme caution." Based on open sources on the mass wedding, Chief Commissioner for Immigration Hon. Leandro Verceles decided to disallow the departure of 286 Filipina "brides."[34]

Meanwhile, one of the "brides" who was recently brought to Korea had been calling the embassy claiming she was being treated

---

[33] See Rodolfo I. Dumapias, "My Journey as Christian Ambassador," in *Scattered: The Filipino Global Presence,* edited by Luis J. Pantoja, Sadiri Joy Tira, and Enoch Wan, (Manila, Philippines: Life Change Publishing) 2004, p. 320.

[34] Continuing controversial opinions on the Unification's doctrines and practices are reflected in a recent response to Wikipedia entry on the Unification Church. The response, entered in March 2015, says, "The neutrality of this article is disputed," in en.wikipedia.org/wiki/unification_church, accessed April 01, 2015.

like a slave although she was supposed to be a "wife." She was made to do farm work, feed the cattle and clean up the den of dung, care for the elderly, and work all house chores, but she was denied the use of the phone and was not given any money for emergency. She could not communicate with anyone, not even her "husband" who could not speak English. So she asked to be rescued from the "Moonies."[35]

Some details of the case are herewith described for the purpose of acknowledging the presence and care of God in delicate and sensitive moments in a person's life.

The Escape

The caller "bride" did not know where she was. She could not speak nor read Korean. She could only describe the large billboard along a nearby road and railroad tracks. When the report reached my desk, I took direct charge of the case.

By asking her to read aloud the full number of the phone she was calling from (no caller ID service yet at that time), the embassy determined her whereabouts by her area code. Working within the EMFK network, I received help in making arrangement with a Korean pastor in that village for her escape. Then, in our next phone conversation, I instructed her to wear a boy's clothing and hat, stand under the large billboard by the railroad tracks at a specified time, and wait for a white Toyota driven by a pastor who would call her by the name I was to give her. I told her to use a new identity – "Aida Santos, a run-away housemaid."

Knowing her situation, I could not help but be impressed with the courage of Aida Santos. The following morning, after her

---

[35] The term "Moonies," derived from the church founder's name Sun Myung Moon, was coined by Western media few decades ago and was used by Church members themselves. Recently, however, it was considered derogatory by the Church and discouraged its usage. It is used here solely for brevity.

"husband" left for work, she rapidly finished her house chores and serviced her "mother-in-law." Then she put on pants, a long sleeve shirt with collar, and a cap, and quietly slipped out of the house. She walked a distance past the store where she had made phone calls to the embassy until she reached the large billboard by the railroad tracks. She must have feared all this time that her Korean "husband" might be coming after her any minute soon. But she managed to maintain her presence of mind as she waited in what seemed an eternity for the white Toyota to appear down the road.

The pastor had in fact parked a distance from the billboard, and when she showed up, he moved. She was quickly taken away and was directly brought to the house of the pastor. In the afternoon, I received a call from my EMFK contact friend that "the bird has flown." I knew what she meant. That evening, after dessert in a sit-down dinner at the Indonesian embassy, I called the house of the village pastor and managed to talk with Aida. The village pastor and his family are nice people, she said, but she recognized a motorcycle that came around in the afternoon belonging to a friend of her "husband." She asked to be taken out from there, fearing she might be discovered soon.

On the following day, I sent two embassy employees (Bro. Rey Castro and Labor Officer Des Dicang) on the three-hour drive to fetch her and bring her to the Labor Refugee Center not far from the embassy. In fact, the same motorcycle (identified by its license plate) was sighted few days later near the Labor center, and I had to move Aida again. From winter to spring, my family and I transferred her from one safe house to another each time other workers or Korean visitors asked details of her background, or when suspicious vehicles were nearby.

One night, Aida noticed a car that remained parked the whole day near her hiding place. Even after we quietly picked her up and had her lie low at the back seat, the car was suddenly behind us. Everywhere I turned, the same car with one headlight at high-beam followed us. So, once I gained some distance, I turned off our headlights, quickly entered a small dark street, parked between cars, and watched the other car drive pass us. After a while, we drove again, but the one-high-beam headlight car was again behind us. I immediately drove into a police station, quickly got out of the car, called the attention of an officer, and pointed toward the one-high-beam headlight car which was idling by the gate.

Whoever he was, he must have watched my actions and concluded I was reporting him to the police. He must have panicked; immediately, he drove away fast. He did not know I was just asking the police for a simple direction to a nearby restaurant.

Who is Aida Santos?

Although her escape and real identity were immediately known to the Unification leaders, the other "brides" did not know who Aida Santos was. Through the phone, she learned from the "brides" Unification moves to look for her. Afraid for her safety, Aida called some politicians and the Philippine media about her plight.

The embassy had also received phone calls from two other Filipino "brides" who wanted to escape. They could not tell us where they were and said they could not use the phone at their home. Their plea for help was seconded by a letter we received from their parents in the Philippines requesting assistance for their escape and return home. Similar to Aida Santos, they also claimed they were being detained against their will. They said there was another Filipina who wanted to leave. I assured them we will help and promised to instruct them of the details of their escape in their next phone call. But they failed to call back.

In Primetime News

Meanwhile, in the Philippines, stories alleging Unification links with some top ranking government officials including military generals and the police were creating media sensation. My article describes what happened next:

"Stories about Aida Santos, 'an escapee from the

Unification,' hit the front page of Philippine newspapers as well as the primetime news on television and radio...The media learned that I knew her whereabouts, so I received long-distance calls from newscaster Noli de Castro (host of *Magandang Gabi, Bayan* who was later elected Vice President of the Philippines) and other broadcasters from Manila as they interviewed me live on the phone...Pressure was building up in the media for in-depth investigation on the activities of the Unification Church in the Philippines. Meanwhile, in Korea, the Unification was becoming restive and defensive to the news reports that the Filipino 'brides' were being treated as slaves and prostitutes."[36]

A New Ambassador Arrives

In January 1996, Brig. General (ret.) Ernesto Gidaya arrived in Seoul to assume his post as the new Philippine Ambassador to South Korea. He was formerly the Undersecretary of National Defense and the Philippine Ambassador to Israel. I felt honored to serve as his No. 2 as I turned over to him the responsibilities of Head of Mission. I briefed him on the Aida Santos case. He seemed to know about the case.

"Do you know where she is?" the general asked.

"I am in contact with her," I replied to convey I knew where she was but she wanted I should be the only line of communication as she was in hiding. I did not want to betray her trust.

"I'd like to see her," he said.

"I'll tell her," I answered, confident that I could bring her to meet him perhaps somewhere but not at the embassy where others could see her.

But when I called and told her of the general, she refused to see him. I was surprised. She explained that he had been seen at the Philippine campus of the Unification in Quezon City, and that his

---

[36] Op.cit., Dumapias, p.321

visit was the talk among the Filipina Moonies.

I was placed in a dilemma, either to please my new ambassador or to honor Aida's plea for her safety. It was not to disrespect my superior, but I decided to stand by her wish and keep my promise not to expose her whereabouts. I was hoping his request for me to present the person of Aida was just a passing curiosity.

But I was wrong. The general insisted to see her and questioned why I could not bring her to him. So, I had to tell him the truth.

"She is afraid of you, sir," I said hesitatingly.

Then, about a week after his assumption as ambassador, a high-ranking official of the Unification Church came as the first visitor to make courtesy call on the general. I was briefly introduced to the guest at the Ambassador's office during which the guest expressed serious concern on how the Philippine media played up the issue. I told him the media had their own sources.

Conflicting Views at the Embassy

Conflicting viewpoints between the general and I regarding Aida Santos became obvious. He took me out from the Unification case and denied me access to the Communications Room. He ordered the relocation of a fax machine out from my office. And he aborted the escape of the two other Filipinas; he summoned them to the embassy, talked with them, and then reported back to the Home Office that the girls no longer wanted to escape. I learned later that other Filipinas who may have planned to leave no longer wanted to ask the embassy for help.

The internal embassy situation, however, did not stop me from requiring the Unification-sponsored "brides" for personal interview and counseling, and to inform them of the legal requirements for marriage with non-Filipinos abroad. I met personally the "brides" and directly heard their stories, and I knew many of them had second thoughts about their "marriage".

To the general, the mass wedding program of the Unification Church gave opportunity for our local girls to go abroad and send money to their families back home. But to me, the mass wedding was a lie: two complete strangers, with different languages, customs and cultures, and seeing each other for the first time—marriage between them would be a farce. In my view, the Filipina would only end up as a slave, or a housemaid without the standard wages. In her predicament, she would not be able to send anything to her family back home.

Nonetheless, the general and I maintained our respect for each other. Eva and I specially admired Mrs. Gidaya for her grace, friendliness, and sweet smile.

Wealthy and Influential "Cult"?

While the media in the Philippines revealed the differences between mainstream Christian beliefs and the Unification Church's theology and practices, I also made further research on the subject.

I read that the church was listed as a "cult." It became a multi-million dollar business organization dealing with products ranging from weapons, munitions, to ginseng. The Unification gained great influence with politicians, police, military and the media. It maintained operation in several countries, especially in the Third World. Although its leader, Rev. Sun Myung Moon, served in prison in the U.S. for tax evasion, the Unification Church remained a powerful, wealthy, and well-connected organization. It owned the Washington Times, a daily publication in the U.S. capital, and maintained newspaper and radio stations in some Asian and Latin American countries.[37] *How can anyone stand against it?* I quietly wondered.

Hired Assassins?

Meanwhile, Aida learned from the Filipina "brides" that Unification hired assassins from Colombia, South America. A week

---

[37] See en.wikipedia.org/wiki/The_Washington_Times. Accessed April 1, 2015.

later, in Soebok Foreigners Church where I was invited to speak, two Latinos suddenly showed up. They were accompanied by a Korean friend of the host church, and were asking for the whereabouts of Dumapias. Although I welcomed them into the house of God, I believe the Holy Spirit urged me to take precautions. Immediately, I thought it was strange that they claimed to be foreign workers; I knew that Latinos go to US, not Korea, for work. And while I met and spoke with them, Aida was hiding.

Later, while the visitors were being served lunch, Pastor Samuel Natividad looked for us, then whispered to me hurriedly: "Sir, *iba na ito* (this is already something else). The two were seen in the bathroom with handguns and they were talking softly about Aida Santos."

My family and I quickly but quietly picked up some of Aida's belongings, rushed her into the car, and drove away to look for a new safe house.

Moonies Demonstrate Before the Embassy

My article describes the next events:

> "But a direct threat to my life came during a violent demonstration staged by the Unification at the Philippine Embassy. In March, more than 300 Unification gathered at the parking lot of the embassy, beating drums and shouting, and carrying placards with slogans such as 'Dumapias Go Home' and 'Verceles and Dumapias, We are Not Prostitutes.' The demonstrators broke the glass front door of the embassy and a glass window, beat up our Korean janitor when they entered the lobby, and ran after the women employees up to the second and third floors."[38]

At the height of the demonstration, apparently unaffected by the continuing noise of beating drums and shouts of the Moonies in front of the embassy, Ambassador Gidaya allowed the leaders to

---

[38] Op.cit., Dumapias, p.322

come up for a frank exchange of views. He invited them to the Conference Room just after the demonstrators damaged some properties of our embassy, forcibly entered an "extra-territorial" building, disrupted the embassy's official functions, and violated the courtesy that was due to representatives of a friendly sovereign state by threatening their safety without cause.

"We Will Kill You"

> "It was during this tense moment that the leader of the demonstration, a young Korean man in red jacket, made his threat. In front of the Ambassador, the Consul, the Military Attache, and the interpreter, he said: 'Dumapias, don't ever think that your life and that of your family is safe in Korea.'
>
> "I told him: 'Don't threaten me while you are at the embassy. If anything happens to my family or anyone in the embassy, I will hold you responsible!'"[39]

After the demonstration, we received anonymous phone calls at my home in the evening saying, "We will kill you."

Diplomatic Protest

The Philippine Government immediately sent a Diplomatic Protest in the form of a *note verbale* to the Korean Embassy in Manila. Simultaneously, my government instructed the Philippine Embassy in Seoul to file an identical *note verbale* to the host Ministry of Foreign Affairs. Almost immediately after the demonstration, the Korean police authorities posted ten fully armed officers to secure my apartment building. Gen. Gidaya did not accept any police protection saying he was safe.

The CNN correspondent in Seoul called me up for an interview. I declined because by talking about the case before the whole world, I might unintentionally hint a rift existed between me and the

---

[39] Ibid.

general. Besides, the more I revealed what I knew to the public, the more I would expose Aida Santos to greater risks. Consequently, CNN used the Manila cable TV news and ran these in its broadcast of world events.

More Unification Demonstrations

The Unification held a second demonstration a week later, but the riot troops prevented the Moonies from coming close to the embassy. Thereafter, the police deployed more forces to put an end to the Moonies efforts.

> "On the third demonstration, eight busloads of anti-riot forces arrived. This time, the leaders, including the young man in red jacket, were chased, surrounded, handcuffed, and boarded on the police wagon. I learned later from reliable sources that the demonstrations aimed to take me out from Seoul so that the plan to bring in more Filipino 'brides' could proceed without hindrance."[40]

Secret Flight of Aida Santos

After the demonstrations, the Philippine government sent a team to Korea composed of NBI (National Bureau of Investigation) Head Agent Mamerto Espartero, Immigration intelligence officer Epifanio Lambino, Jr., and POEA (Philippine Overseas Employment Administration) lawyer Virginia Galvez. The team came with TV newscaster, Julius Babao, and a cameraman from ABS-CBN.

Hesitant at first to appear before the team, Aida finally agreed to see them. So, Eva and I brought her to their hotel late in the night, skipped courtesy visitor phone call, by-passed the front desk, and directly went and knocked at the door of Agent Espartero. When he opened the door in his pajamas, Aida Santos was suddenly before him. After she met the rest of the team, we all agreed on how to

---

[40] Ibid.

bring her back safely to the Philippines.

On the following day, the team spent a sleepless night in my apartment interviewing Aida, giving her advice on her legal rights, and waiting until she could finish writing her affidavit. On the next day, with the help of a Korean police inspector, we secretly boarded her with the team for her flight home. Finally in Manila, her story filled the primetime news of nationwide TV and radio broadcasts, and the headline and front pages of newspapers.

A day later, a second team from Manila, this time from the Department of Foreign Affairs led by Undersecretary Leonides Caday, came to Seoul. They invited the other Filipina "brides" to the embassy and took their statements. The report of this team significantly helped shape the litigation against the Unification Church in violation of mail order bride laws.

Amb. Gidaya and I were summoned to Manila to testify before a joint congressional committee hearing, "in aid of legislation," at the *Batasang Pambansa* (National Assembly), the lower house of the Philippine Congress.

At the House of Representatives

In Manila, two motorcycle police outriders and a car provided by the Office of Intelligence of the Department of Foreign Affairs maneuvered their way through the heavy EDSA traffic and brought Eva and me to *Batasang Pambansa* in Quezon City.

Two opposing groups were already by the main entrance of the National Assembly Building. On one side were placards-carrying Filipino Moonies, shouting and waving their fists. On the other side were born again prayer warriors under Bishop Leo Alconga, also with placards, but they were giving us words of encouragement. Drowned by the shouts and boos from the Moonies and words of support and applause from the prayer warriors, two policemen escorted us as we walked between the two groups and entered the halls of Congress.

The session went on for the whole day, and I revealed all I knew to the legislators. The congressmen—about eight to twelve of them at any one time including my town mate Hon. Ranjit Ramos Shahani—were seated behind three long conference tables across us and by our left and right. Their questions were incisive, intelligent, and direct. Amb. Gidaya, who was seated by the same long table with Undersecretary Caday, Ambassador Susan Castrence, and me, was also thorough, sincere, honest, and direct in his answers to the congressmen. At one time, Gen. Gidaya and I were brought to a private room, "en camara," as some confidential matters were discussed without the presence of the public and the media.

Unification Operations Suspended

About a month later, I assisted four members of Congress led by Congressman Roquito Ablan, Jr. of La Union who came to Seoul for further enquiry into the Unification case. They interviewed a number of Filipino workers and conducted in-depth enquiry regarding other "brides" who wanted to escape.

A few more weeks later, based on gathered evidence, a case was filed against the Unification Church for violation of mail order bride law and other counts. Their operation in the country was suspended.

Aida Santos and her children were placed under witness protection program of the National Bureau of Investigation.

CHAPTER ELEVEN

GOD'S CONTINUING PROTECTION

> *'Because he loves me,' says the Lord, 'I will rescue him; I will protect him, for he acknowledges my name. He will call upon me, and I will answer him; I will be with him in trouble, I will deliver him and honor him.'*
> **Psalm 91:14-15**

The Moonies: Blinded and Made Deaf?

At the start of the first demonstration, I came back from lunch and walked through the middle of the shouting and drum-beating Moonies to get to the embassy building. The language on their placards could enrage the reader against "Dumapias" and "Verceles." I came face-to-face with their leaders and the Filipinas whom I have interviewed days before. It was strange; they looked at me, but did not seem to recognize me.

Again, after the demonstrators broke into the embassy, their leader—the young man in red jacket—ran to the second floor shouting, "Where is Dumapias! Where is Dumapias?"

I blocked his path and shouted back, "I am Dumapias!" as I pointed my right thumb to my chest. But he turned around and went after the female staff and employees running to the third floor, as if he did not hear or see me. And on his way down, he passed me as if I was not there.

I have often wondered. Here was a guy who had just broken the glass door of the embassy and kicked, punched, and pinned to the floor until our Korean employee, Mr. Yu, was bleeding—did he intentionally avoid me? Or was he so enraged he failed to realize he was already facing the person he was seeking? What went on in his mind as he ran to the ground floor and met me again? Nobody else was around to distract him. I shouted, "Get out!" as I pointed to the exit door with outstretched arm, but he seemed unaffected. Did he not hear me or see me, or was he simply momentarily blinded and deaf?

Despite the nightly phone calls we received saying, "We will kill you," my entire household felt comforted by divine protection. Eva, our private staff Lita, our friend and keyboard player Cerich Ponteres, and I continued with the weekly evening Bible study at Masuk. As before, we would leave our apartment and drive long distance, then came home at dawn to the relief of the four armed policemen who were ordered to remain for the security of my family and apartment 24 hours a day, seven days a week.

For Such a Time as This (Esther 4:14)

From the moment I received Jesus Christ into my life, the trials I faced in Korea were meant to prepare me for the Unification challenge. In the 1991 threat to my career, He protected me from "Goliath" for the following reasons:

1. To keep me in Seoul where the Unification challenge was to surface and become a major issue requiring a government decision;

2. To link me up with groups and persons who were to play a role in the crisis; and

3. To strengthen my faith and confidence as my wife and I were to undergo a tough spiritual battle.

The Lord also taught me to be resolute and firm, yet calm and discerning. In the outreach and my ministry at Masuk, He fine-tuned my sensitivity and compassion, leading me to personally see samples of living conditions that awaited the Filipina "brides." He also led me to serve as a minister of the Gospel and thereby provided my credentials, perspectives, and drive to take part in the formation of EMFK.

God's Purpose for EMFK in the Crisis

God's special role for the EMFK became more evident in the Aida Santos experience.

1. EMFK served as an immediate and credible resource on the background and activities of the Unification Church.

2. EMFK played an important role in the escape and safety of Aida Santos.

3. EMFK provided an alternative communication link with my superiors in Manila when I was deprived of a voice on the Unification case especially during the demonstrations.

EMFK role No. 3 is clearly God's plan. Having been taken out of the Aida Santos case and denied access to communication with the Home Office, I would have been effectively neutralized and silenced regarding the fate of a compatriot in distress. However, I saw God's provision even before the need arose. Two months before the demonstrations began, a Korean pastor offered part of his office for the use of the EMFK, without rental and with free use of utilities, including the telephone. In mid-January, the EMFK inaugurated its new office, brought in some of its equipment, and began operation. When the Aida Santos case broke out, the Unification activists and the embassy personnel knew nothing of the EMFK headquarters. It was located only three blocks from the embassy. Denied the facilities at the office, I used to slip out of the embassy and walked unnoticed pass the shouting, placards-carrying, and drum-beating Moonies. From the EMFK office, I observed the goings-on during the demonstrations and sent reports via fax to my superiors in Manila. I brainstormed via phone with Foreign Secretary Domingo Siazon and Undersecretary Rodolfo Severino, discussing with them contingency options to assist those claiming detention against their will. Those options, however, were pre-empted when the general spoke with the prospective escapees and reported "they have changed their mind."

Compassionate Viewpoint

Finally, while pursuing my official function of assisting Filipinos in distress amidst strong pressure from powerful and wealthy parties, God led me to view the crisis with human compassion. Without Jesus, I probably would have taken the easy path of compromise, submitted to pressures, and opted for bureaucratic self-preservation. I would have ignored the pleas of compatriots in distress and risked the safety and life of people I was duty-bound to help.

Help from a Korean Pastor

When Gen. Gidaya and I were required to testify before the Philippine Congress on the Aida Santos case, I travelled with my wife to Manila. As a precaution due to the threats to me and my family, and after two alleged would-be assassins managed to track down Aida Santos and me, I arranged for a friend to meet Eva and me at the airport. When that friend did not show up, the risk of being exposed to any danger became evident.

The hand of God, however, touched the heart of a faithful servant. A Korean pastor, whom we met on board the flight from Seoul, saw us flagging for a taxi. Since he was being fetched by members of his church, he offered us a ride. Who knows what disaster was avoided that night. Nonetheless, my wife and I felt protected and thankful to be in the hands of a man of God. The pastor brought us to the house of another friend, businessman Danny Wong, my buddy since college days.

CHAPTER TWELVE

SHEIKH KHALIFA AND THE PHILIPPINE SCHOOL

> *The man replied, 'You are right in saying that God is one and there is no other but him. To love him with all your heart, with all your understanding and with all your strength, and to love your neighbor as yourself is more important than all burnt offerings and sacrifices.' When Jesus saw that he had answered wisely, he said to him, 'You are not far from the kingdom of God.'*
> **Mark 12:32-34**

His Highness, Sheikh Khalifa bin Salman Al Khalifa, together with his brother, The Amir, Sheikh Isa bin Salman Al Khalifa, ruled Bahrain since the island's independence in 1971. When Sheikh Isa died in March 1999, his son (then Crown Prince) Sheikh Hamad, succeeded him as the Amir (later re-titled His Majesty, the King) of the Kingdom of Bahrain. To date, HH Sheikh Khalifa remains the Prime Minister of the kingdom and is the longest reigning Head of Government in the world today.

In May 1999, I presented my credentials as the Philippine Ambassador Extraordinary and Plenipotentiary to Bahrain. A series of one-on-one conversation with the Amir, Prime Minister, Crown Prince, and other officials of the kingdom enabled me to know them in person, beyond their public image created by the media and history books.

A Ruler's Compassion

Of the 600,000 population of Bahrain in 1999, about 40,000 were Filipinos. They numbered the third largest among the expatriate communities, behind the Indians and Pakistanis. Droves of Filipino workers came to the island since the mid-seventies to fill the kingdom's labor requirements, especially in the service sector. They worked as domestic servants, drivers, and gardeners in private homes, and occupied various positions in hotels, grocery stores, department stores, and restaurants. A good number worked as professionals (engineers, artists, accountants, doctors, nurses, therapists, medical technologists, etc.) in construction companies, banks, hospitals, and the government. Many served in the homes of the royal family.

The Prime Minister said that a number of the children and grandchildren in his family were raised by Filipinos who remained with their household for more than twenty years. At one time in his office, I mentioned to him the number of my compatriots employed by a large Bahraini company. He chuckled and said, "I have more Filipinos in my household alone."

Then he expressed how much he appreciated foreign workers and wished to do something to manifest his sincere gratitude.

Sheikh Khalifa Knew Foreign Worker's Plight

The Prime Minister possessed detailed knowledge of the ordeal foreign workers go through in order to travel abroad. He knew that before the workers left for the Middle East, their respective families sacrificed much to raise the cash for the travel agent's fee, job placement fee, plane fare, and "show money."[41] He understood the emotional anguish the workers suffered when leaving behind young

---

[41] Some job placement and travel agents managed to acquire a tourist visa for the aspiring foreign worker. "Show money" was the cash the traveler carried as proof in case immigration authorities at the destination airport questioned his/her financial readiness as "tourist." The cash was provided by the job and travel agents, and the worker was charged for the use of the show money.

children, aging parents, and handicapped relatives as they looked for "greener pasture" far from home. He was aware of the dangers and risks faced by the women workers, many of whom became victims of sexual and physical abuse. He knew about the "fixers" and the "illegal recruiters" who preyed on the innocent applicants for jobs abroad.[42]

He took the time to listen to their life stories and the problems faced by their respective families. Sheikh Khalifa's knowledge about his employees enabled him to assess their capabilities, and he trusted a number of them to handle delicate and technical financial matters. In several private dinners I attended in his palace, I noticed several Thais, Indonesians, and other foreign nationals, in addition to the Filipinos, in his employ. Sheikh Khalifa's sensitivity and compassion reflected in the efficient administration of his household as well as in the authenticity and richness of the cuisine served to his guests.

A Grateful Heart

I had earlier coursed through the protocol office of the Bahrain Foreign Ministry a request to call on him, so during a cultural heritage event in May 2000, I greeted and informed him of my request. His Highness immediately emphasized that I should visit him again soon because he wanted to know what he could do for the Filipino people in Bahrain. His response surprised me because normally the ambassador waited in line for the protocol office to give the green light for an appointment with the host chief executive. This time, however, no less than the Prime Minister himself urged a foreign envoy to call on him soon. Our conversation, in the presence of other ambassadors and the public, was carried on the national TV news broadcast.

---

[42] "Fixers" are people claiming to be skilled in the processing of passports, visas, and other paper requirements for travel abroad. "Illegal recruiters" are job placement agencies or persons not registered as such with the government. Both fixers and illegal recruiters required money from the applicants but often failed in fulfilling their promise.

I personally saw him give instructions to his staff to arrange a schedule for my courtesy call. His staff moved so quickly that by the time I returned to the embassy that morning, my secretary, Mr. Manny Arbado, reported that Sheikh Khalifa's office will receive me at the Prime Minister's Court on the following morning.

An Expanding School

The appointment to call on His Highness proved timely. It provided me a second chance to pursue an urgent project.

A few days earlier, I called on the Bahrain Minister of Education and discussed the need for a piece of land on which to build a campus for Philippine School Bahrain (PSB). During the visit, I presented him with a thick folder prepared by the school Board of Governors containing the history, growth, future plans, and an artist's perspective of a campus the board desired to build. Due to the increasing number of students, the rented bungalows used for classrooms in Kanoo Gardens (a 35-home residential compound) were no longer sufficient for its needs.

The Minister of Education could not commit land for the Filipino school. He said the government would allocate land once the enrollment reached more than 600 students; PSB had not met that number. At that time, campus land had already been allocated respectively to the Indian, French, and Pakistani schools which had a larger enrollment and been in operation much longer than the PSB.

Urgent Need for School Land

Philippine School Bahrain opened in 1995 with 148 students, three rented bungalows, an acting principal, six teachers, and one administrative staff. A product of dedicated work by the Philippine Embassy and the Filipino community, it continued to grow. Following up on the work of my predecessors Ambassador Leonides Caday and Ambassador Ahmad Sakkam, I received the full accreditation of PSB by the Philippine Department of Education and Culture in March of 2000.

When I met with the Bahrain Minister of Education in mid-April regarding the need for land, PSB had grown to 427 students, five rented bungalows, 19 teachers, and 6 administrative staff. The school prepared to rent the sixth residential bungalow, convert a car park into a kindergarten playground, and build a perimeter wall. PSB opened several high school classes, and its enrollment continued to expand. The need for additional space, buildings, and facilities became more pressing each year the PSB remained in operation. The request for land was unavoidable and urgent.

Promise of the Prince

For the call on His Highness, I was allowed to bring leaders of the Filipino community. I invited PSB Board Chairman Rod Acosta, Vice Chairman Reuel Castro, and Finance Officer Oscar Japitana to join me. I also requested the President of the Filipino Club of Bahrain, Alex Ginete, to join in the courtesy call.

I briefly explained to His Highness the urgent need for a larger campus of the Philippine School, and added that PSB needed 1.5 hectares. Board Chairman Mr. Acosta handed Sheikh Khalifa a copy of the proposal folder.

The Prime Minister expressed delight that the board members were trusted technical professionals employed by the Bahrain government. Rod Acosta was a civil engineer with the construction and development team of the government for more than twenty-five years. Reuel Castro and Oscar Japitana, accounting experts, also served in the government for some years.

H.H. Sheikh Khalifa assured us he would personally look for a place for the school. Thereafter, events happened in rapid succession. By July, during a ceremonial gathering preparatory to the royal wedding of a relative, the Prime Minister personally informed me the government had already found a piece of land, and he would also help the school build the new campus. About a week later, I received an invitation to come to his palace at Riffa for an important meeting.

Land for the School

I will never forget the morning of August 2, 2000. I arrived few minutes before nine o'clock at the Palace of His Highness Sheikh Khalifa, in Riffa. Accompanying me in the official car of the Philippine embassy were Chairman Rod Acosta and Consul Marichu Mauro. We were ushered to a huge guest hall, and were seated on soft lounges and served with Arab coffee in tiny cups.[43] I expected the Prime Minister to discuss in detail the piece of land for the school, but I wondered why the place of the meeting was different that morning. In previous courtesy calls on His Highness, the venue was at the Prime Minister's Court, in the city. Nonetheless, I prepared to engage in deep discussions as I reviewed every detail of the request for at least 1.5 hectares.

A few minutes later, the Prime Minister walked into the room, shook our hands as we stood up to greet him, and took his seat on a sofa next to me. After the usual courtesy exchanges, the Prime Minister opened the topic direct to the point.

"Excellency, Mr. Ambassador," he said, "we found a piece of land for the Filipino school. It is located at A'Ali, not too far from here. It is more than two-and-a-half hectares."

Stunned, I thought, *Two-and-a-half hectares! Fantastic! Much better than we asked for!* So, I hurriedly said, "Yes, Your Highness."

Then the Prime Minister continued, "We are ready to show it to you. We can go there now."

Land! Available now! No longer a dream!

"Yes, Your Highness," I said.

---

[43] The tiny cups, with no saucer and handle, are called *finjaan* or *demitasse*; if an attendant offers a refill, the guest either moves it up and down to say "yes," or shakes it for "no."

The Prime Minister Drove the Car

We then stood up and proceeded to the main door of the palace. The Prime Minister's official car and the embassy car were already lined up on the palace driveway.

"You can all come with me in my car," the Prime Minister said.

Puzzled, I thought, *Normally, the Prime Minister and the Ambassador sit at the back while the protocol officer stays at the front seat. With two additional persons with us, how can we all fit in his car? I must have heard him wrong.*

"Yes, Your Highness."

He gestured to Mr. Acosta to sit at the back of his car. I gave a signal for Consul Mauro to ride in the embassy car.

The Prime Minister said, "Excellency, please sit in front with me. I will drive."

So far, I have been a "yes" man. But this time, I refused to say "yes".

"But Your Highness, you are the Prime Minister. Let *me drive* for you," I insisted. Since he set aside formalities, I wanted to do the same.

But His Highness quickly went to the driver's seat and turned on the ignition. My face must have revealed total astonishment as the security and protocol officers chuckled at the whole event.

His Highness, Sheikh Khalifa bin Salman Al Khalifa, The Prime Minister of the Kingdom of Bahrain, the patriarch of the rulers of the Kingdom, was *himself driving* the car! The prince, not a chauffeur, drove the official carriage. It was out of the usual protocol and very unofficial, but utterly personal.

As he steered the car, I saw in him more than the official image of a royalty who wielded the power of Head of Government. Hidden underneath his flowing robe, headdress, and formal Arabian attire was a heart of flesh that drove his benevolence with extraordinary humility, sincerity, love, and gratitude. Since the recipients were my people, I felt so touched.

"Your Highness, I cannot believe you are the one driving to show us the place," I said.

"I want to do something for your people who are working here in Bahrain. They are like my family. I want to drive myself because I like to directly help and to do it personally. My family has so much to thank such humble people for," he said.

Lease Agreement Signed

We were on the highway towards A'Ali village with no outriders to escort us. Finally, we reached a wide, empty, and sandy piece of real estate. Nearby stood large residential compounds with high perimeter walls. When we stopped the car, the Minister of Finance and National Economy and a number of senior officials were already at the site. His Highness disembarked and was handed the location map. Referring occasionally to the map, he directed my attention to the metes and bounds of the land.

Pointing at some distant pegs with red banners to mark the boundaries, the Prime Minister told me more about the land.

"The total area is 26,000 square meters," he informed. "It was the site of housing for expatriates employed with the Bahrain government. It is a prime lot and located across the municipal office of A'Ali village and a bank. It is a very special property, and since the cabinet could not find any other land, I decided to allocate this portion for the use of the school."

He handed me the location map and introduced the Minister of Finance and National Economy.

"His office will coordinate with you in the drafting and signing of the agreement regarding the land," the Prime Minister said.

"Thank you, Your Highness," I said.

With silent excitement bursting within me, I shook the hand of the Prime Minister and expressed my appreciation. I promised him I would inform my government and the Filipino community of his kindness. As His Highness and the other Bahraini officials left, Rod Acosta, Consul Mauro, and I stayed behind. To absorb the reality of the events that morning, we walked to trace the perimeter of the 2.6 hectares under the seething heat of the Middle East summer sun.

The agreement to lease the school land at a very reasonable, friendly rate was signed in October 2000 between the Philippine School Bahrain Board of Governors and the Bahrain Ministry of Finance and National Economy. Board Chairman Mr. Acosta signed on behalf of the school, with the endorsement of the Philippine Ambassador. A press conference and a reception immediately followed in an adjoining room in Gulf Hotel.

PSB Campus Begins to Take Shape

With a much larger land on which to build the campus, the school board came up with a new plan to build facilities to accommodate 1080 students. The new campus would have a kindergarten block, elementary block, high school block, administration block, sports and other facilities, living quarters, car park, and security stations. After receiving bid offers from various companies, the board decided to engage the services of Ismail Khonji and Associates as consultant. The board also drew up plans for fund-raising and requested the assistance of the Filipino Club and the association of certified public accountants (PICPA) for the campus project. At this point, I requested to see the Prime Minister.

In December 2000, His Highness received me at the Prime Minister's Court. Board treasurer Oscar Japitana and board member Efren Guico accompanied me. We presented to His Highness Sheikh Khalifa a feasibility study and two perspectives of the school plan. The Prime Minister studied the perspectives as I summarized the new plan. He liked the plan and expressed support for the construction project. On the matter of logistics, Mr. Japitana explained that due to financial limitations of the school and the community, the board aimed to complete only portions of the first phase of the four-phase plan. The school could only assure 43 percent of Phase One budget, and thus the next phase would begin in the distant future.

After listening to the financial report, the Prime Minister assured to provide the balance of the project, about 57 percent of the total Phase One budget. Mr. Japitana, Mr. Guico, and I were stunned. But we were delighted. His Highness called it his "personal participation" in the campus construction. Excited to hear his promise, I assured him of the gratitude of the Filipino people for his generosity and extraordinary benevolence.

In the succeeding weeks, I personally conveyed to His Highness updates on the preparations for the construction. By the end of winter, the paperwork and other requirements preliminary to construction were completed. The Prime Minister's Court scheduled my visit on His Highness regarding his "personal participation."

"I Trust You"

On a chilly spring morning, the Philippine flag fluttered on the hood as the embassy car entered the compound of the Prime Minister's Court. Mr. Acosta rode with me while Mr. Japitana, Mr. Castro, and Mr. Guico followed in another car. We arrived fifteen minutes before our appointment at 9 o'clock. A protocol officer escorted us to a waiting lounge and an attendant served Arabic coffee in tiny cups.

Our wait was short and we were ushered into the Prime Minister's office. After the exchange of greetings and photos taken by an official photographer, I made an oral update on the campus project to which His Highness expressed appreciation. Then he motioned to his assistant who took a few steps toward him and handed him a folder.

His Highness Sheikh Khalifa opened the folder, pulled out a

check, and said, "As I promised, Mr. Ambassador, I am giving my personal participation for the construction of the campus of the Filipino school."

Without hesitation, he handed the check straight to me.

Surprised by the simplicity of the handover, I remained speechless. I expected some paperwork before the amount could be turned over to me. And when I read the check, the amount was Three Hundred Sixty Three Thousand Bahraini Dinars (BD363,000), equivalent to about US Dollar Nine Hundred Sixty-Six Thousand (US$966,000), or approximately Philippine Pesos Forty-Eight Million, Five Hundred Thousand (P48,500,000).

"But...but Your Highness, before I accept this, should I not sign any paper first? A voucher, or receipt? As proof that I received it?"

"I trust you," replied the Prime Minister.

The words of His Highness was the greatest compliment and honor anyone could receive, especially coming from someone of his stature.

Just like that. *Without any documentary proof. No paper trail.* Nothing to prove that about one million dollars had left the Prime Minister's hand and placed in anybody's hand. I was not asked to sign anything to compel me to account for such a huge amount of money in case something went missing.

To my mind, Sheikh Khalifa's way of showing his trust was extraordinary. It was unprecedented in the light of the practice and requirements on fiscal matters in the operation of any government unit, civic organization, business establishments, the church, and personal transactions regardless of the amount involved.

Furthermore, he said that this was just the beginning as he wanted to give more help in the future. I assured the Prime Minister his monies would be placed under the stewardship of the Philippine school board and used exclusively for the construction of the school campus at A'Ali. I added, his office would receive accounting reports on the use of the money.

Later, I officially turned over the check to the school board. The board, in turn, deposited it to open a special bank account separate from the rest of the campus fund-raising deposits.

PSB Campus Rises at A'Ali

With added confidence, the board proceeded with the schedule of the construction. In July 2002, work began on the 2.6 hectares at A'Ali. In June 2003, the Philippine school moved from Kanoo Gardens to the new and more spacious campus at A'Ali, on time for the start of the school year. My successor, Ambassador Eduardo Maglaya, held a "soft opening" ceremony on July 20, 2003. The campus was officially inaugurated on December 15, 2003 jointly by His Highness, Prime Minister Sheikh Khalifa bin Salman Al Khalifa, and the President of the Republic of the Philippines, Her Excellency Gloria Macapagal Arroyo.

I visited the school in February 2007, about four years after I completed my tenure in Bahrain. Headed by its new principal, Dr. Geronimo Salem, Jr., PSB had grown to about 700 students attending kindergarten, elementary, and high school levels. A program to welcome me was staged at the main auditorium; all classes attended the occasion.

Although the program was meant to honor me, I sensed a greater significance of the occasion. I saw the dramatic growth of PSB as evidenced by the excellence of the performances, the growth of its academic achievements, the progress of its athletic program, and the professional quality of the administration and faculty. I felt satisfied and fulfilled for having been a part in the making of a respectable educational center for the children of my compatriots living in a kingdom far beyond the shores of our motherland.

An Extraordinary Ruler

In retrospect, his handling of the Philippine school revealed the true character of Sheikh Khalifa. The Bible tells of a wise man who said that to love your neighbor as yourself, as well as to love God with all your heart, understanding, and strength, is more important than burnt offerings and sacrifices. In reply, Jesus told him, *You are not far from the kingdom of God.*[44]

His Highness Sheikh Khalifa bin Salman Al Khalifa proved to be a wise man who loved his "neighbor." And I prayed hence that my government grant him due recognition for his kindness.

---

[44] Mark 12:33-34

CHAPTER THIRTEEN

THE SIKATUNA AWARD

> *But the plans of the Lord stand firm forever,*
> *the purposes of his heart*
> *through all generations.*
> *Blessed is the nation whose God is the Lord,*
> *the people he chose for his inheritance.*
> *From heaven the Lord looks down*
> *and sees all mankind;*
> *from his dwelling place he watches*
> *all who live on earth –*
> *He who forms the hearts of all,*
> *who considers everything they do.*
> **Psalms 33:11-15**

Due to the Prime Minister's benevolence to the Filipinos in Bahrain, I recommended my government invite him for an official visit to the Philippines. During the visit, the Philippine President could confer on him the Sikatuna Award, the highest recognition given to visiting dignitaries. Although the Prime Minister indicated interest each time I discussed with him the President's open invitation, no date was ever set.

The Prime Minister Set the Date

In late September 2001, Bahrain Foreign Minister Sheikh Mohammed bin Mubarrak Al Khalifa called me to his office. He conveyed the Prime Minister's desire to visit the Philippines on 6-7 November. His Highness planned to proceed to Manila after his official visits to Malaysia and the People's Republic of China; then, from the Philippines, he would make an official visit to Thailand on his way back to Bahrain.

"I know this does not give you much advance notice, Ambassador, but the decision was made just recently," the Foreign Minister explained.

As endless details needed to be handled in preparation for the Official Visit, seven weeks advance notice hardly allowed enough time for such an important occasion. Governments normally have six to twelve months lead time. The odds overwhelmingly stood against the proposed schedule.

God Touched Two Presidents

In earnest prayers at the office and at home, I asked the Lord for guidance, wisdom, and His provision for the realization and success of the proposed official visit. I asked, if the visit was of His will, then all obstacles be removed.

I conveyed the proposed date of visit to the Secretary of Foreign Affairs, Vice President Teofisto Guingona, in Manila. Immediately, I received a negative reply. Both the Secretary of Foreign Affairs and the Office of Middle East and African Affairs advised that during the dates in question, President Gloria Macapagal Arroyo would be in Brunei Darussalam for the Summit Meeting of the Association of Southeast Asian Nations (ASEAN). They informed that, according to the Protocol Office of Malacanang, her schedule was full until the next year.

Even within the embassy in Manama, the lady consul (successor to Consul Mauro) who was the only other diplomatic officer with me at the post, echoed the same negative stance and refused to support any effort on the project.

With a clear "no" from the head office, and no support from my own deputy, the situation presented a prospect discouraging enough to dissuade anyone from taking further action.

However, I considered the opportunity for an official Philippine visit too important to disregard because of the mutual economic benefits it could bring to both countries. It would also provide the rare chance for my President to highlight appreciation for the Prime Minister's kindness to the Filipinos in Bahrain.

Thus, I laid my concern before the Lord and asked, "If I should go on, guide me Lord."

As a desperate attempt, I wrote an urgent fax message to former Philippine President, Gen. Fidel V. Ramos. I requested his assistance, hoping that President Arroyo would change her mind.

I learned later that President Ramos went to Malacanang Palace, talked with President Arroyo, and suggested that in her absence on the first day of the visit, the arriving dignitary could be received by Vice President Teofisto Guingona. President Ramos suggested further that on the following day, after President Arroyo would have returned from the ASEAN Summit, she could receive the Bahrain Prime Minister and his official entourage. Also on the second day, President Ramos added, she could confer the Sikatuna Award on the visiting dignitary and conduct bilateral talks at Malacanang Palace.

Within a week after the proposed date was turned down, I received a message from the Foreign Department conveying the affirmative response of the President. The "No" became "Go."

Delighted that the earlier negative response was reversed, I eagerly worked long hours to provide the Home Office with embassy inputs needed for the visit. Within a few days, the embassy sent to Manila protocol, substantive, and administrative data including draft briefing papers on bilateral issues, bios of the visiting dignitaries, and personal trivia such as dietary requirements.

Clearly, God touched the hearts of two presidents to open a shut door, winking to assure His interest in the affairs of sovereigns and nations. Through the Holy Spirit, God leads men, spirit to spirit, toward taking certain measures and connecting His servants with people whose hearts are also in tune to fulfilling His plans.

Some foreign ambassadors in Bahrain asked how I managed to arrange the visit despite the short notice. I told them, "It wasn't I. Thanks to two presidents, and to the grace of the Almighty." I added, *"Competence comes from God"* (2 Corinthians 3:5).

Dilemma over Two Invitations

Diplomatic protocol requires that the President's invitation must come in the form of an official letter as basis by both governments to allocate fiscal, security, and administrative support for the visit.

The embassy received a copy of the invitation letter via fax and the original copy arrived later by special pouch. I immediately sent a copy to the Protocol Office of the Bahrain Ministry of Foreign Affairs and presented the original letter to the Foreign Minister.

Unknown to me as Ambassador to Bahrain, another invitation letter of the President was acquired earlier by Filipino businessman Dr. Amable "King" Aguilus V, owner and CEO of AMA University and AMA Computer Institute. To his credit for his initiative and on the strength of his personal closeness with President Gloria Macapagal Arroyo and Vice President Teofisto Guingona, he managed to get the aforesaid letter perhaps around the time the Bahrain Foreign Minister conveyed the dates for the Prime Minister's visit. I first learned about this letter when the PM's Court asked me to convey to King Aguilus that, in reply to his request to come to Bahrain to personally give the other invitation to His Highness, no schedule was available.

Thus, I faced a dilemma. Should I push, nonetheless, for King's request to see the Prime Minister as a second letter personally handed by a prominent compatriot businessman could emphasize importance of the invitation? But why was there no word about this from my superior, Foreign Secretary Guingona?

At this point, I asked in prayer for the Lord's guidance. I was led to Proverbs 19:21: *Many are the plans in a man's heart, but it is the Lord's purpose that prevails.*

To me, the Bible verse assured the visit would inevitably push through in accordance with His will, not because of my personal insistence or of any man's desire.

"God's provision is all man needs," this thought lingered in my mind as the PM's office called again asking me to emphasize to King Aguilus there was no appointment made and that "it was not necessary" for him to come. Thus, when King called me from Manila and informed me about the President's invitation letter, I had the painful role of conveying a "bad news" to an influential, wealthy, and well-connected businessman.

In any case, when the Bahraini officials were already in Manila, King Aguilus hosted a grand dinner on 7 November at his mansion in Corinthian Gardens in honor of the Prime Minister and his entourage. Vice President Guingona headed the list of special guests that included a number of senators, foreign affairs officials, foreign diplomats, and businessmen. The presentation of an artist's oil portrait of the Prime Minister highlighted the evening. On the sprawling lush garden where we enjoyed the dinner, in a fitting ceremony before all the guests, King officially handed over his gift to His Highness. So, whatever he wanted to personally say to the Prime Minister had he made the trip to Bahrain, he had all the opportunities to do so in Manila, and with style.

One Last Piece

"When I checked, there was only one last piece of Sikatuna medal left," said Ambassador George Reyes, Chief of Protocol for the Office of the President. "You were lucky. Due to short advance notice, we did not know if the incoming order would arrive on time." When I heard him say this, I shuddered with the thought the awarding almost *could* not happen.

The availability of that *one last piece* was not due to good planning given the hurried, narrow lead time for the PM's visit. By the time the President decided to accept the date of visit, the protocol people could only work on the reality of that time—either a medal existed or there was none. The protocol office would not have any other option but to say "no" to the proposed Sikatuna awarding if they had no more piece of the medal left even if the President wanted to honor the visiting dignitary.

The situation assured me God was in control of the events, and His purpose could not be frustrated. Many times, we do not factor-in the role of God in the affairs of men, especially in high level State affairs. When things go well, we credit it to good works, good planning, and good fortune. In this case, the margin of success was so narrow and the smell of failure so near. I believe the one last piece of medal was there because God wanted to honor Sheikh Khalifa with a deserving recognition.

A Successful Official Visit

On the morning of November 6, 2001, the aircraft carrying Prime Minister Sheikh Khalifa and his entourage touched down at the Ninoy Aquino International Airport in Manila. Accompanying the Prime Minister were the ministers for foreign affairs, finance, trade, oil, transportation, and officials of the Prime Ministers Court as well as the Bahrain media. Events that day proceeded in quick succession: a warm welcome led by the Presidential Chief of Protocol and the attending cabinet minister at the tarmac; a brief reception at the airport VIP room with more Philippine officials, ambassadors from the Gulf countries, and other guests; and check-in at the Shangri-la Hotel Makati. In the afternoon, the Prime Minister received courtesy calls by the Philippine Senate President and the acting Speaker of the House. In the evening, a welcome dinner for the guests was hosted by Vice President Guingona at the Mandarin Hotel in Makati.

Sikatuna Award to the Prime Minister

On the next day, after laying a wreath at the Rizal Monument in Luneta, the Prime Minister and his party proceeded to Malacanang Palace, seat of the President of the Republic of the Philippines. A brief courtesy call on President Arroyo was held in a function room.

Then, in a larger hall, the President conferred the Sikatuna Award to the Prime Minister. In the presence of Philippine cabinet members and their Bahraini counterparts, media, and Foreign Affairs officials, the President extolled the Prime Minister for his major role in forging close and friendly relations between the two countries, and cited his generosity in providing land and financial support to the Philippine School in Bahrain.

Bilateral Talks

A bilateral discussion was held in the conference hall of Malacanang with the Bahraini Prime Minister and his accompanying cabinet ministers sitting on one side while the Philippine President and the counterpart cabinet ministers sat on the other side. On top of their mutual concern and common position on political and economic issues, Prime Minister Sheikh Khalifa offered to give the first financial contribution to President Arroyo's development plans in Mindanao. The Philippine Finance Secretary, seated next to me, was the first to applaud.

During the luncheon at Malacanang hosted by the President, more informal exchanges transpired especially on trade, oil, and the resumption of Philippine Airline flights to Manama. Sheikh Khalifa assured his appreciation of the Filipinos and "your good ambassador" in Bahrain. Across the table, I smiled when I heard him say those words to my President.

Two Agreements Signed

In a separate function, two bilateral documents—the Philippine-Bahrain Agreement on the Promotion and Reciprocal Protection of Investments, and the Philippine-Bahrain Agreement on the Avoidance of Double Taxation—were signed to conclude years of negotiations.

Again, just before boarding for his departure flight, Sheikh Khalifa assured Vice President Guingona of Bahrain's financial contribution, a remark which caused a bright look of contentment on the face of my Foreign Secretary.

A Prophetic Word of Caution?

As I watched the plane rise higher into the clouds, I stood wondering how a project faced with seemingly insurmountable obstacles ended up with so many accomplishments. Indeed, officials of both governments deserved the credit, especially the unsung protocol, intelligence, and security officers who labored silently, as well as the diplomats and technical staff who drafted the substantive briefing papers. But hovering above two presidents, a prime minister, a vice-president, and everyone involved in the event stood a higher power who removed the hindrances and allowed the rekindling of relations between two nations.

In the visit, the Lord showed two kingdom principles. First, a prayer request is granted because of God's grace and man's faith. Psalm 37:4 says: *Delight yourself in the Lord and he will give you the desires of your heart.* Second, God is Sovereign and can direct the affairs of leaders and nations. Isaiah 14:24 reflects His will, *The Lord Almighty had sworn, 'Surely as I have planned, so it will be, and as I have purposed, so it will stand.'*

"It was a successful visit—despite the odds against it," commented Presidential Chief of Protocol, Ambassador Reyes. "But be careful *from now on*," he added.

Were his words prophetic, or just a usual parting expression after we thanked each other? I wondered.

Let all the earth fear the Lord;
let all the people of the world revere him.
For he spoke, and it came to be;
He commanded,
and it stood firm.
Psalms 33:8-9

CHAPTER FOURTEEN

SHADOW OF AN INVISIBLE FORCE

> *If anyone would come after me, he must deny himself and take up his cross and follow me. For whoever wants to save his life will lose it, but whoever loses his life for me will find it. What good will it be for a man if he gains the whole world, yet forfeits his soul?*
> **Matthew 16:24-26**

Faith at Risk

Faith is being sure of what we hope for and certain of what we do not see (Hebrews 11:1). Faith holds man's belief, trust, hope, and confidence in God through Jesus Christ. Faith is man's deliberate response to the grace of salvation that God offers as a gift to each person. Faith serves as the foundation of man's relationship with the Creator, his "citizenship card" in the kingdom of God.

Since man's exile from Eden, the devil subjected him to constant deceit and oppression in order to deny his return to God's realm. He knows that faith through Jesus Christ is man's ticket back to his home in the kingdom of heaven. In his spiritual battle over the loyalty of man, the devil considers man as a contested territory, a *terra nullius,* a piece he wants to keep in a zero-sum game. One rule exists and remains unchanged: whoever is not inside is outside. Those outside the kingdom of God belong to Satan and are subject to his manipulation.

But Satan's greater goal is to destroy the faith of the believer. Snatching Jesus' disciple is a greater reward for the devil.

Narrated in this chapter is an attempt of a formidable spiritual force to destroy my faith in Christ. From the start, however, the reader is requested not to search for personalities behind the events. The following personal experience is narrated in the light of its spiritual, non-material dimension. The reader is directed to focus on the interplay between the Lord's faithfulness and purpose on one side, and man's faith on the other, as the narrative offers crucial principles revealed in a deeply sensitive period of my life.

Defenseless Target of a Powerful Force

By the stroke of a pen, a very powerful political figure in my country became the leading character in a cast whose action caused an attack on my official position, denial of my material support, depletion of my savings, and an assault on my faith.

The Premature Recall

In May 2002, I received a fax message recalling me to the Home Office, Manila, effective immediately. It was signed by a political personality whose governmental powers exceeded all other officials except the President of the Republic. No reason was given for the recall.

I considered the order premature because it cut short to three years the normal tour for career diplomats of six to eight years in foreign assignments before serving again in Manila. It was arbitrary since it did not pass through the usual administrative route in the foreign affairs department. In the absence of legal procedures leading to the recall of an ambassador, the directive circumvented the President of the country who had the sole authority to appoint and recall ambassadors. I never received any reply to my requests for the basis of the premature recall. Yet, before, during, and after the recall directive, no investigation or hearing on any allegation ever took place even after my repeated request for such an inquiry.

The recall caused emotional, financial, physical, and spiritual stress on me, a career, non-political, merit-based public servant on whom several lives depended. It deprived me of material support while in a foreign land. And since the premature recall suggested a punishment, it served to destroy my credibility as a minister of the Gospel. At the time, I have been preaching in three churches and a number of house congregations. In fact, the recall encouraged two non-evangelical, non-Muslim members of the embassy to ridicule my faith and call me *pastor ng kadiliman* (pastor of darkness). It emboldened them to display disrespect to their superiors as they were assured of protection by higher officials and influential personalities in Manila.

The directive also served as basis for denying my request for vacation leave to attend the Haggai Institute-sponsored Christian leadership training course in Maui, Hawaii. The leave could have given Eva and me time for a medical check-up by her brother in Indiana as she was already under stress due to the premature recall.

Compared to the challenges I faced in the past, the directive promised a devastating threat to my career, finances, honor, faith, and the life of loved ones.

Powerful Personalities

A free-lance TV commentator who came to interview me in Bahrain intimated that based on his research before he left Manila, several personalities laid behind the directive. These persons included a network of wealthy and influential people strategically positioned in the government and private sectors who could do harm if they wanted to and easily cover their tracks. In his view, there would be no way that I, being alone, could frustrate their agenda, resist, or escape them, much less win over them.

Added Cut to an Open Wound

Submit yourselves for the Lord's sake to every authority instituted among men, says 1 Peter 2:13. But if those in authority contradicted God's will, Acts 5:29 insists, *We must obey God rather than men!* I sensed the truth needed to be exposed so my superiors could consider retracting the order.

What Price Truth?

Some acquaintances suggested Eva and I should stop asking for the truth but instead leave immediately for Manila before the 60-day grace period expires. But to me, leaving my post at that point in time was tantamount to admission of guilt.

Any hint of falsehood could lead some foreign workers to stumble in their faith; a preacher should be *above reproach* and *set an example for the believers in speech, in life, in love, in faith, and in purity* (1 Timothy 3:2 and 4:12). On such principle, I had risked my life and the safety of my family. Years ago, pistol-carrying men came at night to my Manila residence with bribes and demanded I approve, as Head of Intelligence and Security, illegal passport applications. But I denied them. I ordered my maid to bring their basket of "gifts" outside of our gate, and on the following morning, I had the person who accompanied the armed men dismissed from DFA employment. In Bahrain, a real estate agent came to give part of her commission (consistent with Middle East practice? or "kickback"?) for the rent of the embassy building, but I refused to accept. She cried (of embarrassment?) in front of Eva and me.

While I waited for reply to my requests for investigation of any question concerning my official actions or my integrity, I used my savings for my household sustenance. Meanwhile, Eva's health deteriorated.

Between Life and Death

On the morning of September 4, 2002, my wife suffered a stroke. She went into a coma, and lingered between life and death. The doctor at the intensive care unit of Salmanya Medical Center in Manama was direct and honest, saying he did not know if she would wake up. If she survived, he predicted she would have some permanent physical disabilities and serious mental incapacities. He explained that Eva suffered an infarction at the brain stem, or cerebellum, affecting all nerves.

"At this point," he added, "healing of your wife is in the hands of God."

From subsequent conversations with the nurses and other doctors, I learned more details about my wife's condition. They all confirmed: within forty-eight hours, most patients with brain stem hemorrhage die.

The hurt I felt that day was the most painful I suffered in my life. In my heart, the stroke was an added—yet deeper—cut to the open wound already inflicted by the recall directive. The two events led me to asked whether justice reigns at all in life. *Is this the price for my faith, Lord?*

Pawns in Spiritual Battle?

I never intended to fight back whoever were behind the recall directive, not then or afterwards. Perhaps for reasons unknown to me and the Office of Personnel and Administration, the powerful political figure who signed it and anyone else who may have brought him into it, probably had compelling motives to do what they did. However, being an official who attained his position through merit, I should have been informed of the basis of the recall—if any, indeed. On the spiritual level, I wondered: *Weren't the instigators aware of the pain the directive would bring to a career official? With the ill-timed recall order, didn't they not realize they have turned into pawns in the battle against my faith in God?*

Why no Investigation?

Looking back at the events, I am convinced the justification for the recall—whatever it was—could not be sustained at all from the start. Otherwise, I would have been required to explain within 72 hours if there was truly any adverse report. I considered the aforesaid assumption a logical conclusion because I never received any reply to my numerous requests for investigation. As a fact, no administrative case was filed against me in my entire thirty-two years of service as a public servant.

A reliable source told me that whatever the instigators had

planned to do after pulling me down, they no longer could pursue their agenda because of some tragic turn of events. *First,* the person the instigators planned to put in my place as ambassador to Bahrain suddenly became incapacitated and never recovered. *Second,* the powerful political figure who signed the recall lost his cabinet position two months after issuing the directive. *Third,* the two critics at the embassy who ridiculed my faith also were shortly removed from their posts. After the Filipino community and some embassy members filed a petition against them, the two critics were recalled and left for Manila before Eva and I left Bahrain.

Watching my wife lying motionless at the hospital, I wondered whether all the machinations to remove and insult me, and mock my work in sharing the Gospel, were worth anything to those behind the directive. Though painful, I forgave them all. My struggle was not with men, but against *dark spiritual forces.*

Foretastes of Things to Come

The premature recall and the stroke of Eva served as foretastes of what believers will encounter as the world rotates deeper into the End of the Age.

The twin crisis suggested features inherent in the prophesied final days. 1 John 2:18 says, *...in the last hour, the antichrist is coming.* Also called *the beast out of the sea,* such dark spiritual force of Antichrist *was given power to make war against the saints and to conquer them* subjecting believers either *to go into captivity* or *to be killed.*[45] Based on the preceding biblical description of the End of the Age, believers will be accused by powerful persons of authority, pursued and condemned for their faith, deprived of material resources, and punished without due process. Although such persecution persisted throughout the ages, its extent in the final days will be worldwide. Today's surveillance and control techniques make the fulfillment of the prophecies on "the beast" real. The

---

[45] Revelation 13:1, 7, 10, 12-18; see also 2 Thessalonians 2:3-4

pursuers' power will penetrate deeper into every aspect of every person's life, their resolve more relentless than ever, and their effectiveness based on digital technology.

Revelation 13:10 adds that the aforesaid situation *calls for patient endurance and faithfulness on the part of the saints.* As world condition worsens, believers need to endure, learn from their trials, prepare for tougher days, and stand firm in their faith.

Jesus' forewarning to His disciples of tough times ahead as He assured them of ultimate salvation reverberates to believers in our time. He said,

> *On my account you will be brought before governors and kings as witnesses to them and to the Gentiles. But when they arrest you, do not worry about what to say or how to say it. You will be given what to say, for it will not be you speaking, but the Spirit of your Father speaking through you...All men will hate you because of me, but he who stands firm to the end will be saved* (Matthew 10:18,19, and 22).

Christian Rules of Engagement

While a dark shadow loomed to destroy my faith in Jesus Christ, the Bible offered me the strength to override the ominous force. Spiritually, I was fitted with the "armor of God" which I call a Christian's Rules of Engagement. While soldiers and policemen have rules on combat response to a situation, believers are also given predetermined response vis-à-vis the devil. The Christian's rules are heavily founded on faith, the Word of God, and prayers.

Spiritual Battle

The Bible cautions the believer to brace for spiritual battle as his faith is constantly under threat by the evil one. Man's struggle is not against the person but against the spirit behind his action, perception, and motive. *For our struggle is not against flesh and blood, but against the rulers, against the authorities, against the powers of this dark world and against the spiritual forces of evil in the heavenly realms,* reminds Ephesians 6:12.

The Full Armor of God

The Bible tells us to *be strong in the Lord and in his mighty power. Put on the full armor of God so that you can take your stand against the devil's schemes* (v.10-11).

Then it continues:

> *Stand firm then, with the belt of truth buckled around your waist, with the breastplate of righteousness in place, and with your feet fitted with the readiness that comes from the gospel of peace. In addition to all this, take up the shield of faith, with which you can extinguish all the flaming arrows of the evil one. Take the helmet of salvation and the sword of the Spirit, which is the word of God. And pray in the spirit on all occasions with all kinds of prayers and requests. With this in mind, be alert and always keep on praying for all the saints* (v. 14-18).

The Rules

With the preceding passages, the Bible at once gave me a guide on how to stand against the trauma I faced. The principles are:

a) *Be strong in the Lord and in his mighty power.* Be firm, steadfast and consistent in your faith. Trust and believe in the Lord as the source of your strength and protection.

b) *Take your stand against the devil's scheme.* Taking a stand means guarding against any vulnerability you may have to sexual, wealth, power, and all other temptations and fears as the devil can exploit these to destroy your faith. Hold on to your faith in the face of the devil's attacks; it is enough that Jesus had already won the battle for you. You need not pursue and attack the "spiritual forces of evil" for the devil is already defeated.

c) *Frustrate the assault of the devil with the truth and righteousness of God.* With your heart, mind, and behavior rooted on the Gospel of Jesus Christ, be ready always to parry the enemy's attack. Read, learn, remember, and live the word of God, plant these in your heart, and *speak* them in defense against deception, temptation, and intimidation.

d) *Deal with the evil forces with your faith on the Lord.* Avoid the use of physical force unless clearly commanded by the Lord to do so. Do not doubt the salvation you received through Jesus Christ, and always be ready to justify your defense with the scriptures from the Holy Bible which is the word of God.

e) *Pray in the spirit for the protection of other believers and the salvation of the unsaved.* Pray on all occasions with supplication, not with shallow incantations but a from-the-heart exchange with God. Meditate on His word and listen with your heart for His answer. *Ask and it will be given to you; seek and you will find; knock and the door will be opened to you* (Matthew 7:7).

f) *Be informed.* Keep abreast with events in your time, in your community, church, family, nation, and the world.

I stood firm and did not engage in a quarrel with anyone, but sought the truth. I lived by the Word of God, and submitted with humility to my superior although in my view the directive was unjust. *For it is commendable if a man bears up under the pain of unjust suffering because he is conscious of God,* advised Christ's apostle in 1 Peter 2:19. Then Apostle Peter added, *To this you were called because Christ suffered for you, leaving you an example that you should follow in his steps* (v.21).

Although some friends suggested I should retaliate or file a lawsuit, my spirit sensed that was not my role. But even if the issue was not brought before a human court, I believed justice would still be rendered by the highest authority. Revealed in Romans 12:19 is God's word, *It is mine to avenge; I will repay.* And Hebrews 4:13 adds: *Nothing in all creation is hidden from God's sight. Everything is uncovered and laid bare before the eyes of him to whom we must give account.*

The Kingdom principle I learned is this: if you are not called to do the physical battle, just be concerned with remaining within God's righteous boundaries. Let Him be the judge of others and the administrator of divine justice. The full armor of God is sufficient to give you protection, strength, humility, and confidence to overcome the crisis as you gain spiritual strength.

CHAPTER FIFTEEN

FAITH IS A CHOICE

> *I have set before you
> life and death, blessings and curses.
> Now choose life, so that you and your children
> may live and that you may love the Lord your God,
> listen to His voice, and hold fast to Him.*
> **Deuteronomy 30:19-20**

As the serpent enticed Adam and Eve in Eden and caused them to fall from grace, I sensed a dark spirit was tempting me to question God's promise of love as it whispered, "Are you sure?"

The Pitfall: Self-Pity

Self-pity was the trap.

"If he really loves you," said the faint voice, "he would have saved you from all these. Go ahead. Cry. It's normal." Then the dark spirit whispered closer to my ears, "Deprived. Persecuted. Abandoned. Unfulfilled promises of God."

An unfounded punishment of a recall, my wife in a coma, ridiculed for my faith, my savings gone—I was drowning in a maelstrom of panic. At the edge of losing control of my emotions, I knew that once I give in to self-pity, there was more than enough pain, fear, and hurt to break down the floodgate holding back the accumulating dam of tears, anger, hatred, bitterness, recrimination, loneliness, and even distrust in God.

By crying, I would get the sympathy of other people. But feeling sorry for myself would accuse God of being absent and leaving us alone in the midst of mounting agony. Self-pity would have been tantamount to accusing Him of breaking the promise, *The Lord is good, a refuge in times of trouble. He cares for those who trust in Him* (Nahum 1:7).

Self-pity waited as the door to breaking my faith in God.

The Crossroad

I faced a crossroad. Should I accuse Him of being a fake, unfaithful, and insensitive? Or should I hold on to the trust, confidence, and hope in Jesus I held for many years?

Isaiah 1:18 invites us to use our intellect when faced with a dilemma: *Come now, let us reason together.* The wages for either choice are made clear. Verse 19 assures: *If you are willing and obedient, you will eat the best from the land.* But verse 20 warns: *If you resist and rebel, you will be devoured by the sword.*

Furthermore, in Deuteronomy 30:15-16, God says:

> *See, I set before you today life and prosperity, death and destruction. For I command you today to love the Lord your God, to walk in His ways, and to keep his commands, decrees and laws; then you will live and increase, and the Lord your God will bless you.*

Without God's protection, man is defenseless against the devil:

> *But if your heart turns away and you are not obedient, and if you are drawn away to bow down to other gods and worship them, I declare to you this day that you will certainly be destroyed* (v. 17).

The necessity for choice is clearly stated in verse 19, *I have set before you life and death, blessings and curses. Now choose life, so that you and your children may live.*

In that September morning in ICU, the dilemma grew clear: death if I rejected God, but a chance for life—Eva's life—if I chose to follow Him.

Faith: Man's Free Will

God gave man free will. Therefore, He allows man freedom of choice. In my reading of the Word of God, I have not encountered any hint that the Almighty intervenes to tempt, compel, threaten, trick, lie, or somehow pressure anyone into believing in Him. He leaves it to man to make the choice. He presents the consequences, but permits him to use his will to make a decision. Faith not founded on man's free will is not faith at all.

God's Unfailing Love

More than my fear of losing Eva, I could not turn against Him. Through His Word and in my actual personal experiences, I knew His character—He is a loving God. Deep in my heart, I knew He loved me.

In a piece of paper that I kept in my pocket since the recall issue began, I read His promise taken from Isaiah 54:10, *Though the mountains be shaken and the hills be removed, yet my unfailing love for you will not be shaken nor my covenant of peace be removed.*

In the years since I received Jesus Christ as my personal Savior, through the series of trials Eva and I underwent, we had personally witnessed the reality of His love, grace, power, and faithfulness. God was too real for me to deny. His Love was too engulfing to forget. He was present to help us overcome when we suffered.

Choose Faith, Choose Life

The word of God is clear. *If you do not stand firm in your faith, you will not stand at all* (Isaiah 7:9).

Thus, I chose to still believe in God. I chose to keep my faith. I chose life. At that crossroad of my spiritual journey, I resolved: "Yes, I am sure."

I was sure of God's love. My choice was a sober, conscious, and deliberate response, free from emotionalism and self-pity.

Prayer of Righteous Men

The prayers of a righteous man, although alone, will still be heard by God. James 5:16 tells us, *The prayer of a righteous man is powerful and effective.* But the prayers of many also delights the Almighty if their requests are in accord with His will. Jesus promised: *Again, I tell you that if two of you on earth agree about anything you ask for, it will be done for you by my Father in heaven. For where two or three come together in my name, there I am with them* (Matthew 18:19-20).

Nightly Prayers Began

Touched by the Holy Spirit in a dream, OFW Ms. Emma Bacaron suggested to her pastor and me to start a series of prayers for the recovery of Mrs. Dumapias. Thus, five days after the stroke, nightly prayers at my residence began. The congregation of the Good Shepherd Christian Fellowship (GSCF) led by Pastor Jay Dare and Pastor Koshy Eapen, and some members of the Bahrain Christian Fellowship (BCF), Word of Life International Ministry (WOLI), Jesus is Alive Community (JIA), and The Shepherd's Flock joined in the prayers. Some leaders of the Filipino community and a few Muslim Bahraini friends of Eva and me were also present. My daughter Myra, her son Daniel, Eva's sisters Lethie and Merlee, and her brother Dr. Munding Vitug, arrived in the afternoon from the U.S. on time to be with us for the prayer that evening.

In the nightly prayers, Pastor Jay led the GSCF congregation, composed of Indian and Filipino believers, in praise and worship. Pastor Koshy led the prayer for the awakening of Sis. Eva from a coma. The prayers were not formula incantations memorized or read from written script. Rather, they came from the heart and were based on biblical passages. They invoked the authority of the name of Jesus Christ in healing the sick.[46]

---

[46]In Matthew 10:8, Jesus said, "Heal the sick, raise the dead." In John 14:14, He assured His believers, "Ask me anything in my name, and I will do it."

Prayers of Church Congregations

I also requested via email ministry leaders in several countries with whom Eva and I became personal friends.[47]

In Bahrain, the Filipino, Indian, and American Christian congregations also included in their Sabbath (Friday, not Sunday in Muslim States) worship service a prayer for the recovery of Eva.[48]

In Philippians 4:19, Apostle Paul assures, *My God will meet all your needs according to his glorious riches in Christ Jesus.*

And Hebrews 4:16 directs, *Let us then approach the throne of grace with confidence, so that we may receive mercy and find grace to help us in our time of need.*

---

[47] Bishop Fred Magbanua, Chairman of the Council of Christian Bishops of the Philippines and President of Christ Jesus our Life Ministry; Bishop Efraim Tendero, Chairman of Philippine Council of Evangelical Churches; Bishop Eddie Villanueva, Chairman of Philippines for Jesus Movement and President of Jesus is Lord Ministry; and Rev. Dr. Joy Tira of the Canada-based Filipino International Network (FIN); and a number of churches in South Korea and America replied assuring that the prayer request was passed on to their respective churches, and that prayers for Sis. Eva were said on regular basis.

[48] The Sacred Heart Catholic Church of Bahrain under Fr. Felicio Denis from Kerala regularly prayed for her. Intercessor prayer teams from the BCF under Pastor Fred Cudiamat, WOLI under Pastor Boni Villanueva, JIA under Pastor Ignar Reyes, Shepherd's Flock under Pastor Jesse Cordova, Church of Philadelphia under Pastora Marilyn Pinto and her husband Bro. John Pinto, as well as other Filipino and Indian ministries included Eva in their prayers and in their hospital visits.

CHAPTER SIXTEEN

THE HEART OF A PRINCE

> *As water reflects a face, so a man's heart reflects the man.*
> **Proverbs 27:19**

The Lord knew I was practically penniless by the time Eva suffered a stroke. Seen from the eyes of the material world, the accumulated costs of Eva's confinement could bury me in debt for life.

Eight Months in the Hospital

Eva stayed at Salmanya Medical Center for more than eight months. Within this period, she underwent CT Scan nine times, was brought to the operating room four times, and remained in the intensive care unit for about three weeks connected to a respirator and other equipment. A team of specialists, headed by the country's top neurologist, operated on her. A shunt was inserted under her skin to drain into her stomach any liquid that may accumulate in her cranial. She was later transferred to a private room, and a special nurse was assigned overnight duty exclusively for her. A feeding tube was introduced directly to her abdomen; she was brought to the operating room twice for this purpose. A team of doctors visited her every day.

Half a Million Dollar Debt?

If Eva was confined in a top U.S. hospital, it would cost about half a million dollars as estimated by an accountant after considering the use of a private room and other facilities, high-tech equipment, medicine, and the services of specialists. Even if the figure was exaggerated, anything close to that amount would take half of my lifetime to pay. After my financial support abroad and medical insurance terminated due to the mysterious recall, my personal savings drained out fast. How could I ever cover such mounting cost?

Touched by God

How much did I pay?

ZERO!

The Almighty God touched the heart of His Highness, Sheikh Khalifa. As soon as he learned of Eva's stroke, he instructed the Minister of Health that all hospitalization, medical, and doctors' bills due to me shall be sent instead to his office, the Prime Minister's Court.

A few days after Eva was rushed to the hospital, the Prime Minister instructed that a special nurse be assigned for overnight duty. In a phone conversation, the Minister of Health conveyed to me Sheikh Khalifa's instruction that Eva could transfer to the VIP ward of the medical center. However, I assured the Minister that the regular private ward was sufficient. I thanked him and the Prime Minister for their kindness.

I was so overwhelmed and humbled by the unsolicited generosity and kindness welling out from the heart of His Highness, Sheikh Khalifa. I have heard of the generosity of the Al Khalifa family to the Bahraini people and to foreign guests. But for my family to be the recipient of such benevolence was deliriously euphoric.

Beyond Diplomatic Courtesy

Salmanya Medical Complex was a government institution under the supervision of the Minister of Health who sat with other cabinet ministers in the Council of Ministers headed by the Prime Minister. On the basis of humanitarian considerations and diplomatic courtesy, His Highness could choose to grant a foreign guest the rare full exemption from payments. A few years earlier, he granted such a courtesy to the previous Bangladesh ambassador who suffered a heart attack. The gesture was not automatic, and he could have ignored my predicament. He made a deliberate choice as he issued the order for all the hospital bills to be settled by the Prime Minister's Court. No bill was charged against me.

Beyond diplomatic courtesy and his friendship with the Philippine Ambassador and Mrs. Dumapias, the Prime Minister possessed a heart sensitive to the will of the Almighty. Despite the height of his power and office, Sheikh Khalifa acted with kindness in response to the needs of one who placed his full trust in Almighty God.

Return of the Rain

Eighteen days passed since Eva fell into a coma. Every morning, I closely examined her fingers, toes, and eyelids, but observed no movement. Relatives and friends cheered whenever they saw a muscle move, only to be told it was just a twitch—an involuntary muscle movement. Still, scores of Filipino community leaders, acquaintances from various churches, some ladies of the diplomatic corps, local businessmen, and people we had not previously met, came to visit her and comfort me.

Third Week in a Coma

While evening group prayers for Eva's healing continued nightly at our residence, guests at the hospital visitors lounge expressed pessimism. The longer Eva remained in coma, they said, the less likely she would wake up. It seemed that some guests had already given up hope and expected the worst, hurrying to visit her "before it is too late." A well-meaning group came to sing soothing melodies to comfort me, yet concluded the serenade with "*Hindi Kita Malilimutan*" (I Will Never Forget You), a song usually sung to someone about to depart.

The Eyeball

My brother-in-law, Dr. Munding, relied on facts in his profession. In his life and education, he would not believe unless he could base his belief on facts. Until he accepted Jesus Christ as his personal Savior a few evenings earlier, he could not understand how I could hold on to my hope that Eva would snap back from her coma and be restored to normalcy. After all, the facts indicated a negative prognosis.

Doing his routine each time he came to the ICU, he raised his sister's eyelid. Previously, he would see no movement except the pupil which dilated whenever a light was flashed on it. This time, the whole eyeball rolled.

A moving eyeball, though an ordinary and common motion of a healthy person, revealed the unexpected. For the first time, I saw my brother-in-law cry even as he tried to hide his shock. He knew the rolling eyeball signaled the end of the coma. His sister was on her way back from the edge of death.

As I watched him, I understood immediately what he had seen. Then, I noticed the ventilator machine and the monitor showing her breathing normal and her vital signs stable.

God's Intervention

I felt the same elation that seized Prophet Elijah when a fist-sized cloud rose above the sea, signaling the end of drought in Israel. After the earnest prayer of this man of righteousness, courage, and conviction, the sky grew black with clouds, the wind rose, and heavy rain fell. Because of Elijah's prayers, God intervened in the course of nature.[49]

To me, the moving eyeball in the vast universe of the human body stood for the fist-sized cloud that marked the end of drought in Eva's condition. It signaled God's intervention in the course of nature, a sign that He heard the prayers, assuring me of the

---

[49] 1Kings 18:41-45

overwhelming power of the Holy Spirit to heal and restore Sis. Eva.

I shouted, "Hallelujah! Thank you, Jesus!" I turned to my daughter Myra and grandson Daniel and told them, "Mama is waking up. She survives!"

Within three weeks since her coma, my family saw the faithfulness of many friends, the benevolence of a human prince, and the mercy of the Divine Prince of Peace, the King of Kings!

Road to Restoration

Eva's vital signs remained normal, so she was moved to a private ward. From there, she continued to receive treatment and therapy. When she gained enough strength to travel, I brought her to America where her three sisters and brother, Dr. Munding, resided. We stayed at her sister Nora's house.

She Would not Stop Talking

Shortly after Eva's arrival in Cincinnati, Ohio, the Lord showed us another miracle. Even before any doctor could see her for any treatment or speech therapy, one morning she began to speak, not just one syllable between gasps but long sentences.

When told to slow down to rest, she said, "I have not spoken for eight months, why stop me now?" Since then she had not stopped talking. She was back to her old self, relating stories and giving instructions. I knew then she had not lost her memory, language skills, comprehension, wit, and sense of humor. She still knew everyone's birthday and read more books than ever.

Haggai Institute and FIN

God's grace of restoration also covered me. Although the recall directive prevented me from attending the Christian leadership training in Maui, I was invited to the same executive seminar a few months later at the Haggai Institute in Singapore. At HI, I finally received formal training in Christian ministry. When I returned to

Manama where my wife waited at Salmanya hospital, Dr. Rev. Joy Tira invited me to join the International Committee of the Filipino International Network (FIN), which further exposed me to the ministry for the diaspora, especially for the Filipinos working in the Middle East. In every message I shared with congregations that invited me, I talked about the love and power of God in the recovery of Sis. Eva and the blessings we received.

More God's Blessings

Sen. Blas Ople, the new Secretary of Foreign Affairs, granted almost immediately my request for foreign assignment. While there was no position available in the US for my rank, I opted for Mexico as the next best choice.

God's love continued to manifest when I brought Eva from Cincinnati to Mexico City. Despite the high elevation of the capital city, her hypertension did not worsen. Instead, even without any treatment by a doctor, her blood pressure went down to normal. Her blood sugar reading also decreased, so her insulin injection was stopped. Her speech and general condition continued to improve.

With the urgings of supportive embassy staff, primarily Administrative Officer Rene Canlas, his wife Sis. Tess, and my secretary Maria Annette Aquino, I began a Bible study in which Eva shared her testimonies from her wheelchair. We were later joined by Pastor Angel and Sister Elma Ignacio who shared their knowledge of the word of God.

The Philippine government extended my service as a career diplomat beyond my retirement date, perhaps as a way to compensate for the damage caused by the arbitrary recall. And I regained the savings lost due to the recall order even as I maintained my rank, dignity, and honor.

I will repay you for the years the locusts have eaten, assured the Lord in Joel 2:25.

I believe He did.

CHAPTER SEVENTEEN

THE KINGDOM OF HEAVEN AND YOU

> *If anyone thirsts, let him come to Me and drink. He who believes in Me, as the Scripture has said, out of his heart will flow rivers of living water.*
> **John 7:37-38**

In winter 2013, Eva and I reminisced those critical moments we experienced in various postings. We marveled at the consistently lavish protection, provision, and affection shown by the Lord especially in those times we faced formidable threats. With His love and power, the impossible became possible. Confident in the faithfulness of the Almighty, we viewed the events in today's world from a vantage point different from that of most people.

World Focus on Human Supremacy

Understandably, the world looks with alarm at the present trend of global events, especially the conflicts in the Middle East and the international financial crisis. Indeed, the prognosis is dim as most people limit their focus to the physical dimension of today's headlines. While they fear the effects these crisis would have on their lives, they suppress their apprehensions through entertainment in their high-tech lifestyle. And they look to the world leaders—Kings, Presidents, Prime Ministers, United Nations Secretary-General, economists, diplomats, and other decision makers—as they leave in their hands a blank check to look for solutions. In the face of persistent global instability, many today believe the high level of technology speaks of man's competence to save himself. They place their hopes on human drive for world unity, intercultural understanding, interfaith harmony, global economic cooperation, and international comity—all contained in the capsule of "political correctness"—as the avenue for a peaceful and safe future. "Man is the master of his destiny" is their motto.

Natural Disasters: Beyond Human Control

But despite his increased knowledge and advanced technology, nature flutters beyond man's ability to overcome or escape. Natural forces persist to bring destruction as the magnitude, intensity, frequency, and location of earthquakes, flashfloods, super typhoons, tornadoes, hurricanes, sinkholes, and tsunamis in recent years proved to be rare, if not unprecedented. Man generally considers these earth-bound disasters as unwanted phenomena to avoid, overcome, or totally eradicate. However, scientists generally admit that the more they learn, the more they realize they don't know enough. Man remains overwhelmed by these forces beyond his control.

Look Beyond the Human Box

While it is commendable to acknowledge the abilities of man, the world should also recognize his limitations. The track record of man clearly suggests he does not measure up to the towering magnitude of today's impending global calamities. While technology and societal unity propped up Nimrod in building the Tower of Babel, his project came to nothing.[50] Hence, history has been filled with examples of empires and civilizations that rose and fell due to internal human frailties.[51]

---

[50] Genesis 11:1-9

[51] The Roman Empire is an example. Read www.history.com/news/history-lists/8-reasons-why-rome-fell. See also Will and Ariel Durant, *The Lessons of History,* Simon & Schuster: 1968 (New York, London, Toronto, Sydney).

Shouldn't man now look beyond the human box and consider the reality of a power above and beyond human sovereigns?

God's Long-Range Plan

If viewed in a wider perspective, natural movements are not separate nor contradictory to man's well-being; instead, they complete the greater scenario and are very much linked to man's future. Man needs to consider that his Maker may have greater perspective—and plans—beyond present mortal capabilities. Isaiah 55:9 reflects the dichotomy of man's perception and God's: *As the heavens are higher than the earth, so are my ways higher than your ways and my thoughts than your thoughts.*

The Lord allows natural disasters to visit humanity even as man achieves today's high-tech lifestyle, in order to deliver a point.

Man: Engineered for Higher Goal

Evolutionists' theory of adaptation and natural selection claim certain qualities of species are either acquired or lost due to requirements imposed by the physical environment. Believers of the Bible, however, take issue with evolutionists on the matter of man's intellectual potential. Creationists insist that from the moment of his creation, man—the homo sapiens species—has been endowed with a brain possessing the same capacity and potential he now has. Man's intellectual capacity is inherent in his DNA and is not a product of, nor can it be degraded through, adaptation. If the evolutionist theory were correct, any high intellectual capacity man may have initially possessed would have deteriorated due to non-use for millions of years as he survived through the Stone Age. On the principle of atrophy, man's high-tech potential would have further degraded through the hunting and agrarian periods which required muscular, but less of mental, prowess for survival. On the other hand, the biblical account of Noah's ark suggests man possessed the propensity for technical calculations, resiliency, and meditation without the process of evolutionary adaptation.

God fashioned man to have the mental capacity and physical dexterity to administer His creation on Earth and transform his environment. Man's high-level intellectual potential remained untapped for millions of years and began to surface only during the industrial revolution. By the twentieth century, man confirmed he possessed the brain for higher mathematics ("non-linear tensor calculus, relativistic quantum theory, and higher dimensional geometry"), logic, analysis, and communication.[52] His reserved capacity for high-technology led him to produce computers, digital imaging, cybernetic inventions, rockets for space travel, and other innovations. The fact that thirty-five percent of the whole blood flow in the human body services the brain reveals God's provision and purpose from the moment He created man.

Nature: God's Provision—and Warning

God's foresight and purpose are also evident in the timely provision of natural elements that man needed to achieve a high level of technology. Among these is fossil hydrocarbon fuel, especially petroleum. The main ingredients of the fossil fuel were deposited some 500 million years ago in the Cambrian Age, and the geological process involved pressure, heat, and millions of years to produce hydrocarbon fuel, petroleum. God's timing was impeccable as the petroleum stage came at the time man appeared on earth as if by predetermined appointment. Had man came too soon, there would have been less petroleum but more of kerogen; had he came too late, petroleum would have degraded into methane, or natural gas.[53]

In addition, certain sedimentary and tectonic processes must occur through millions of years to produce the right reservoir

---

[52] For a detailed presentation of man's God-given intellectual gift, see Hugh Ross, PhD., "Equipped for High-Tech Society," in *Connections: Linking Science and Faith,* a publication of Reasons to Believe, Vol. 6, No. 3, Third Quarter 2004, p. 4.

[53] "God's Well-Timed Gift to Mankind," Hugh Ross, PhD., ibid., pp. 2-3.

structures for collecting and storing fossil hydrocarbons. Again, had man appeared on Earth too late, the deposits of these fuels would have leaked so that there would be less or no fossil hydrocarbon left to support industrialization and modern civilization.

Although both kerogen and methane are important in sustaining modern industries, petroleum is still the mainstay of today's high-tech society. Alternative fuel is now being discovered, but until a viable option becomes operational, petroleum would remain the platform for the next rung of science and technological lift-off.

In fact, earlier generations saw God's control over nature. Jesus' disciples recognized and marveled at His power. *In fear and amazement, they asked one another, 'Who is this? He commands even the winds and the water, and they obey him'* (Luke 8:25).

If today's generation recognizes God's control over nature, shouldn't people also credit Him for the provision of the natural elements made available for modern living? Shouldn't they also recognize that He is capable of unleashing inescapable disasters to underscore the truth that God remains the master of man's fate?

The Message

The foregoing factors convey the following divine message: *God holds control over nature to help as well as to warn mankind. As the Creator, He designed and engineered man for a much higher achievement. But to reach it, man must remain within the parameters of God's will, provision, and purpose.*

Purpose for Man

The Maker has a sublime, ultimate purpose for man. As God created the whole universe to reflect His glory and majesty, man's role is to glorify Him and to acknowledge His deity. *Let them praise the name of the Lord, for he commanded and they were created,* the psalmist declared.[54]

Every person is intended to radiate as a mirror, reflecting the glory of God. Each of us is *predestined according to the plan of him who works out everything in conformity with the purpose of his will, in order that we...might be for the praise of his glory.*[55]

For this purpose, God made man with spirit, body, and soul, equipping him with the ability to fellowship with Him. Created in the image of the Creator, man is intended to reflect His love, power, and righteousness. However, after man's disobedience in Eden, his spirit wandered away from his Master. For man to regain his luster, his spirit must be reconciled with the Will of his Maker so he can reflect the glory of God and fulfill the purpose for which he is created.

God Has a Plan for Each Person

In line with His purpose for mankind, God also devised a plan for each individual. Every person is uniquely made for a purpose that is reserved and designed only for that person. The Bible gives numerous examples of men and women who were born for a specific purpose and plan for God's glory: Moses, Samson, Esther, Joseph, Samuel, Jeremiah, Mary, and others .

Before I formed you in the womb, I knew you, the Lord told prophet Jeremiah as He revealed His plan for his life. *Before you were born I have set you apart; I appointed you as a prophet to the nations.*[56]

Those words of God reveal several principles applicable to everyone. *First,* He equipped every person with talents, gifts, and capabilities enabling him/her to fulfill God's specific plan and purpose. *Second,* He has foreknowledge of every situation that

---

[54] Psalm 148:5. Verses 1-14 reflect God's purpose for all creation.
[55] Ephesians 1: 11-12
[56] Jeremiah 1:5

would confront each person, but leaves it to man to choose whether to obey Him and fulfill his God-given role. And *third*, His plan for a person's life is for his/her benefits and in line with His goodness.

Although at first we may not understand, the plan of God is always for our own benefit and is better than what we can achieve without Him. The Lord declared, *For I know the plans I have for you, plans to prosper you and not to harm you, plans to give you hope and a future* (Jeremiah 29:11).

The Bible also teaches that no other person is best suited to assume your role in God's plan except you. And no other plan is reserved exclusively for you but His plan, which can be made perfect only with your participation. *God had planned something better for us so that only together with us would they be made perfect* (Hebrews 11:40).

The aforesaid verse underscores the importance of putting your faith into action in order to fulfill the role reserved for you. *Faith, by itself, if it is not accompanied by action, is dead* (James 2:17).

God assures protection to those who come into His kingdom and act to fulfill His plan for their lives: *No weapon forged against you will prevail, and you will refute every tongue that accuses you. This is the heritage of the servants of the Lord, and this is their vindication from me* (Isaiah 54:17).

Everybody is Invited

God has a special place for each of us in His grand design and *wants all men to be saved and come to a knowledge of truth,* whatever social, political, and economic backgrounds we come from (1 Timothy 2:4). Nobody is under-qualified, overqualified, or exempted from His offer of salvation. The invitation to His kingdom is for all, but God does not force His plan and blessings on those who reject His offer of redemption through His Word.

To anyone with faith in Jesus Christ, God reveals His plans and purpose for his or her life, *having been predestined...in conformity with the purpose of His will, in order that we* (believers), *who were the first to hope in Christ, might be for the praise of His glory.*[57]

How About the Non-Believers?

Don't the non-believers also deserve to receive God's plan to prosper them and give them hope and a future? Indeed, there is a plan waiting for them, for God loves them as much as He loves everyone else, and the gifts of salvation and blessings are waiting for them.[58]

By divine grace, even non-believers are endowed with one talent or another, which are gifts from God. But such gifts must be used in line with His purpose. By their denial of the Son of Man, non-believers remain blind to God's purpose for their gifts and therefore failed to attain the blessings prepared for using these gifts. Many are misled as they erroneously misuse their gifts in art, music, literature, sports, leadership, business, etc., for crime, immorality, and all sorts of corruption. They prefer to listen to false teachings and believe the lie that God has nothing to do with their talents. But the rewards they receive through the corruption of God-given abilities are counterfeit "blessings" that destroy them in the end.[59] Jesus offers the true, priceless blessings to those who rightly use His gifts in accordance with His purpose. But those who rejected Him, they have also rejected His blessings.

It is Not Too Late

But it is not too late. A choice can free an unbeliever from darkness and a pointless, dead-end existence. By coming into the kingdom of God, he can rise above the deception of Satan.

To open the door to a new life, the unbeliever may now

---

[57] Ephesians 1:12

[58] Romans 5:8

[59] 2Timothy 3:8-9 says: *...these men oppose the truth—men of depraved minds ...But they will not get very far because...their folly will be clear to everyone.* See also Titus 1:15; Psalm 53:1; 2Timothy 3:1-9.

reconsider the call of Jesus Christ: *Seek first the Kingdom of God and His righteousness and all these things will be given to you as well* (Matthew 6:33).

Jesus and the Salvation of Man

When God made man, He delegated him to have dominion over the Earth.[60] But by the disobedience of Adam and Eve, they lost their spiritual fellowship with God and, by man's default, Satan took over the administration of the planet. Driven out of Eden, Adam and Eve and their descendants became subjects to sin, death, sickness, decay, violence, greed, envy, and all kinds of corruption.

Because wickedness prevailed on earth in Noah's time, God destroyed all living things except those on board the ark. But as man replenished the planet, God saw he still tended to fall for Satan's deception. God so loved the world He took another step to fulfill His plan to redeem mankind to His spiritual kingdom.[61]

God's Covenant with Abraham

Through Abram of Ur of the Chaldeans (now part of Iraq), God planned to create a nation through which He could channel the message of redemption of man. The Lord made Abram, whom he later renamed Abraham, the promise:

> *I will make you into a great nation*
> *And I will bless you.*
> *I will make your name great,*
> *And you will be a blessing.*
> *I will bless those you bless you,*
> *And whoever curses you I will curse;*
> *And all peoples on earth*
> *Will be blessed through you."*
> (Genesis 12:2-3)

---

[60] Genesis 1:28

[61] Ibid., 3:15

The promise serves as a framework for understanding God's role and judgment in the affairs of men and nations. His commitment is unchanging, absolute, guaranteed, and eternal despite the imperfection of the human recipients. The pledge was to persist through all generations of the Israeli nation.[62] But His promise also extends to anyone whose faith is birthed with the fervor of Abraham's obedience to the Word of God.

Jesus: Fulfillment of God's Promise

The fulfillment of the final portion of the covenant—*all peoples on earth will be blessed through you*—is Jesus Christ. The Almighty Father sent Him to earth to live fully as man even as He remained God, so that through Him, man may accept the principles of the kingdom. Though Jesus suffered death on the cross, He came back to life in a glorified existence so that those who believe in Him may be reconciled with the Maker and have eternal life. From Jesus flows the river of life and through Him leads the road to salvation and the kingdom of Heaven.

Apostle Paul attested, *If you belong to Christ, then are you Abraham's seed, and heirs according to the promise* (Galatians 3:29).

God's principle of redemption offered to the Israelis applies not only to the biological descendants of Abraham but to all who choose to come into His kingdom:

> *I will give you a new heart and put a new spirit in you; I will remove from you your heart of stone and give you a heart of flesh. And I will put my Spirit in you and move you to follow my decrees and be careful to keep my laws.*[63]

---

[62] Abraham's covenant is given through his offspring through Isaac, according to Genesis 17:21.

[63] Ezekiel 36:26-27

Courage and Truth

I wonder how many of the youths knew the story of this man. At first, he was like many people of today who do not know Christ.

He was among the elect in his society, well-educated, wealthy, and a leader whose decisions affected the lives of many. He knew that his peers would ostracize him, and perhaps remove him from his position, for what he was about to do. But what others would think did not stop him from seeking the truth.

In this man, courage and integrity prevailed over what was "politically correct" in his time. Unlike many leaders in our time, he did not have an excuse to accept the lies, cowardice, deception, abuse of authority, conformity for its own sake, and the rot of traditionalism he saw in many of his peers. Though a member of the Sanhedrin, Nicodemus gathered the courage to go in the cover of night and seek a man who was unemployed, uneducated, and homeless—Jesus Christ, a former carpenter-stone cutter.[64]

Nicodemus' Encounter with Jesus

His encounter with Jesus is found in the Book of John, Chapter Three. To many people, the episode is an eye-opener. It is the basis of the principle of spiritual regeneration, an experience of a person when he accepts the promise of redemption and salvation made through Jesus.

Nicodemus felt rewarded when Jesus revealed to him a heavenly wisdom, *'I tell you the truth, no one can see the kingdom of God unless he is born again'* (John 3:3).

The glare of truth blinded momentarily the mind of Nicodemus. He wondered how a grown person be born again from a mother's womb. So Jesus added, *'No one can enter the kingdom of God*

---

[64] Dr. Chuck Bagby, *Born to Die, The Jesus Story: What I Wish I Had Known (Book 1),* Burning Heart Bible Studies Publishing: San Antonio, TX (2014), p. 37, believes Jesus and Joseph worked more on stones, which were more numerous and cheaper than wood.

unless he is born of water and the Spirit. Flesh gives birth to flesh, but the Spirit gives birth to spirit' (v.5-6).

Nicodemus was shown the first thing that happens when a person enters the kingdom of God: immediately, the new believer is freed from spiritual blindness. The veil of lies and deception imposed by the devil suddenly drops off, and the new believer begins to see the brilliant truth of God's realm.

Then, in the same encounter, Jesus revealed to him more of the basic truths regarding the kingdom, *'For God so loved the world that he gave his one and only Son, that whoever believes in him shall not perish but have eternal life'* (v.16).

Jesus emphasized God's promise of salvation by saying, *'For God did not send his Son into the world to condemn the world, but to save the world through him'* (v.17).

As he walked home, Nicodemus mulled over every word of Jesus. He thought of the other members of the Sanhedrin and the Chief Priest; he wished they, too, had heard those words. Yet, he knew most of them were instead devising trump up charges for a farce trial against Jesus. They made up their mind to reject Jesus. But not him. Nicodemus decided to follow Jesus.

Spiritual Journey to the Kingdom

There are no preconditions for entering the kingdom of God. Regardless of your past and present lifestyle, whether you were a hardened criminal, persecutor of Christians, an atheist, drug addict, adulterer, or a murderer, God is willing to overlook all those things. He looks at you for what He made you to be, not what you made of yourself without Him. But your decision is needed.

The only requirement is to repent of your sins and accept Jesus Christ as Lord and Savior—not a ritualistic, shallow repentance and acceptance, but a deliberate decision to receive Jesus Christ's offer of salvation. Decide to turn away from spiritual wandering, and come home to where you truly belong. As the father in Jesus' parable ran to meet his returning prodigal son, so will heaven celebrate when you return to His kingdom.[65] The earthly father hugged his wandering son with compassion and joy, and said to his servants,

> *'Quick! Bring the best robe and put it on him. Put a ring on his finger and sandals on his feet. Bring the fattened calf and kill it. Let's have a feast and celebrate. For this son of mine was dead and is alive again; he was lost and is found'* (Luke 15:22-24).

Many have been led to Christ through prayers with a pastor or other believers, or evangelism programs on television and radio, while others just pray on their own.

The following is a sample prayer you can say as you repent:

"Almighty Father, thank you for sending Jesus Christ to redeem me. I repent of my sins, and I ask for your forgiveness. I invite Jesus into my life as my Lord and Savior, and I receive the Holy Spirit. Amen."

Prepare to Face the End of the Age

God will forgive you and cleanse you of your sins—*though your sins are like scarlet, they shall be as white as snow* (Isaiah 1:48). Through the Holy Spirit, He will transform and strengthen you to overcome trials. And Jesus will equip you with authority to fulfill His plan and your role in our time. He promised:

Anyone who has faith in me will do what I have been doing. He will do even greater things than these…I will do whatever you ask in my name, so that the Son may bring glory to the Father. You may ask me for anything in my name…I will do it (John 14:12-14).

As a new creation, you can proceed in life assured of salvation and confident to face the challenges of the End of the Age.

---

[65] Luke 15:11-32 tells the story of a young man who, after finding false security in a worldly lifestyle, decided to return home to find assured provision, love, acceptance, and protection.

PART THREE

END OF THE AGE

*The coming of the lawless one
will be in accordance with the work of Satan
displayed in all kinds of counterfeit miracles, signs and wonders,
and in every sort of evil that deceives those who are perishing.
They perish because they refused to love the truth and so be saved.
For this reason God sends them a powerful delusion
so that they will believe the lie and so that
all will be condemned who have not believed the truth
but have delighted in wickedness.*

2 Thessalonians 2:9-12

CHAPTER EIGHTEEN

SIGNS OF THE END

> *Jesus answered, 'Watch out that no one deceives you. For many will come in my name, claiming, I am the Christ, and will deceive many. You will hear of wars and rumors of wars, but see to it that you are not alarmed. Such things must happen, but the end is still to come. Nation will rise against nation, and kingdom against kingdom. There will be famines and earthquakes in various places. All these are the beginning of birth pains.'*
> **Matthew 24:4-8**

The Days of Noah, Sodom and Gomorrah

The Bible foretells that at the End of the Age, the world would be like it was as in the days of Noah when the big flood came,[66] and of Lot when Sodom and Gomorrah were destroyed.[67]

Abraham bargained with God to spare Sodom and Gomorrah but there were not even ten righteous people in the cities. Men had sex with other men and indulged in incest.[68] In those days, men ignored God's laws and authority, and believed their own lust, greed, and arrogance were right and wise. They devised multiple standards of

---

[66] Luke 17:26

[67] Ibid., 28-29

[68] Genesis 19:4-5; v. 30-38

right and wrong contrary to God's righteousness. People were wicked and violent and *their sins so grievous* God decided to destroy the two cities.[69] Engrossed in their wanton lifestyle, they were not prepared when their end came.

Spirit of Rebellion in Our Time

In today's world, we see the same spirit of rebellion against God displayed in the affairs of men and nations. The continuing justifications for same-sex marriage and abortion reflect the persistence of the spirit that brought destruction to Sodom and Gomorrah. Furthermore, as the people in Noah's time ridiculed him for being out of touch with reality in building the ark, many today malign believers of Christ as out of touch with "politically correct" culture. It is tragic enough that in many countries millions of Jews and Christians are persecuted, killed, and sold as slaves, yet no government had come forward to effectively put a stop to it. Furthermore, some Western societies have introduced legislations and jurisprudence that overturn many biblical principles, even as these precepts are re-interpreted and repackaged beyond recognition by self-appointed spiritual media. Laws are issued that limit public expression of the Judeo-Christian principles even in countries that were founded on these same principles. God's commandments are openly criticized as some politicians, entertainment industry, main stream media, and public education introduce alternative standards of morality.[70]

Consequently, many young people no longer see the distinction between right and wrong, good and evil. Non-believers fail to see the truth while some believers are induced to doubt their faith. The

---

[69] Genesis 18:20

[70] See Brad O'Leary, *America's War on Christianity*, WND Books: Washington DC, 2010.

New Age movement, for example, claims that there is no evil and man can metamorphose to attain divine spirituality of God.[71]

Some social, cultural, and statutory pressures now conspire to make the perversion of God's laws acceptable and enforceable, while the people faithful to His commandments are punished. What used to be right is now questioned, and what used to be wrong is now right. The world is flying upside down. Instead of reaching to the stars, it is rushing to a crash.

Warning Signs

God's judgments on Sodom and Gomorrah and on the wicked world in Noah's time are previews of the catastrophe that will fall on a world that rebels against the sovereign Creator. The image of fire and sulfur raining down and destroying all things including men, women, and children in the sinful cities forewarns that the fate of the insolent will be horrifying. The cries of drowning humanity and all living creatures except those in Noah's ark deliver the graphic warning of God's sweeping, total, and inescapable wrath.

To the non-believers, the message is this: *Unless you repent, you too will all perish* (Luke 13:5).

And against backsliding of the faithful, the message is this: *See to it brothers, that none of you have a sinful unbelieving heart that turns away from the living God ... so that none of you may be hardened by sin's deceitfulness* (Hebrews 3:12-13).

War in Heaven, War on Earth

Each person remains the prize as well as the battlefield in which the devil wages his war against God. In the last days of the age, Satan is desperately fighting his final battles. And he knows he will lose.

---

[71] See https://en.wikipedia.org/wiki/New_Age. Accessed June 30, 2013.

Revelation 12 describes how he was thrown down from heaven:

> *And there was war in heaven. Michael and his angels fought against the dragon, and the dragon and his angels fought back. But he was not strong enough, and they lost their place in heaven. The great dragon was hurled down – that ancient serpent called the devil, or Satan, who leads the whole world astray. He was hurled to the earth, and his angels with him* (v. 7-9).

Without any more access to heaven, Satan is frantic for he knows Jesus is about to return to Earth, and his time on this planet is coming to an end. Even the devil's power in the underworld has been compromised as Jesus now holds the power of life, resurrection, and forgiveness as a result of His crucifixion. The Son of God now has the keys of death and Hades.[72] With Jesus' second coming, Satan is destined to a bleak future of condemnation in the lake of fire. *He is filled with fury because he knows that his time is short* (v. 12).

Why is Satan waging the battle even when he knows it is futile? He wants to bring as many souls into hell with him, in his kingdom of eternal damnation. He still tries to convince gullible mortals and his fallen angels that his kingdom is greater than God's, that he is greater than the Creator. Even to his very end, he still insists his lies on others.

Old Warfare Strategy

In waging his battle, the devil is using the ancient warfare strategy. In his attempt to conquer "territory" which is man, he employs both force and propaganda. He targets the physical defenses as well as the will of his target. Once his "enemy" surrenders, he then occupies and sets up his rule.

In ancient warfare, the invader first used catapults and archers to send a rain of rocks, fire, and arrows to inflict havoc against the shields and fortifications of the city. But parallel to Sun Tzu's thesis

---

[72] Revelation 1:18

in his writing, *The Art of War*,[73] Satan also views spiritual warfare as a contest of the will. Likewise, the surprise attack on Pearl Harbor to destroy America's fortification and capability to strike back was also meant to destroy American will to resist. The concepts of "counter value," "assured destruction," and "overkill" in the Cold War era aimed to weaken the enemy's strike capability as well as his psychological fiber.

Therefore, expect the devil to increase efforts in destroying the institutions intended by God as foundations and vessels of His righteousness: marriage, family, church, and leaders of the faith. Simultaneously, he sows fear, temptation, and confusion through gross misinterpretation of the Bible as he employs intimidation, persecution, murder, and pillage to discourage the believers.[74] To prevent non-believers from knowing the Creator, the devil will impress the world with *counterfeit miracles, signs and wonders, and in every sort of evil that deceives those who are perishing.*[75] When we consider today's upside down morality and values in a number of societies, the devil appears to be winning.

However, as a lesson in the history of warfare, the attacker does not always win the war. On the strength of his psychological foundation, the defender can turn the tide of battle. The Minute Men, for example, resorted to guerilla warfare against a better armed and trained adversary. American independence was won on the basis of the defenders' familiarity of the terrain as well as on their resilience, perseverance, faith, and determination. Many crucial

---

[73] An ancient Chinese military treatise, "war is an extension of politics by other means," is made famous by a high-ranking military general, strategist, and tactician. *The Art of War* is well known among military historians in Asia and had inspired strategists such as General Douglas McArthur, Mao Tse-tung, and Vo Nguyen Giap.

[74] See Matthew 24:4-25. Jesus warned that in the last days, the devil will use a combination of deception and persecution to deny people of true salvation.

[75] 2 Thessalonians 2:9-10

battles were won not by attrition and deception of the attacker but by the high morale and spirit of the defender.

Satan's Lie: "There is no sin."

The strategy of the devil is deception and remains unchanged since he tempted Adam and Eve in the Garden of Eden. In our time, the popular term "politically correct" serves as a convenient tool by which the devil channels his spiritual thrust. He asserts that sin is merely an invention of the "narrow-minded," that there is really no difference between good and evil. He tries to convince man that sin is a matter of personal opinion and its meaning relative and cultural; and since there is no universal standard of sin, he insists there is no sin. No sin, no evil. Therefore, he concludes, man is free from the moral limits imposed by God and can instead formulate his own morality as he adapts to changing conditions. With a suggestive wink, the devil then whispers to man, "You need not look to God for approval of your actions, for you can become god yourself."

In Satan's strategy, whoever does not believe in God belongs to him. Jesus warned against the devil's strategy: *'He who is not with me is against me, and he who does not gather with me scatters'* (Matthew 12:30). As long as a person is kept from knowing the truth, the devil can manipulate him with deception and oppression, and can deny him his God-given purpose and blessings.

Warning to Non-believers and the Apostates

Jesus urged the non-believer to choose wisely. He said, *'The thief comes only to steal and kill and destroy, I have come that they may have life, and have it to the full* (John 10:10).

The gullibility of the weak, undiscerning, and wavering believer is foreseen in 1Timothy 4:1, *The Spirit clearly says that in later times some will abandon the faith and follow deceiving spirits and things taught by demons.* And Jesus gave a loving warning against apostasy: *'If anyone does not remain in me, he is like a branch that is thrown away...into the fire and burned* (John 15:6).'

"What's the Big Deal?"

Despite my busy schedule, I found time to turn on the television for an update on world events and local news, and I could not avoid seeing parts of other programs. I was shocked at some of the comedy shows for their storyline, language, and scenes. I came across a scene of two women in a ladies room confessing to each other that they were lesbians, and as they approached each other the scene was cut off. A canned laughter followed. In another program, the dialogue was filled with the words "v..." and "p..." referring to the private anatomy of woman and man, not as cuss words but in regular conversation to spice up the "funny" storyline. A canned laughter also followed. But when I expressed my shock, some folks questioned: "What's the big deal? It's only entertainment."

But that is precisely the problem. It is a big deal.

Desensitizing the Audience

While people laugh, they are unaware that their thoughts and attitudes are being transformed by the ideas they tolerate. Since these "mere ideas" are presented to them in light entertainment mode, the audience will eventually accept them as part of normal life. It wouldn't be long when they begin to believe them as new standards of morality. Many TV programs today have the effect of desensitizing the audience, especially the youth, in matters that used to be exclusively personal, private, and sacred between husband and wife.

Satan is using a technique that is tried and tested: seeing is believing. Through today's technology, he promotes lifestyles opposed to long-accepted standard of family and social relations to plant disbelief in the word of God. What is "just entertainment" has turned morality upside down and released the rebellious spirit in our time. For example, statistics vary as some show homosexuals comprise only 1.6 percent of the total US population compared to higher figures claimed by LGBT advocates. Yet, Hollywood, mainstream media, President Obama, and the U.S. Supreme Court have legitimized LGBT sub-culture and made it enforceable over ages-long Bible-based values.[76] And while God's moral prescription and His warning remain unchanged, many people do not seem to care whether what they watch or listen to is right or wrong, as long as it makes them laugh.

Another technique used by Satan is telling half-truth. Some people, for example, peddle the claim that Jesus loves all men even the violators of God's righteous standards, suggesting that they are also saved, and that "Christians" are therefore wrong in "hating" the "sinners." The full truth, however, is that Jesus also calls on violators to *Repent, for the kingdom of heaven is near* (Matthew 4:17)—to turn from their violations and obey God's righteousness. Violators must respond positively to His offer of salvation. Jesus' love in dying for the violators is the guarantee that if they repent, they shall be forgiven and can partake in the glory of the kingdom of heaven. If they do not believe in Him and repent, Jesus still loves them and will not overturn their choice; but by their decision, they remain outside of God's kingdom and are denied of His promises. And true followers of Jesus do not hate; like Him, they also love everyone and wish all men choose to enter the kingdom of God.

Preparing World Mindset

Some TV talk shows occasionally suggest New Age ideas promoting the lie that man can metamorphose into god, or is a part of a universal god himself. In these talk shows, some episodes promote the Universalist view that there are many paths to salvation not only through Jesus Christ; the idea is, of course, contrary to the Bible. The devil wages his spiritual warfare also in movies with themes that idolize witchcraft and make sorcery, sexual immorality, murder, and lies acceptable and justifiable as "politically correct,"

---

[76] A 2013 NHIS data released by the Center of Disease Control and Prevention claimed 96.6 % self-identified as straight and 0.7 % as bisexual. See Eugene Volokh, *What Percentage of the US Population is Gay, Lesbian, or Bisexual?* July 15, 2014, *Washington Post,* Washington , DC.

themes that are in violation of God's warning.[77] Also popularized in movies and cable shows are stories of superheroes with superhuman abilities. Unaware, the young audience is being set up to accept a mortal leader who will claim to be God with supernatural powers, as savior of the world.[78]

One must be discerning in choosing the CDs and radio programs to listen to, and what to watch on television, movies, you-tube, Netflix, and internet on-line. Ultimately, it is one's knowledge of, and belief in, the word of God that can guide the believer away from the temptation and intimidation directed by the devil. A Scotland Yard expert on transnational crimes once said, "To know the counterfeit, you must first know the REAL money." One must first know the TRUTH in order to see the lies behind the programs people watch or listen to. It is therefore essential that a person should honor his or her inner urge to read the Bible, commune with the Maker through prayers, and fellowship with other believers. By doing so, their spiritual integrity will be secured and strengthened. If values commanded by the Almighty are taken for granted, what is left for man to care about?

Daniel accurately prophesied the devil's work in our time: *With flattery he will corrupt those who have violated the covenant, but the people who know their God will firmly resist him* (Daniel 11:32).

Against Man's Faith, Satan is Guaranteed to Lose

In spiritual battle the devil is guaranteed to lose if only his intended victim knew the Christian Rules of Engagement and invoked the power of the kingdom of God. The devil's targets—the believer and non-believer alike—have in their power to win or lose, to surrender or reject the harassment, temptation, and deception of Satan. Even a non-believer is equipped by God with the ability to

---

[77] Revelation 22:15

[78] 2 Thessalonians 2:3-4 warns that a mere human will *oppose and will exalt himself over everything that is called God or is worshipped ... proclaiming himself to be God.*

recognize the reality of the Creator, and he can outright repulse the attacks from the devil by accepting the offer of salvation through the Messiah.[79] The universe is filled with evidences of the reality of the Creator, *so that men are without excuse* (Romans 1:20). The battle is waged in the mind of man, and overcoming the devil's onslaught is a matter of choice, of decision. The anchor for every man in the spiritual war is still faith in the Sovereign God through his Word, Jesus Christ.[80]

The Face of the Sky

The signs of the times are among us now, and they pulsate with the warning of the coming End of the Age. But many people today fail to recognize these signs, much less understand how they relate to the present world condition and their personal lives. Jesus' warning to the Pharisees and Sadducees echoes today: '*You know how to interpret the appearance of the sky, but you cannot interpret the signs of the times*' (Matthew 16:3).

The Almighty confirmed that the prophecies will happen. Specifically on the war described in Ezekiel 38 and 39 as a result of the devil's scheme and manipulation, the Sovereign Lord declared: *It is coming! It will surely take place* (Ezekiel 39:8). And after describing the signs of the end of the age, Jesus told His disciples, *When you see all these things, you know that it is near, right at the door. I tell you the truth, this generation will certainly not pass away until all these things have happened* (Matthew 24:33-34).

When the prophecies unfold and converge in rapid succession, God's judgment on this generation is indeed near.

---

[79] A study on tribes and past civilizations unreached by the Gospel showed their awareness of the one true God and a Messiah. See Don Richardson, *Eternity in their Hearts,* Regal Books, 1984.

[80] John 1:1-5

CHAPTER NINETEEN

END TIME TECHNOLOGY

> *But you, Daniel, close up and seal the words of the scroll until the time of the end. Many will go here and there to increase knowledge.*
> **Daniel 12:4**

Mark of the Beast

Signs of the End of the Age are also revealed in today's technology. One of the most intriguing issues in end time prophecy is the mark of the beast, 666.[81]

RFID Chips

Through the centuries, people used to conclude that the three digits would be etched or tattooed on the forehead or the right hand in order for a person to buy or sell. In the past, however, manual monitoring and enforcing its implementation in a global scale was physically impossible. It is only in the recent years that accuracy and enforcement are achievable due to advances in technology.

The early answer came in the form of a tiny glass capsule, about the size of a grain of uncooked rice, containing a microchip that could be implanted under the skin. The RFID (radio frequency

---

[81] In Revelation 13:1-18, the *beast out of the sea,* together with his chief ally, *the beast out of the earth,* will require everyone to receive on the right hand or forehead his mark, 666, without it *no one could buy or sell.*

identification) chip contained electronically stored information that can be transferred to a reader device within an electromagnetic field.[82] But the capsule was just the early version.

Being developed among the recent inventions is an RFID that can be painted on the skin, invisible, which cannot be removed and can contain information from the recipient's bank account, medical history and condition, police records, driver's license, social security, credit records, and everything about the person including genetic properties. Furthermore, the painted transmitter can be re-programmed even after its introduction on the skin, and it is permanent.[83]

The RFID technology can be a major component of a new global currency system if and when such "new money" is implemented. In his book, *The Day the Dollar Died*, (paperback, published January 2009) author Paul McGuire expounded on the theme that the American dollar will be superseded; he mentioned the statement of multi-billionaire George Soros that the world banking elite will introduce by 2018 a new global currency known as The Phoenix.[84] For the system to succeed, they would require people to have microchip in their body to be able to conduct commercial, legal, or any transaction that involves identification, credentials, and one's monetary worth.. Apparently, this new money will be guaranteed and acceptable throughout the world, unlike the dollar which is at times less stable than the Eurodollar, the Japanese yen, and the Chinese Renminbi. The uniform standard of currency would also make possible the use of the microchip anywhere in the world.

---

[82] Terry Watkins, "Is the Microchip the Mark of the Beast?" http://www.av161.org/666/biochip.html. Accessed 29, August 2014.

[83] Christie Weick, "The Mark of the Beast – RFID Chip or Tattoo?" http://www.explainthis.us/index.php?option=com_content&view=article7id=100:the-mark-of-the-beast-a-rfid-chip-or-tattoo&catid=44:free-articles. Accessed 15 August 2014.

[84] Paul McGuire, *The Day the Dollar Died,* paperback, January 1, 2009. See also http://www.paulmcguire.com/newarticlesdaydollardied.htm.

One's commercial value would no longer be limited within national borders, and transaction abroad can be as easy as buying groceries in one's local supermarket— cashless and worry-less.

RFID: Increasing Feature of Today's Lifestyle

The RFID is rapidly becoming perennial in today's lifestyle like cell phone and laptop. In 2004, the US authorized the use of embedded microchip on humans allowing hospitals and healthcare institutions to implant RFID for identification and immediate access to the patients' medical information. Since then, there has been steady increase in the use of RFID in commerce, trade, airport security, police work, banking, and schools. Some educational institutions in the US, England, Japan and the Philippines are already using the technology in student ID, backpack, entry/exit gates for tracking students, attendance monitoring, security against unauthorized personnel, and the use of the library and bookstore.

Controversy over RFID had already begun. In San Antonio, Texas, a local court suspended a student for refusing to wear the ID due to religious reason. A higher court, however, reversed the decision and prevented the school from harassing the student. But the rest of the students remained subjected to being monitored wherever they go. Unlike a credit card, the microchip cannot be misplaced or stolen. It is convenient, painless and affordable, and people can only become more dependent on it in the long run.[85]

Recently, digital tattoo has been made a feature to make mobile phone more secure. In a partnership, two major companies introduced a system in which a cell phone can be unlocked by simply passing it through a digital tattoo placed near the wrist of the user. The new feature is free, but to enjoy it, the buyer needs to get a pack of 10 super thin flexible adhesive materials for $10. The nickel size tattoo is taped on the body and can last for five days even

---

[85]Kevin Bonsor and Wesley Fenlon, "How RFID Works," http://electronics.howstuffworks.com/gadgets/rfid7.htm. Accessed August 20, 2014.

through shower, swimming, and rigorous activities, and is made attractive with intricate design and shimmering glow. If the tattoo or phone is stolen, the owner simply changes the program, according to the promoters.[86] With such a come-on, would not this new feature make the people of the earth become more receptive to the mark of the beast?

Critics of RFID technology warn that it is subject to hacking by identity theft as it can be read within a certain magnetic field area even without direct "eyesight."[87] However, cell phones, computers, and credit cards also had early hitches, but these did not prevent them from becoming necessary features in today's lifestyle. And if a hack-proof system is devised, will this not be a currency sanctuary "trusted" globally? Perhaps, with a pin code "666"?

RFID's Permanent Feature

In order to survive in the Antichrist economy, some people entertain the idea of receiving the chip but with the intention of removing it later. Spiritually, however, once they submit to the Antichrist, they will be so convinced of its benefits that they lose the capacity to see the truth, and they will also be condemned. Warned the third angel in Revelation 14:9-10,

> *If anyone worships the beast and his image and receives his mark on the forehead or on the hand, he, too, will drink of the wine of God's fury, which had been poured full strength into the cup of his wrath.*

There is also the physical dimension of the aforesaid Bible verse. The microchip capsule has the tendency to migrate to other parts of the body making it very difficult to trace and extract. Even the

---

[86] Tom Olago, "Digital Tattoos to Unlock Your Phone," August 7, 2014. http://www.prophecynewswatch.com/2014/August07/074html. Accessed August 7, 2014.

[87] Phil Elmore, "Experts Warn RFID Risks Outweigh Benefits," in *Whistleblower*, Vol. 21, No.3, March 2012 issue, pp. 36-37.

paintable version is said to be non-erasable, supposedly for the protection of the recipient. So once the person receives the mark, it would indeed be a permanent element in his system.

Obamacare: A Precursor?

Some people believe that the Affordable Health Care Act, or HR 3962, otherwise known as Obamacare, which was declared constitutional by the US Supreme Court in 2012, contains the legal basis for the US federal government to require everyone to receive the mark of the beast when it is implemented in full. The Democrats claim that the term Class II refers mainly to pacemakers, and that the chip is not obligatory. Legislating the implanting of the chip, however, suggests the use of the government as an institution for the implementation of the mark of the beast if and when the time of the Antichrist comes. Wouldn't the Obamacare add legitimacy to the enforcement of the mark of the beast by a future world government?

Surveillance Technology

Research in surveillance techniques is advancing so fast that new discoveries and inventions are made by a wider-than-ever field of scientists and researchers. Methods of monitoring people on their whereabouts, and collecting and keeping information about them, are now in use for commercial and security purposes. Devices are also developed for listening to conversations and "seeing" every move of persons, and identifying them by their voice, face, and iris. Perhaps suggestive of future trends, the surveillance technology has attracted the interest of dictators in the Third World as they have been among the valued customers of the products.[88]

---

[88] David Kapellian, "How Dictators Get Our Latest Surveillance Technology," *Whistleblower,* op.cit., pp.14-15.

Monitoring thru Facebook, Twitter, Social Network

In the US, users of Facebook, Twitter, and personal blogs can attract government investigators if they use any word in the Department of Homeland Security "watch list." Reportedly, communication through the ordinary laptop and PCs, especially in the social networks, are monitored and analyzed. Any "relevant and appropriate de-identified information" is shared with "federal, state, local and foreign governments and private sector partners."[89]

As one can recall, during the Arab Spring protests in Egypt, the Cairo government shut down Twitter, Facebook, You Tube, and Google to clamp down on the crowd, and there was hardly any international outcry against the measure. The Egyptians may have reinforced the resolve of some governments to monitor and control the social media to keep track the movements of their political opponents.

Carrier IQ

The smart phone has become indispensable to most people as it has multi-functions enabling the user to call friends, send email, visit friends on Facebook, send a text message, or log on to a bank's website and pay a bill. These functions are done through a program called Carrier IQ. While people enjoy the conveniences, Carrier IQ, however, has a downside: it records the user's full name, password (which people thought is exclusive), location, and anything that is said on the phone, and these data can be accessed by the provider company. Even as the user is worried about compromising his privacy, the Carrier IQ cannot be turned off. In addition to Android phones, the aforesaid software is also used on iPhones with iOS3 operating system and above.[90]

---

[89] Editor's note, "Feds Monitoring Personal Social Network Accounts," ibid, p.35. Read also article by Steven Wyer, "Government Paws on Our Every Tweet," pp. 24-25

[90] Floyd and Mary Beth Brown, "You Have No Privacy" ibid., p. 46.

Then there is also the tracking device known as "Stingray" that can track a cell phone even if it is not being used to make a call.[91] In fact, a number of major commercial establishments have been tracking the movements of people in shopping malls via their cell phone signals even when these are not in use, for the purpose of monitoring the flow and interest of customers.

X-ray Van

There is also the unmarked white van travelling on busy city thoroughfares, or the freeways, or on a dusty country road. To the observer, it looks like an ordinary delivery van, but inside at the back are two men operating an X-ray machine capable of "seeing" the contents of the other vehicles. Known as Z Backscatter X-ray vans, they are now deployed by governments to combat smuggling, drugs trafficking, human trafficking, and gun-running. The US military is also using them now in the Middle East against terrorists. Watch out, ladies, it can also "see" through clothing.[92]

Insect Spies

With the rapid advance in research and development, more sophisticated though strange devices can be expected in the near future. For example, the US Defense Advanced Research Projects Agency, or DARPA, is reportedly funding research for the use of live insects such as beetles, dragonflies, bees, and butterflies in intelligence gathering. The research intends to enable an insect to carry micro-cameras, micro-transmitters, and micro-generator. Progress is reportedly made in harnessing the extra energy released by the insect and converting this through the micro-generator to fuel the other loads carried by the insect. In another project of DARPA, researchers are inserting computer chips into moth pupae so that

---

[91] Editors' note, "Stingray Can Find You by Tracking Your Cell Phone," ibid., pp. 38-39.

[92] Michael Carl, "Government Peering at You with X-Rays on Highway," ibid., pp. 6-7.

when hatched, the new butterfly would literally be a "cyborg moth." The aim of the project is to create insects "whose nerves have grown into the implanted micro-processor so that operators can control them in flight."[93]

The bugs with cameras and microphones can be used in places that humans cannot go to, and they can also be used to spy on highly sensitive subjects like the President of the United States. The downside? Bugs with multi-million equipment may easily be eaten by birds, house lizards, and reptiles, or caught in spider web.

Identification Technology

Technology for identifying a person has now reached higher sophistication. The products are widely advertised and used by the government and commercial sectors. They are used on arriving foreign passengers at the airports and other entry points in many countries, and are also featured in some laptops as alternative to pin code of the user. Their technical mechanics are available in open sources as their websites can be quickly accessed by clicking in Google search for "facial recognition," "voice recognition," or "iris recognition." Supposedly used only against law violators—terrorists, drug traffickers, and the like—the technology, however, can pick any person from a crowd as a subject. Data from Twitter, Facebook, You Tube, Google, and Smartphone can be integrated with the biometrics, algorithms, and the RFID. Tapping on the details already stored in data banks, the government can accurately access every information about the target person in matter of seconds.

---

[93] Steve Elwart, "Government Eyes Turning Bugs into Spies," ibid., pp. 10-11.

Mind Control and Brainwashing

If the above-said gadgets are already reminders of George Orwell's warnings in his book, *"1984"* (a dystopia science-fiction novel published in 1949), how much more fearsome it would be when more research in mind control and brainwashing eventually succeeds. At the MIT (Massachusetts Institute of Technology), for example, a team of scientists have succeeded in implanting false mental reactions in a mouse. Known as "Optogenetics," the technique involves the use of chemicals to manipulate the neurons—and thereby implants mental responses—in the rodent's brain. Although it is still a long way from hacking the human brain, that day will eventually come. The sponsor DARPA is reportedly funding also other research projects on mind-control and brain/computer interface.[94]

When the mind control technique is finally developed, a way to incorporate it in the RFID microchip may soon follow. What is there to stop a global dictator from using the technology to go after some "politically uncooperative, narrow-minded, judgmental bigots" which is how some people sometimes falsely and derogatively label Christians?

/[94] Daniel G.J., "The Frightening New Mind Control Technology Can Hack Your Brain," http://storyleak.com/mind-control-technology-hack-your-brain/ . Accessed July 29, 2013.

CHAPTER TWENTY

DIPLOMACY: RISE OF THE ANTICHRIST

> *The whole world was astonished and followed the beast.*
> *Men worshipped the dragon because he had given authority*
> *to the beast, and they also worshiped the beast and asked,*
> *'Who is like the beast?*
> *Who can make war against him?'*
> **Revelation 13:3-4**
>
> *At that time if anyone says to you,*
> *'Look, here is the Christ!' or, 'There he is!' do not believe*
> *it. For false Christs and false prophets will appear and*
> *perform great signs and miracles to deceive even the elect –*
> *if that were possible.*
> *See, I have told you ahead of time.*
> **Matthew 24:23-25**

The Antichrist

The books of Daniel and Revelation warn against the "lawless one," "beast that rises out of the sea," and "abomination that causes desolation," a character referred to by a number of writers as the Antichrist.[95] Prophesied to attain power as ruler of the world, the

---

[95] Daniel 7:2-7, 24-27; 8:4: 11:36; Revelation 13:1-18; 17:11-17. 1 John 4:3 warns of the spirit of antichrist that denies Jesus, and 2:18 predicts that *in the last hour*, there will be *many antichrists*. However, apostle John also affirms that *the antichrist is coming (2:18)* to suggest that an individual will rise in the

Antichrist will be given by Satan *power to make war against the saints and to conquer them,* and the authority over *every tribe, people, language and nation* (Revelation 13:7). Presenting himself as a spiritual and secular leader, his rule will be *terrifying and frightening and very powerful,* and he *will devour the whole earth, trampling it down and crushing it* (Daniel 7:7, 23). His appearance in the world stage will be with the work of Satan who will be behind *all kinds of counterfeit miracles, signs, and wonders, and in every sort of evil that deceives those who are perishing* (2 Thessalonians 2:9-10).

The world's view of the Antichrist will be the result of manipulation. He is in fact *not* what people think he is. His life wrapped in mystery, his personal past and agenda will at first be intentionally hidden from the public. Despite the lies, he rises to rule the world when the planet is engulfed in a crisis that the devil himself created.

A second beast, also known as "the false prophet," will serve as the prime ally of the first beast (Antichrist). He will perform counterfeit miracles to deceive the world into worshipping the Antichrist and his image, and causing everyone to receive the mark of the first beast – 666 – on the right hand or on the forehead, *so that no one could buy or sell unless he had the mark.*[96]

The Bible says that the beast's followers perish:

> *...because they refused to love the truth and so be saved. For this reason God sends them a powerful delusion so that they will believe the lie, and so that all will be condemned who have not believed the truth but have delighted in wickedness* (2 Thessalonians 2:10-12).

---

final days to personify such spirit and epitomize the many antichrists.

[96] The activities of the second beast, and his relationship with the first beast, are in Revelation 13:11-18.

Diplomatic Feat Elevates the Antichrist

The verse Daniel 9:27 suggests that the Antichrist will attain legitimacy and position as world leader through diplomacy: *He will confirm a covenant with many for one 'seven.'* Bible scholars believe that the Antichrist will be credited for making a seven-year peace treaty with Israel, apparently within the context of today's geopolitical problems in the Middle East. Perhaps the prophesied war in Psalm 83 will occur after which the would-be Antichrist steps in to broker the peace treaty.[97] Because of such a feat, he will be acclaimed by the nations of the world as a peace-maker and the answer for global problems. Unaware that Satan staged the scenario, many people on the planet will be so impressed and hail the beast as they shout, *"Peace and Safety!"* (1 Thessalonians 5:3).

After the echoes of delirious exaltation have subsided, there will be no peace. The signing of the treaty marks the beginning of the last seven years of this age. It will also mark the start of the tribulation when destruction will come suddenly on insolent people *as labor pains on a pregnant woman, and they will not escape* (1 Thessalonians 5:3). Lawlessness will intensify, the first five of the seven seals will be opened, and the world will witness unprecedented distress.

It is not clear whether he makes the treaty already as head of a global government, or as head of a multilateral organization such as the UN, or as the sovereign of a powerful country. It appears, however, that the treaty will either be a non-aggression pact or a

---

[97] Psalm 83 describes the nations uniting to destroy Israel as a nation. Since Israel still exists in the succeeding events of the End Time, it is concluded that she will prevail over the coalition and become the chief beneficiary of the peace treaty. The nations listed when the psalm was written are now in Palestinian territories (Gaza, West Bank), portion of northern Syria, southeastern Turkey, northern Iraq, Lebanon, Jordan, and Saudi Arabia. Visit Joel Richardson, "Which Nations Does Psalm 83 Really Include?", www.com/2012/08/which-nations-does-psalm-83-really-include, accessed June 15, 2014.

defense umbrella guarantee to Israel. In any case, the Antichrist's role in a landmark accord will propel him to a new height of power as he gains great prestige, worldwide influence, and global acceptance that seals his rise to head a global government.

The New World Order

On the basis of the people's enchantment over him as "savior" of an endangered world, the "beast" would then implement his plan of world domination. He would pursue the unfulfilled dream of Nimrod, Alexander the Great, Napoleon Bonaparte, and Adolf Hitler to unify all nations under one global authority. To a world where many believe man can evolve into a god, and to a global audience of young adults that have not outgrown their fictional "superheroes," idolatry to a mere human being is possible.

Considering the extent of power the Antichrist is prophesied to have, and consistent with the nature of the Antichrist's regime, his purpose, and the manner of implementing the mark of the beast as described in the Bible, the system of his world rule will necessarily have to be a totalitarian dictatorship.[98] The New World Order (NWO), as some writers call this feature of the prophecy, will be more powerful, pervasive, and invasive than any rule in human history.

The economic system to support such a global government will necessarily be a centralized world economy similar to socialism as practiced by the debunked Soviet Union where the means of production and distribution are controlled by the government. Free

---

[98]"Totalitarian dictatorship" is defined as a rule without the consent of the governed; the ruler's power extends to all aspects of his subjects' life. See examples in https://www.boundless.com/sociology/textbooks/boundless-sociology-textbook/goverment-15/types-of-states.

enterprise will not be allowed to flourish as it will be considered an economic sanctuary of those opposed to the Antichrist.

The global leader will institute social programs that would buttress his image as "savior of mankind." To keep his subjects loyal to him, he will implement socialist "welfare state" measures such as socialized medical care, unemployment benefits, some kind of "food stamps," and the like on a global scale.

The biblical reference to the *ten kings who have not yet received a kingdom, but who for one hour will receive authority as kings along with the beast* (Revelation 17:12), gives hint to the power structure of the global government. Where power emanates from the top and center of the world government, the Antichrist will be buttressed by a select group of like-minded followers (call it a cabinet, or secretariat, or council, or central committee, or junta). These ten "kings" will probably be leaders appointed by the Antichrist to supervise ten regions of the world. The ten "kings" will likely be selected from among heads of nation-states, or multinational organizations, or major industries. They can be a mixture of political and economic world elites. Whatever may be their background, they will be influential and powerful people in their own right, next only to the Antichrist.

Enmeshed in the administrative structure will likely be a network of technocrats and bureaucrats to implement and manage the mark of the beast, and to administer worldwide propaganda, surveillance, brainwashing, and religious affairs. There will also be those empowered to control the world banking system, global media, internet, and phones. Others will direct medical research, science and technology development, world police, NWO peace-keeping military forces, etc.

The global government will have knowledge and control over every aspect in the life of individuals: his thoughts, feelings, beliefs, preferences, behavior, utterances, private conversation, travel, and all personal relationships. Surveillance gadgets of all kinds can be expected to be installed in public places, highways, malls, department stores, groceries, airports, schools, churches, and even in private homes' living room and bedrooms. People will be made to believe this is for their own good. Expectedly, all communication media such as phones, internet, radio, and TV will be utilized as they are now beginning to be used to monitor the consumers. Food and drinks may even be programmed not only to provide financial gains for the NWO elites but also to keep the world citizens docile.

Among the socio-economic and political systems devised by man, the societal structures forged by Hitler, Mussolini, Stalin, and the communist dictators in the former Soviet Union are historical examples that come close to the rule of the Antichrist as described in the Bible. Furthermore, in each of the samples of totalitarian dictatorships, an escape goat existed on whom the ills in the society were blamed. Today's criticism, persecution, beheading, and pillage against Christians and Jews in some countries reflect the devil's scheme in setting them up as the escape goat when the Antichrist assumes his world rule.

The Antichrist Declares He is God

In his global rule, he will be in alliance with the "false prophet," the second beast that comes "out of the earth," who will perform miraculous signs to deceive the world into worshipping the Antichrist and his image as god.[99] Anyone who refuses to worship the Antichrist will be hunted down and killed.[100] The false prophet, as prime advocate of the Antichrist, will require everyone to receive the mark of the beast "666" on the right hand or the forehead without which a person will not be able to buy or sell.[101]

The Bible says that three-and-a-half years after the signing of the treaty, he breaks the agreement and reveals his true identity as the

---

[99] Revelation 13:11-12

[100] Ibid., 15

[101] Ibid., 16-18

Antichrist. He will stand in the holy temple in Jerusalem and proclaims himself as god.[102]

The Great Tribulation

Then the world will see the start of the worst calamities of all times in the Great Tribulation, the last three-and-a-half years of the treaty. There will be *great distress, unequaled from the beginning of the world until now – and never to be equaled again* (Matthew 24:21). In this period, most destructive cosmic, natural, and human disasters such as the effects of nuclear blast, fallout, and radiation will kill a large portion of world population. The seven bowls of God's wrath includes ugly and painful sores on those who had the mark of the beast and worshiped his image, sea turning into blood killing all marine life, rivers and springs becoming blood, the sun scorching people with fire, and prolonged darkness over the earth. The great tribulation will continue until the Second Coming of Jesus Christ to destroy the Antichrist and his coalition.[103]

> *Then there came flashes of lightning, rumblings, peals of thunder and a severe earthquake… The great city split into three parts, and the cities of the nations collapsed. God remembered Babylon the Great and gave her the cup filled with the wine of the fury of his wrath. Every island fled away and the mountains could not be found. From the sky huge hailstones of about a hundred pounds each fell upon men. And they cursed God on account of the plaque of hail…*
> **Revelation 16:18-21**
>
> *…but they refused to repent and glorify him.*
> **v. 9**

---

[102] 2Thessaloneans 2:4; Matthew 24:15

[103] See Revelation 9:15-16; 14:14-20 for more description of God's wrath..

PART FOUR

THE KINGDOM AND IMMORTALITY

Jesus said, 'My kingdom is not of this world...
My kingdom is from another place.'
'You are a king, then!' said Pilate.
Jesus answered, 'You are right in saying I am a king.
In fact, for this reason I was born, and
for this I came into the world,
to testify to the truth.
Everyone on the side of truth listens to me.'

John 18:36-37

CHAPTER TWENTY ONE

TRUTH BEHIND THE LIES

> *So you also must be ready, because the Son of Man will come at an hour when you do not expect Him.*
> *Who then is the faithful and wise servant, whom the master has put in charge of the servants in his household to give them their food at the proper time? It will be good for that servant whose master finds him doing so when he returns. I tell you the truth, he will put him in charge of all his possessions. But suppose that servant is wicked and says to himself, 'My master is staying away a long time,' and he then begins to beat his fellow servants and to eat and drink with drunkards. The master of that servant will come on a day when he does not expect him and at an hour he is not aware of. He will cut him to pieces and assign him a place with the hypocrites, where there will be weeping and gnashing of teeth.*
> **Matthew 24:44-51**

Sir, what must I do to be saved, a man asked Peter and Silas.[104]

The same question is in the heart of many people today. But like the Pharisees and Sadducees who could not discern the signs of the times, today's non-believers are blinded by their own fears, arrogance, and escapism as events unfold leading to the fall of the last domino chip. Though aware of the physical magnitude of the global distress, they "whistle in the dark," blind to the forces moving

---

[104] Acts 16:30

these events. They seek instant microwave—but not true—salvation.

Dark Spirit Behind the Rumors

On the spiritual level, above and beyond the physical dimension, the current events radiate the same ungodly forces prevailing in Noah's time and in the days of Lot in Sodom and Gomorrah. The spiritual forces behind today's "wars...rumors of war" reflect Satan's desperate attempts to "fire all his cannons" in his *last gasp* before he goes down.

Satan Setting the Stage for Antichrist Advent

The devil has expanded spiritual warfare to a global scale, and is waging material assaults on his targets at physical warfare mode. Revelation 12:17 describes Satan's rage, saying he *went off to make war against...those who obey God's commandments and hold on to the testimony of Jesus.*

His grand scheme is to cause worldwide anxiety and panic while he attacks the institutions and principles of God. It is the same ancient warfare strategy he uses to subjugate persons he can bring to hell with him. He intends to destroy alternative options that offer salvation to man, cause the world to look for escape from man-made disasters, then convince the unsuspecting planet to accept his "solution" to the "problems" he created.

The present events in the Middle East and in many Western countries may be viewed from the perspective of the aforesaid Satan's scheme. While Christians and Jews are being executed, enslaved, raped, sold, and beheaded for their faith in Syria, Iraq, and other places in the region, their sacred institutions and beliefs such as man-woman marriage, sanctity of human embryonic life, and family unity are being eroded in the West. The global political, economic, social, and psychological atmosphere is being readied by the sinister invisible force. Satan is about to present to the world his prescription to "save" the world: a human "savior" empowered by a "universal god"—the Antichrist. Sponsored by Satan, the mortal "messiah" in our time, the human "Mighty Mouse,"—the Antichrist, the "instead" Jesus Christ—will justify the desires of many for a "politically correct savior" although he is opposed to the Creator

If seen only in their material, physical instance, the events can easily be misunderstood and the truth missed. Meanwhile, unaware of the devil's sinister scheme, millions will stand by and allow him to wage his campaign dissuading them from the only force that offers true salvation to humanity—God and His only begotten Son.[105]

The Unbelievers' Crossroad

Satan's determined warfare against God is reaching the critical point by which *those days will be shortened* for the sake of the *elect, otherwise no one would survive.*[106] At this momentous time, the Father will determine the day and the hour of Jesus' return to put a stop to Satan's machinations, render His judgment on this generation, and release His wrath on an insolent world.

The outcries of God's people are now heard by Him as He did before the destruction of Sodom and Gomorrah,[107] and He is about to release His wrath on a world turned "upside down."[108] As burning sulfur rained down on Sodom and Gomorrah since there were not even ten righteous people in the city, He will command His angels to open the seventh seal and blow the seven trumpets.[109] The period

---

[105] 2Thessalonians 2:7-8 reveals Satan's threat, and verse 3:3 promises, "… the Lord is faithful, and He will strengthen and protect you from the evil one."

[106] Matthew 24:22

[107] Genesis 18:20-21

[108] God will avenge the saints' death when the number of believers who were to be killed was completed (Revelation 6:11). But God only knows the number.

[109] Revelation 6:1-17, 8:1-13; 9:1-21; 11:15-19

of tribulation will come, and world conditions will worsen in the final three-and-a-half years of the fallen world.

Before fire reduced the city to ashes, angels urged Lot and his family to leave and escorted them out of Sodom and Gomorrah. Lot's family was saved, but not his sons-in-law who thought he was joking, and his wife who turned into salt because she looked back as her heart was attached to the corrupt lifestyle in the city.[110] The same voice of concern urges today's generation to leave the Sodom-and-Gomorrah lifestyle and reach out to receive Jesus' offer of salvation.

I have set before you life and death, blessings and curses. Now choose life so that you and your children may live (Deuteronomy 30:19). These words that echoed in my heart when Eva's life hanged between life and death now whisper behind today's headlines. She lived because I chose to believe in Christ. The same choice is now offered to nonbelievers.

The unbelieving person may wish to consider the answer of Peter and Silas when they replied to their jailer: *Believe in the Lord Jesus and you will be saved, you and your household* (Acts 16:31).

Reminders Against Apostasy

Believers who may have entertained the deception of the dark spirit may wish to consider the reminder of the Almighty. The following passage guided me to resist the pressure to break my faith as I faced the twin crises: *If you do not stand firm in your faith, you will not stand at all* (Isaiah 7:9).

The Truth Remains

Today's generation should consider looking above and beyond the material, worldly dimension of present-day headlines. The

---

[110] Genesis 19:14, 26

stakes are so high: if one chooses the wrong road, he spends eternity in damnation; if the right path, eternity in heaven. Salvation of mankind rests in the hands of the Almighty, not in the machinations of a loser, the devil.

Not the End of the World

One must be cautious not to be taken in by reports of impending global destruction such as large meteors hitting planet Earth. Claims that hydrocarbon emission causes global warming and melts the ice caps leading to a "waterworld" in our time proved exaggerated and controversial.[111] What better way for the advocates of New World Order to place all nations under one rule than to convince them they all face extinction from a common threat? And what better time to compel the world to accept the Antichrist than when people believe a "messiah" in this generation—a superhero, a human "Mighty Mouse"—has come to save the world?

The Bible does not teach that the world will end following the tribulation. Although cosmic disasters and natural calamities are prophesied in the last days, mankind and the earth will continue to exist. Man-made troubles such as global financial crisis and threats of war will continue to unfold, leading to the fulfillment of the prophesied mark of the beast and wars in the end time. Satan will exploit the crisis he created to justify the rise of the Antichrist. So, even if the fallen world ignored the inevitability of God's wrath, the threat of implosion or self-destruct proves a convincing argument for evil to make the world accept the global government under the New World Order Dictator. And the Antichrist will put the blame on the Christians for the calamities.

The biblical term "end of the age" simply means the end of the present Church Age, not the planet Earth.[112] We live in an age when

---

[111] Read Brian Sussman, *Climategate: A Veteran Meteorologist Exposes the Global Warming Scam,* WND Books: Washington D.C., 2010.

[112] The Greek words *aion suntevleia* can mean "completion or consummation of eternity, world/universe, or period of time/age." Other than to God's promise

man acquires salvation through faith in Jesus Christ in response to God's grace, His gift to man for his restoration to His kingdom.

So, if there is going to be an end to anything, it would be the end of Satan's machinations on earth, the end of his campaign to win souls he can bring with him to hell. It would be the end of a world as we now know it.

Beyond the End of the Age, the upside down world will be turned right side up. And there will still be men and nations.

It Matters Still

The truth that there is life and earth beyond the End of the Age should have a profound impact on anyone's expectations, plans, and activities especially at this time-side of the final days.

To each person. What you do, say, create, publish, build, think, and believe today will matter still beyond the end time. The End of the Age does not provide an excuse to ignore or abandon God's righteousness; one does not disappear but will face the judgment for eternity. It matters still to choose courage and truth over what is "politically correct" despite the pressures to conform to those of different values and beliefs. If others choose to live a different lifestyle, let them exercise their free will. But a believer ought to be ready to justify his faith with the word of God, and continue to love—but not follow—them. Live your life as the salt and light of the world. Choose to invest today on a future life in tune with God's kingdom beyond the end of this age.

To each nation. There is reason why one should look beyond the Antichrist's diplomacy. Surely, there will still be nations after the end of this age. After destroying the armies that joined the Antichrist in the final battle, Jesus will gather the nations as He makes judgment on the survivors, and He shall rule with "iron

---

of "eternal life," the term can only refer to the "completion" of a period of "time/age" since the Bible teaches there is judgment and Jesus' rule over men and nations after His Second Coming. See also Footnote 12, p. 41.

scepter" over them in the age to come.[113] Thus, it matters how a nation conducts diplomacy at this time side of the end time, whether or not it takes a stand against the persecution, killing, and enslavement of people on the basis of their faith.[114] There is judgment still on the conduct of nations. National leaders, decision makers, and diplomats must therefore carefully steer their nation's foreign policy with regard to the Middle East. The prophecies in the Bible on the outcome of the Antichrist's assault on Jerusalem should serve as a warning to guide a nation on what to avoid. If a nation refuses alliance with the Antichrist in the assault on Jerusalem, it can mean survival of that country in the age to come.

The Authenticity of Christ

In today's "politically correct" culture, many young people do not know who Jesus Christ really is. There are volumes of literature they can read, and various internet websites, on the authenticity of Jesus Christ. In bookstores and libraries, there are also millions of testimonies of people experiencing the relevance of Jesus in their lives. The stories in the previous chapters of this book are actual events that convinced Eva and me the Jesus Christ in the Bible is real.

No human description can completely describe the extent and fullness of the love and power of Christ. Jesus is a transcendent that can live in man's three dimensional world as well as in many other dimensions of time and space. Thus, no matter how sophisticated are man's inventions, mankind can only have a limited view of the total extent of His deity. Nonetheless, God endowed man with

---

[113] Revelation 19:15

[114] In Matthew 25:31-46, at the end of the age when all nations are gathered, those who showed kindness *for one of the least of these brothers of mine* (believers of God in the Bible) He sends to eternal life, while those who *did not do...did not do for me* (Jesus), to eternal punishment.

intellect sufficient to peek into revealed portion of the truth about the Creator, that he may believe the reality of his Maker and His only begotten Son.

Science's Glimpse into Creation

In our generation, the explosion of knowledge enables man to see more of the truth through science. For example, more than twenty years ago, in 1992 when the hot big bang origin of the universe was detected by COBE (Cosmic Background Explorer), a host of scientists, including big names in astrophysics such as Stephen Hawking, considered it "the discovery of the century, if not of all time." Scientists of unquestionable credibility even called the hot big bang the "Holy Grail of cosmology," while Dr. George Smoot (UC Berkeley), project leader for the COBE satellite, declared it as evidence of the birth of the universe. "It's like looking at God," he added.[115]

As can be recalled, the hot big bang theory acknowledged the truth that the universe had a beginning and, therefore, its first cause. The theory asserted, the universe expanded from a volume very much smaller than a tiny dot, and it continues to expand. It did not recognize evolution, nor a static, unchanging universe, but instead supported the creation account of the Bible. The theory coincided with Genesis 1:1 which states, *In the beginning, God created the heavens and the earth.* From God's first act of creation, all matters and energy, and the dimensions of space and time, came into being.[116] From a void, stars and galaxies and all cosmic matters assumed material reality. Although some theologians refuse to entertain science, I believe scientists just had a glimpse of a portion of God's eternal truth and unlimited power.

---

[115] Hugh Ross, *The Creator and the Cosmos: How the Greatest Scientific Discovery of the Century Reveal God*, p.19.

[116] Isaiah 40:28; 42:5; 45:18; Mark 13:19; Ephesians 3:9; Colossians 1:16; Hebrews 1:2; Revelation 10:6

The Higgs Boson: God Particle?

For centuries, skeptics questioned the Bible's account of creation. How can anything come from nothing, they asked.

In 1964, Dr. Peter Higgs and other scientists presented a proposition that a subatomic particle, a certain boson, is responsible in the formation of the mass of anything. On 4 July 2012, the existence of the Higgs boson was independently confirmed and announced by two experimental teams of the Large Hadron Collider (LHC), at CERN (European Center for Nuclear Research), home of the most powerful particle accelerator in Geneva, Switzerland. The existence of the Higgs boson confirmed the existence of the Higgs field.

The significance of the aforesaid discovery is that the Higgs field, which exists throughout the universe, is the factor that enables elementary particles to acquire mass.[117] But in addition to the formation of mass, the Higgs field also holds together the particles and atoms of the new material. The existence of the Higgs field may not tell the whole story of creation, but it demonstrates the reality of creating something from nothing, of producing visible matter from invisible emptiness. It points to the practicability of creation, especially of the formation of the universe from a volume smaller than the atom, and no larger than a lightweight subatomic particle, until there exists the vast expanse of space containing millions of galaxies and other heavenly bodies.

In June 2014, after nearly two years of further research, scientists at LHC have not gotten beyond confirming the presence of the Standard Model boson. They said they may not be able to confirm any theory on the property of boson until after LHC's 60-mile

---

[117] For details on discovery confirming the existence of Higgs boson, see *The Higgs Boson*, home.web.cern.ch/topics/higgs_boson. For simplified technical data, see *Higgs Boson,* whttp://en.wikipedia.org/wiki/higgs_boson and Jonathan Ateberry, *What Exactly is the Higgs Boson?* Science.howstuffworks.com/higgs-boson1.htm, accessed December 20, 2013.

successor is built in 2015 or later, when the collider is upgraded with double its present collision energy.[118]

The new finding is expected to open up fresh perspectives in physics and would greatly affect human understanding of the universe. What is "new," however, has already been written in the Bible some two thousand years ago. *The universe was formed at God's command, so that what is seen was not made out of what was visible* (Hebrews 11:3).

The Higgs boson discovery supports the Biblical description of the power of Jesus Christ to create. *Through Him all things were made; without Him nothing was made that has been made* (John 1:3). And Colossians 1:15-17 is even more specific:

> *He is the image of the invisible God, the firstborn over all creation. For by him all things were created; things in heaven and on earth, visible and invisible, whether thrones or powers or rulers or authorities; all things were created by him and for him. He is before all things, and in him all things hold together.*

Laminin: The Cross that Holds Things Together

Jesus' historical role is symbolized through a recent scientific discovery—laminin. In all organic living things, the cell is part of the building blocks that make up the whole being, whether human, animal or plant. Laminin is a protein network foundation that holds together the cells and organs of all organisms.[119] It's shape? Cross.

Since Jesus Christ is described as the power in which all things hold together, is it more than a coincidence that laminin is shaped like a cross, that a series of crosses hold together the cells of all living things? Is there a parallel between a living organism and the

---

[118] Amir Aczel, "Confirmed: That Was Definitely the Higgs Boson Found at LHC," June 25, 2014. http://blogs.discovermagazine.com/dbrief/2014/06/25/d-confirmed-definitely-higgs-boson-foundlhc/ Accessed June 27, 2014.

[119] Visit https://en.wikipedia.org/wiki/Laminin. Accessed February 1, 2012.

"body of Christ" which is held together through faith in Jesus who died on the cross? Is laminin symbolic of Jesus' love, sacrifice, suffering and death on the cross, that whosoever believes in Him is guaranteed salvation through re-attachment with the Creator?

"I am the gate; whoever enters through me will be saved," Jesus said.[120] The Bible displays the words of *the Christ* whose powers and truth the Higgs field and laminin may now be acknowledging. Apostle Peter corroborated the claim of Jesus: *Salvation is found in no one else, for there is no other name under heaven given to men by which we must be saved* (Acts 4:12).

Finely Tuned Universe

Jesus' claim is supported by other scientific discoveries. The finely tuned characteristic of the universe reflects the love and care of the Maker for living things, particularly the human race. The more accurately and extensively scientists measure the elements of the universe, the more finely tuned they discover it to be. An astrophysicist asserted, "God invested heavily in living creatures. He constructed all these stars (about a hundred-billion-trillion no more and no less) and carefully crafted them throughout the age of the universe so that at this brief moment in the history of the cosmos humans could exist and have a pleasant place to live."[121]

Astrophysicists observe that, for life of any kind to exist, there are more than twenty-four parameters the universe must have values falling within narrowly defined ranges. For example, "the first parameter of the universe to be measured was the universe's expansion rate. In comparing this rate to the physics of galaxy and star formation, astrophysicists found something amazing. If the universe expanded too rapidly, matter would disperse so efficiently that none of it would clump enough to form galaxies. If no galaxies form, no stars will form. If no stars form, no planets form, there's no place for life. On the other hand, if the universe expanded too

---

[120] John 10:9

[121] Hugh Ross, op.cit., p.118.

slowly, matter would clump so effectively that all of it, the whole universe in fact, would collapse into a super-dense lump before any solar-type stars could form." Also, such delicately balanced expansion rate must be maintained for life to exist. "It cannot differ by more than one part in 10x55zeros from the actual rate." Electromagnetic force also must remain constant relative to gravitational force: if increased by one part in 10x40zeros, only small stars would form. If decreased by one part in 10x40zeros, only large stars would form. "But for life to be possible in the universe, both large and small stars must exist." Only in the thermonuclear furnaces of large stars are most of the life-essential elements produced, and "only small stars like the sun burn long…and stable enough to sustain a planet with life."[122]

God So Loves the Intellectuals

The Lord is unraveling in our time more of his mysteries in proportion to the persistent indifference in the science age to the truth about Him. For God so loves the intellectuals—scientists, academicians, and other thinkers—as much as He loves the rest of mankind. He reveals to them Divine Truth, so that by their acceptance of Jesus Christ's authenticity, they, too, may choose to enter the kingdom of God and be saved.

- **Beyond the End of the Age, the upside down world will be put right side up.**
- **Choose to invest today on a future life in tune with God's kingdom in the age beyond the end time.**
- **Higgs boson points to the practicality of creation, especially of the formation of the universe from a volume smaller than the atom until there was the vast expanse of space containing millions of galaxies.**
- **With laminin, is God assuring the world that Jesus' death on the cross and resurrection guarantee re-attachment with the Creator and salvation to those who believe?**

---

[122] Ibid., pp. 109-111. The list of parameters is found on ibid., pp. 106-114.

CHAPTER TWENTY TWO

THE HIGHEST KINGDOM

> *Now have come the salvation and*
> *the power and the kingdom of our God,*
> *and the authority of Christ.*
> *For the accuser of our brothers, who accuses them*
> *before our God day and night,*
> *has been hurled down.*
> **Revelation 12:10**

The Gospel Reaching All Nations

In our time, the devil wants people to believe Christianity is on the decline while he discredits the faith and persecutes the followers of Jesus. Though Christians face mounting challenges and risks, Christianity is far from declining. On the contrary, an unseen power is presently sweeping across the globe, and many divine manifestations continue to encourage and strengthen believers around the world.

Jesus: Salvation not Number

To begin with, God is not in the business of numbers. Jesus' primary concern is the salvation of each person. He did not command His disciples to go and make converts of everyone and kill those who refuse, nor did He require the disciples to establish a worldwide theocratic authoritarian rule. Jesus' commission to the believers is to simply preach the Gospel and allow the listeners to decide for themselves without intimidation. Christians are to make disciples of those who believe, baptizing them in the name of the Father, the Son, and the Holy Spirit.

He knew there will be those who would refuse Him, but He reserved to Himself—not to mortal men—the role of judging over men. He commissioned the believers to *go into all the world and preach the good news to all creation. Whoever believes and is baptized will be saved, but whoever does not believe will be condemned* (Mark 16:15-16).

Despite the pessimistic prognosis played up in some surveys, Christianity is far from extinction. Although some surveys say the percentage of total number of self-identified Christians is declining, still one out of three persons in the world believes in Christ. Christianity remains the largest religion in the world and Christians continue to be the majority in 157 countries. Furthermore, statistics taken in a number of "restrictive" countries may not really tell the full story; state religion in these countries discourages individuals from openly declaring their beliefs.

Reversal of Roles

Alarmist outlook prevails more in Western countries than elsewhere, but this is understandable. A decline indeed existed in the percentage of Christians in Europe and North America in relation to the total population of their respective countries. In 1910, 93 percent of Christians in the world lived in these two regions, but by 2010 their standing went down to 63 percent. Meanwhile, the percentage of Christians compared to their respective country population in these two regions also went down: for Europe, from 95 percent in 1910 to 76.2 percent in 2010, and for America, from 96 percent to 86.6 percent in the same period.[123]

---

[123] The statistics on the Global North and Global South in this section are from the article, "Global Christianity – A Report on the Size and Distribution of the World's Christian Population," December 19, 2011. http://www.pewforum.org/2011/12/19/global.christianity. Accessed December 01, 2013.

Although the aforesaid trend may be partly due to apostasy and disillusionment among young people in these two regions, the downturn is also due to low-to-zero birth rate growth among most Europeans and some North Americans. Furthermore, these two regions allowed the continued flow of immigrants of other religions including the Muslims who do not practice self-imposed limit on their birth rate.

Compared to the Western countries, the people in developing countries are more receptive to the Gospel. In Sub-Saharan Africa, for example, only 9 percent of the total population was Christian in 1910, but they grew in number to 63 percent by 2010. In Asia-Pacific, the growth rate may not be that dramatic, from 3 percent to 7 percent in the same period, but this includes Christian growth in China where millions of souls were saved.

When viewed from another presentation made by Pew Forum, the reversal of roles becomes more glaring. In 1910, the Global North (Europe, North America, Australia, New Zealand, and Japan), had 82.2 percent of the total world Christians, while the Global South (the rest of the world) only had 17.6 percent of world Christians. But by 2010, Global North only had 39.2 percent of the total world Christians while the Global South was the host to 60.8 per cent of the world Christians. And among the top ten countries with the largest number of Christians, the US and Germany are the only ones in the Global North while the rest are from the Global South including Russia (behind US, Brazil and Mexico), Philippines, Nigeria, China, DR Congo, and Ethiopia.

The two regions—Sub-Saharan Africa and Asia-Pacific—had the fastest growth rate especially achieved only within the last few decades. By 2010, they had a combined total of more than 800 million Christians that almost equal the Christians in the Americas (804 million in North America and Latin America).

The Gospel in Former Soviet Union and China

Even in countries of the former Soviet Union, the growth rate of Christians had been phenomenal. In Russia, for example, Christians numbered 66.90 percent of the population in 2010, compared to the second largest religious group (Muslims) which had 20 percent.[124] By the same year in Romania, 96.96 percent of the population was Christian with the Evangelicals growing faster at annual rate of 2.3 percent compared with other Christian groups (-0.2%). Christian churches in Romania grew from 12,000 in late 1980's to more than 20,000 in 2013.[125]

From the historical perspective, the preaching of the Gospel in Global South (including the former Soviet Union) is relatively new. Since these regions have four times the total population of Global North, there are still hundreds of millions that have yet to hear the Good News, especially in countries such as China, Russia and India. In fact, China is expected to have the largest Christian population by 2030 at 247 million, based on an estimate by Prof. Fenggang Yang of Purdue University, author of the book, *Religion in China: Survival and Revival Under Communist Rule*. A professor in Sociology, Dr. Yang said about 100,000 Chinese come to Christ every day, and that there may be more Christians now than Communist Party members. Furthermore, the website of Christianity receives more visitors than that of the Party.[126]

The aforesaid statistics testify to the truth that even in the most stringent situation, the soul of man searches for the quenching of his spiritual thirst. In Mother Theresa's word, "You'll never know that Jesus is all you need, until all you have is Jesus."

---

[124] www.operationworld.org/russia. Accessed August 23, 2013.

[125] www.operationworld.org/romania. Accessed August 23, 2013.

[126] Jim Denison, "Will China Be World's Largest Christian Nation by 2025?" August 29, 2014.
http://www.prophecynewswatch.com/2014/August29/295html. Accessed August 29, 2014.

Amazing Growth

Presented in the following narratives are facts, most of which have been missed by mainstream media—"under the radar" in a sense—but are nonetheless true and verifiable.

At present, Christianity has a slightly less growth pace than Islam, but this does not tell the full story. According to World Religion Database (WRD), the rate of growth of Christianity from 1910 to 2010 was 1.32 percent while Islam grew by 1.97 percent. But in 2000 to 2010, Christianity's growth went down very slightly at 1.31 percent while Islam experienced a deeper fall at 1.86 percent. The long-range projection of WRD is even more encouraging to Christians: the prognosis for year 2200 is 37.9 percent of total world population for the Christians, which is an increase from the present estimate of 32-33 percent. Meanwhile, in year 2200, the projection for Muslims is 22.6 percent of world population which is a decline from the present estimate of 23+ percent.[127]

Core Apostolics

James Rutz, in his book, *Mega Shift: Igniting Spiritual Power,* offers an even more amazing, if not fascinating, perspective. From available statistics, mainly from David Barrett and Todd Johnson, *World Christian Encyclopedia 2001,* (New York, Oxford University Press), he isolated the born-again charismatic, Pentecostals, and Evangelicals and separated their numbers from those of the mainstream Christian denominations. The aforesaid group, which he called "Core Apostolics," had a meteoric increase from 71 million in 1970 to ten times their size in 2000. Of the total 2 billion Christians worldwide, the core apostolics numbered 707 million in 2000, growing at 8 percent a year.

---

[127] "Growth of Religion," in *Wikipedia, http://en.wikipedia.org/wiki/growth of religion. Accessed March 5, 2014.*

Here is his annual growth rates list:[128]

World population   1.2 %

Buddhists   0.9 %

Hindus   1.1 %

Muslims   1.8 %

All "Christians"   1.1 %

All Protestants   1.4 %

Core Apostolics   8.0 %

Theoretically, if the above growth rates are maintained, the entire world population would be core apostolic by 2032, at about 8.2 billion. In a humorous way, Rutz jokingly said there would then be more apostolic Christians than people on earth. As a measure of the speed of core apostolic growth, in 1960 Western Evangelicals outnumbered non-Western Evangelicals (mostly Asians, Latin Americans, and Africans) by two-to-one, but by 2000 the non-Westerns reversed the ratio four-to-one, and by 2010 the estimate was seven-to-one non-Western over their Western brothers. In fact, some non-Western countries such as the Philippines that used to be missionary-receiving are now missionary-sending countries.

Throughout the world, fantastic beginning and increase of believers have recently been witnessed. For instance, in Cambodia, Christians grew from 200 to 400,000 from 1990 to 2004. In Hainan Province, China, believers of Christ grew from zero to 255,000 in eight years, by 1995. In Nepal, Christians grew from 5,200 in 1970 to 543,340 by 2000, while in the Congo, believers among the Pygmies grew from about zero to 300,000 from 1972 to 1997. It has been claimed that the fastest growth is in Latin America. In

---

[128]James Rutz, *Mega Shift: Igniting Spiritual Power*, WND Books, Washington DC., 2011, p. 14.

Guatemala, 44% of the country is born-again Christian while El Salvador is 53.6% born-again Christians, and this figure does not include the traditional non-born-again Christians. In the Middle East, millions are believed to have become Christians through hearing evangelistic transmissions, and that "more Muslims have turned to Christ in the last ten years than in the previous 1,000 years." In India, about 25% of the people would like to become Christians if they could stay in their family groupings, according to a 1995 confidential survey.

All the preceding data are reported by Rutz on pages 81-82 in his book, and he insisted, "I will defend my statistics to the death, or until the numbers change, whichever comes first."[129]

To most people, the above figures are too "out of this world" to believe. Sorry. With a thousand apologies, these are presented only as SAMPLES of a worldwide phenomenon that seems unstoppable. I even heard of confidential reports (the sources of which I cannot disclose at this time) that in Iran, Christians are increasing in number so fantastic that it could indeed fulfill the prophecy in Jeremiah 49:38, *'I will set My throne in Elam (Iran), and will destroy from there the king and princes,' says the Lord.*

My Personal Witness

While I was serving in Mexico, I personally witnessed the power of the Holy Spirit and how fast the Gospel spread as it transformed the lives of individuals, families and communities. In-between diplomatic functions and office work, I took the time to go with my missionary friends Pastor Angel and Sis. Elma Ignacio of International Missions Board in their various activities. Within one year before I met them, they had already planted several house churches, even as they gained mastery of the Mexican-Spanish language.

---

[129] Ibid., p. 44, End Note #15.

I also had the privilege of meeting another missionary, born-again Gloria Sloan, whose weekly routine included mentoring to leaders of thirteen house churches she had planted in the previous years. Still, she continued to encourage more new converts to pastor their own house churches. As a footnote, Gloria lost her missionary husband and a daughter in one day in a tragic drowning at a western beach of Mexico (two other mission volunteers also died as they tried to save the girl), but by her surrender to God's will and purpose, she gained more strength and has been an inspiration to many people. According to Facebook and Twitter, she is now serving in Honduras.[130]

Through my exposure to the life of missionaries, and in my personal experiences as Eva and I went deeper into sharing the Gospel even as a diplomat, I have come to know the truth of the spiritual hunger of millions of people. I saw the immeasurable dedication of core apostolics and the faithfulness of Jesus Christ to His promise, *I am with you always, to the very end of the age* (Matthew 28:19).

The Bible foretold this explosive growth in Joel 2:28-32, and reiterates it in Acts 2:17-21, as follows:

> *'In the last days,' God says, 'I will pour out my Spirit on all people. Your sons and daughters will prophecy, your young men will see visions, your old men will dream dreams...Even on my servants, both men and women, I will pour out my Spirit in those days, and they will prophecy...before the coming of the great and glorious day of the Lord. And everyone who calls on the name of the Lord will be saved.'*

---

[130] See Alan James, *Tragic Day Leads Missionary to Find Peace in God's Sovereignty,* imb.org/main/news/details.asp?StoryID=90.8,11/2/2010. Accessed December 20, 2014.

Go and Make Disciples of All Nations (Matthew 28:19)

The Spirit of the Lord sweeps across the planet in these last days, mobilizing faithful Christians to share the Good News to all nations by internet, TV and radio programs. How exciting it must be for the millions positioned to welcome the return of the Messiah as they take part in the movement now spearheaded by the Holy Spirit in preparing the Second Coming of Jesus Christ.

If you are not yet on board the chariot now cruising throughout the nations, you may wish to be among the multitude of people on the move to bring the Gospel to every corner of the globe.

Jesus' Call to Action for Believers

When Jesus described the global conditions at the End of the Age, He tried to get the believers to take action in response to the signs of the times.[131] Jesus' parable on the unprepared servant delivers the importance of His call for action:

> *The master of that servant will come on a day when he does not expect him and at an hour he is not aware of. He will cut him to pieces and assign him a place with the hypocrites, where there will be weeping and gnashing of teeth.* [132]

As He encouraged His followers to strengthen their faith to face persecution, death, and hatred by all nations on account of their belief, He also called them to play their role in these critical times as given them by the Creator.

Jesus urged His followers to go beyond themselves, to help their fellow believers overcome the false teachings, antichrist culture, persecution, and apathy that lead many into apostasy and loss of love.[133] He further warned that in our time, millions of non-believers

---

[131] Matthew 24:36-51

[132] Ibid., 50-51.

[133] Daniel 11:35 says, *Some of the wise will stumble, so that they may be*

will be kept in captivity from knowing the kingdom of God and will not receive salvation unless someone brings to them the Good News.

Daniel 12:3 gives assurance and encouragement to those believers who take up their role in the end time: *Those who are wise will shine like the brightness of the heavens, and those who lead many to righteousness, like the stars for ever and ever.*

Preach the "Sermon of your Life"

Does it mean all believers should take a formal course, be ordained, and become priests or pastors? No, that is not demanded in the Great Commission. Instead, Jesus meant for each believer to manifest—or "preach"—in his/her life the message of the Gospel. He wants the Gospel to come alive in the life of a believer as he thinks, speak, and behave according to His righteousness.

Preach the sermon of the Gospel in your life founded on the measure of faith you have—in accordance with the gift the Holy Spirit had given you.[134] I believe there is a continuum of roles, from the least obvious to the most visible, but all for the same purpose—the advancement of the kingdom of Heaven—and founded on the same spirit of God.[135]

To start, ask for God's guidance as you set your sight on the spiritual conditions of your family, relatives, and friends who remain unsaved. Be the "salt and the light" to people around you, at work, in school, at the playground, wherever you are, without going out of your way to impress. Live the Gospel as "ambassador

---

refined, purified and made spotless until the time of the end, for it will still come at the appointed time.

[134] Ephesians 4:1 says, *live a life worthy of the calling you have received.* Verse 11 added that Jesus *gave some to be apostles, some to be prophets, some to be evangelists, and some to be pastors and teachers, to prepare God's people for works of service...*

[135] Ibid., 4-6

of Christ," reflecting the image of Jesus. Or you can also do what I did. While I performed my secular job, I conducted Bible study and preached the Gospel in my personal time wherever I was assigned. The Word of God greatly helped the overseas workers and their families.

Or you may serve in any capacity in your church community:

> *If a man's gift is prophesying, let him use it in proportion to his faith...if it is serving, let him serve; if it is teaching, let him teach; if it is encouraging, let him encourage; if it is contributing to the needs of others, let him give generously; if it is leadership, let him govern diligently; if it is showing mercy, let him do it cheerfully* (Romans 12:7-8).

The task of bringing the Gospel beyond our local community is no longer limited to serving as a missionary abroad. There are now several roles. As world migration is made easier, one can go abroad as contract worker and share God's message to other foreign workers as well as to any interested person. Going abroad as "tent-maker"[136] has been a common choice for those going to "limited access nation" (LAN) where missionary visa for a Christian is not granted. Some denominations train for pastoral work their members slated to work abroad, especially in LAN. But there is still the role of a missionary sent to FAN (free access nation) such as those in Sub-Saharan Africa, Asia-Pacific, and Eastern Europe where the Gospel has been touching and transforming lives by the millions a year. One can also work under any of the several missionary-sending organizations accessible through local churches.

While millions of Christians in Syria, Iraq, and some other countries are driven out or murdered, their fellow Christians may have to bear the burden of providing for their safety, shelter, food and clothing as the world seems to have closed its eyes to such daily horror. More challenging but equally urgent is the ministry to

---

[136] Like Apostle Paul who traveled as maker of tents for livelihood, many ministers find employment abroad while sharing the Gospel.

Western Europe, North America, and the Middle East (expatriate communities) where undercurrents of spiritual hunger is prevalent among those who are weary of political, social, and economic stress. But even in one's neighborhood, foreigners have moved-in and many of them have not heard of the Gospel.

Diaspora Ministry

There is now a movement that ministers to the modern-day diaspora as fluidity of migration and importation of labor brought millions of foreign workers to Europe, Middle East, North America, and the Dragon countries (China, Taiwan, Japan, and South Korea) in the Far East. The Global Diaspora Network (GDN) has been formed and is now working with evangelical leaders, denominations, and para-church organizations in various countries such as the Philippines, China, Japan, and Ukraine. Linked to the Lausanne Committee for World Evangelization through the Senior Associate for Diaspora, Dr. Rev. Sadiri Joy Tira, the GDN is an example of core apostolic.[137]

As to what specific role a follower of Jesus shall assume is an individual choice arrived at thru prayers, visions, dreams, experiencing God's presence, or other manifestations of the Holy Spirit. But anyone who answers the call of the Lord is assured of a role in God's battle strategy in the end time and will receive reward as he translates his faith into action.

How about the unbeliever? By accepting Jesus Christ's offer of salvation, a person then begins his spiritual journey towards a new life, and assumes his role reserved for him before time began. As a new partner of Jesus, he can then partake in the thrill of seeing and experiencing the most exciting events of the centuries as the Creator brings to a dramatic climax the present Church Age. He can join the thrill in the final harvest through the Good News proclamation, and

---

[137] Visit www.lausanne.org. or www.globaldiaspora.net, or email info@globaldiaspora.net

be among the privileged to prepare the world for the return of the Messiah and the dawning of a new era.

More Evidences of Holy Spirit's Work

Miracles still happen in our time. The works of the Holy Spirit manifest assuring today's generation that the Bible is true, and Jesus Christ remains relevant in our lives. The following are just samples of such occurrences, as collected by Rutz in *Mega Shift*:

1. Resurrection cases have increased to about a thousand by now, and reported in at least 52 countries, including those who have been dead for three days (p.30).

2. Healing of all kinds of illness and restoration of missing body parts continue in large number (p.29).

3. Millions of Muslims, Hindus, and Buddhists have turned to Christianity after having encounters with Jesus through dreams and visions, angelic appearances, hearing God's voice, TV/radio broadcasts, ***Jesus*** film, Billy Graham's My Hope country-to-country projects, and social media like Facebook, You tube and Twitter (p. 79).

4. Miracles involving individuals led millions to Jesus. Examples:

    a) Athet Pyan Shinthaw Paulu. He was a Burmese Buddhist monk who was dead for three days in 1998. He came back to life during his funeral and declared he saw Buddha and other Buddhist "holy men" in hell. As his story was consistent with the Bible although he had not read it, some 300 monks and many others turned to the Lord, Jesus Christ (pp. 32-33).

    b) Hawa Ahmed. She was a Muslim college student in 1990's in North Africa when she became a Christian. Her father, who was an emir (Muslim ruler), and her brothers stripped her naked, tied her to a chair, and tried to electrocute her for becoming a Christian. But the current would not flow. They then beat her severely and threw her out into the street without any clothing on. She ran crying in pain and humiliation to her Christian friend's apartment. On the following day, her friend Sarah apologized to neighbors who might have been offended after seeing Hawa naked, but the neighbors insisted Hawa was wearing a beautiful white gown (p.33).

c) Wang Xin Cai, leader of one of the seven main strands of the true (non-government) church in China, was dying after 13 years of hard-labor imprisonment, so he was released to die with his family. But God healed him. At the time, there were only four strands of Christians in the country, but they were at odds over minor differences. So, Wang called for unity meeting in Henan city to save the Christian church in the country. But on the morning when the other leaders were arriving for the meeting, Wang's baby daughter fell three floors down to instant death, with head split wide open. He wrapped her in a blanket, laid her on the couch, and prayed, "Lord, if this unity meeting is of You, then You have to heal my daughter." Then he left for the meeting. When he returned, she was still dead but her head was now in one piece. The following day, after his meeting, he came home to find the baby breathing, but she was in a coma. On the third day, after praying, he left again for the meeting which successfully resulted to unity and cooperation, and the salvation of the body of Christ in the country. When he got home, Wang radiated the joy of a happy father as he saw the baby awake, alert, and eating heartily (pp. 104-105).

CHAPTER TWENTY-THREE

JESUS RULES IN THE MILLENIUM

> *For the Lord himself will come down from heaven with a loud command, with the voice of the archangel and the trumpet call of God, and the dead in Christ will rise first. After that we who are still alive and are left will be caught up together with them in the clouds to meet the Lord in the air. And so we will be with the Lord forever.*
> **1Thessalonians 4:16-17**
>
> *To him who overcomes and does my will to the end, I will give authority over the nations...just as I have received authority from my Father. I will also give him the Morning Star.*
> **Revelation 2:26-28**

Eternal Life

Eternal life is more than the absence of death. Those who believe in God's only begotten Son will also receive more rewards, equipping them to fully live and fulfill the purpose for which they are given the gift of immortality.

Abundant Life in Eternity

Whoever has will be given more, and he will have an abundance. Whoever does not have, even what he has will be taken from him. This principle expressed in Matthew 13:12 and 25:29 gives the promise to those who have faith, that by believing, they will have abundant life. But those who have no faith, the devil will corrupt and destroy whatever God-given gift they have since birth.

I have come that they may have life, and have it to the full, assured Jesus.[138] The believer is guaranteed to be filled with his needs in the three areas of his existence—spirit, body, and soul—in his spiritual journey, physical sustenance, as well as emotional health and intellectual pursuits.

The gift of abundant life is the realization of God's promise of restoration to man, a "return to Eden" in a way, for those with faith in Jesus Christ. But the gift package contains more. Whereas Adam and Eve were denied the fruit of the Tree of Life,[139] believers in the Son of God shall receive the gift of eternal life wrapped with abundant existence. Such abundant life that is promised while a believer lives on earth shall be carried over in full into the thousand years beyond the End of the Age—and into eternity.

The Rapture: Escape from the Wrath

The "rapture"[140] is the event that saves the believers in Christ from the coming wrath during the great tribulation. While

---

[138] John 10:9 The *Spirit Filled Life Bible: New King James Version* text is: *I have come that they may have life, and that they may have it more abundantly.* Strong's #4053 defines "abundantly" as excessive, more than sufficient, superabundance, overflowing, surplus, extraordinary, over and above, more than enough, profuse, and above the ordinary.

[139] The fruit of the Tree of Life would have given Adam and Eve eternal life. Genesis 3:22-24

[140] The word "rapture," a derivative of Latin word *raptu,* is commonly used as a translation of the Greek word *harpazo* in 1Thessaloneans 4:17 which means "caught up."

describing the pressures His followers will face in the last days, Jesus promised, *he who stands firm to the end will be saved.*[141]

In Revelation 3:10, Jesus was more specific in His assurance to those who overcome. He said: *Since you have kept my command to endure patiently, I will also keep you from the hour of trial that is going to come upon the whole world to test those who live on the earth.*

The rapture event will prove to be the most spectacular and rewarding experience to all believers. In an instant, they will vanish from the earth and join Jesus in the air between heaven and earth:

> 1. *For the Lord himself will come down from heaven, with a loud command, with the voice of the archangel and with the trumpet call of God, and the dead in Christ will rise first. After that, we who are still alive and are left will be caught up together with them to meet the Lord in the air. And so we will be with the Lord forever* (1Thessaloneans 4:16-17).
>
> 2. *We will all be changed—in a flash, in the twinkling of an eye, at the last trumpet* (1Corinthians 15:51-52).
>
> 3. *The dead will be raised imperishable, and we will be changed. For the perishable must clothe itself with imperishable, and the mortal with immortality* (v.52-53).

Jesus' promise of eternal life transcends the fate of the believers at the End of the Age. Believers who have died before the rapture will resurrect first and be lifted up. Those who survive the onslaught of the Antichrist will be caught up in the air and be clothed with immortality, *in the twinkling of an eye*; they will never experience

---

[141] Matthew 24:13; Mark 13:13

physical death. Those who are killed in the tribulation because of their faith in Jesus will be resurrected and given imperishable body.

Nobody knows the day and time of the rapture, *not even the angels in heaven, nor the Son, but only the Father.*[142] The believer must therefore *be ready, because the Son of Man will come at an hour when you do not expect Him.*[143]

Some Bible scholars believe the rapture will happen before the tribulation, while others believe it will occur mid-way of the tribulation or at the start of the great tribulation when the "abomination that causes desolation" demands all to worship him as god. Still others believe the rapture will be in the great tribulation just before Jesus descends to defeat the Antichrist and the coalition of nations. Eschatologists all have convincing arguments to support their varied views, but ultimately the timing is of less importance. Being prepared for Christ's return should be the believer's priority.

Unbelievers will be caught by surprise at the timing of the Lord's coming. 1Thessaloneans 5:3 describes, *While people are saying, 'Peace and safety,' destruction will come on them suddenly, as labor pains on a pregnant woman, and they will not escape.*

The unbelievers like Lot's sons-in-law, as well as the apostates like his wife who looked back at the lifestyle of Sodom and Gomorrah, will be left behind to suffer the wrath of God. The moment following the rapture begins God's wrath. *For then there will be great distress, unequaled from the beginning of the world until now – and never to be equaled again,* Jesus described the coming wrath to His disciples.[144]

---

[142] Matthew 24:36. The rapture is unscheduled, the first phase of Jesus' return preparatory to His final descend to defeat the Antichrist at the end of the age.

[143] Ibid., 44

[144] Matthew 24:21. The coming wrath makes it vital and urgent to bring the Gospel to all, including the young and the people in unreached places.

Believers will face the most difficult testing and challenge to their faith until the day of the rapture. It should be understood, though, that these pre-rapture trials and difficult times will be imposed on the believers by unbelieving authorities, not by God. Believers *will be handed over to be persecuted and put to death,* and be hated by all nations because of their faith (Matthew 24:9). Employing the Christian's Rules of Engagement, everyone with faith must be prepared to endure and strengthen his spiritual muscles in response to the major trials.

Final Moment, Final Choice for Eternity

Every person's eternal fate hangs on his choice of beliefs and lifestyle during the pre-rapture period. Revelation 21:6-8 gives a contrast of the consequences of one's decision:

> *I am the Alpha and the Omega, the Beginning and the End. To him who is thirsty I will give to drink without cost from the spring of the water of life. He who overcomes will inherit all this, and I will be his God and he will be my son. But the cowardly, the unbelieving, the vile, the murderers, the sexually immoral, those who practice magic arts, the idolaters, and all liars—their place will be in the fiery lake of burning sulfur.*[145]

Some basic factors, therefore, require serious considerations. Among these are:

1. Every believer must take action appropriate to the role he is intended to fulfill preparatory to Christ's return. Believers are called to preach the Gospel. With courage, perseverance, and dedication, they must remain faithful to the Word of God,

---

[145] See also 1Corinthians 6:9-10 which says, *Do you not know that the wicked will not inherit the kingdom of God? Do not be deceived: Neither the sexually immoral nor idolaters nor adulterers nor male prostitutes nor homosexual offenders nor thieves nor the greedy nor drunkards nor slanderers nor swindlers will inherit the kingdom of God.*

rely on the power of the cross, and share their testimony on the love of Jesus even in the face of death.[146] Believers must guard against falling into apostasy, and non-believers must make up their mind to accept salvation through Christ before it is too late. Non-believers who choose to receive Jesus during the tribulation will join the rapture; those who are martyred because they received Him will resurrect and receive rewards.[147]

2. After the rapture, the apostates, like the non-believers, will no longer be saved. Like the unfaithful servant who failed to do his master's will, the apostate will be *cut into* pieces, and assigned *a place with the unbelievers* (Luke 12:46). Those who have heard Jesus' offer of salvation but opted to believe the lies of Satan will be subjected to God's wrath.

3. The wrath of God comes on the rebellious world with the same fury and completeness as the destruction of Sodom and Gomorrah and the wicked world in Noah's time.[148] On the other hand, as earlier mentioned, believers will escape the wrath of God through the rapture; the dead in Christ will resurrect into imperishable existence, while the surviving believer will be clothed with immortality.

---

[146] On the parable of the unfaithful servant, read Luke 12:42-47. Verse 48 adds, *From everyone who has been given much, much will be demanded, and from the one who has been entrusted with much, much more will be asked*.

[147] Revelation 20:4 assures, *"They had not worshipped the beast or his image and had not received his mark on their foreheads or their hands. They came to life and reigned with Christ a thousand years."*

[148] Revelation 19:15 says Jesus will *"strike down the nations ... rule them with iron scepter ... and treads the winepress of the fury of the wrath of God Almighty."* See also 2 Thessalonians 2:10-12.

Resurrection into Glorified Body

Christianity is unique among world religions in that Jesus Christ came back from death not to the corruptible state of mortal man but to an incorruptible life with ability to traverse to other dimensions.

In His resurrected body, Jesus passed through walls as He suddenly appeared before the disciples in an enclosed room.[149] He appeared by a lakeside, caused a big catch of fish, and ate with the disciples (John 21:1-14). He appeared and talked with Peter in one place, then reappeared in another place as He talked with two other disciples on their way to Emmaus (Luke 24:13-35). He ascended to heaven as He rose higher and higher until He could not be seen anymore—without space suit.[150] It is clear the resurrected Jesus was a transformed being that defied the laws of today's physics.

The believers' resurrected body will be like Jesus' resurrected body.[151] Their new body shall be adapted to the conditions of the next age, new heaven, and new earth.[152] Their glorified body will be free from decay and disease, and from the laws of nature.[153] Their immortal and imperishable body will, however, still be recognizable,[154] and they can eat and drink with their friends and relatives.[155]

---

[149] Although the doors were locked, Jesus was suddenly with the disciples while they were eating (Luke 24:36-43). Again, Jesus suddenly came into a locked room to show Thomas the wounds on His hands and side (John 20:24-29).

[150] Ibid., 50-51; Acts 1:9-11

[151] Romans 8:29; 1Corinthians 15:20, 42-44, 49; Philippians 3:20-21

[152] 1Corinthians 15:47-49; Revelation 21:1

[153] Luke 24:31; John 20:19

[154] Luke 16:19-31

[155] Ibid., 14:15; 22:14-18, 30

The Second Coming of Jesus Christ

Most writers believe a two-stage return of Jesus Christ. First, He comes to receive the believers during the rapture. Second, He descends to defeat the Antichrist and his allies. The length of the interlude depends on the timing of the rapture. Although the day and hour of the first phase is unknown, the second phase will be seven years after the signing of the peace treaty, or 3.5 years after the Antichrist stands at the temple and declares himself god.

From heaven, Jesus Christ descends riding on a white horse as the Warrior-Messiah with eyes like a blazing fire. On His head are many crowns, and on His robe and thigh are written "King of Kings and Lord of Lords." He is followed by the armies of heaven who are also riding on white horses and dressed in white and clean linen to confirm they are the saints who are already in heaven.[156]

The world will see what many had rejected: the Truth that the battle between good and evil belongs to God. Jesus and His army swiftly defeat the Antichrist and all his troops and allies who are poised to take Jerusalem. They capture the beast, or Antichrist, and also the false prophet who had deluded many into receiving the mark of the beast and worshiping the Antichrist and his image.[157]

The beast and the false prophet are *thrown alive into the fiery lake of burning sulfur. The rest of them were killed.*[158] But punished together with the invading forces are men and nations that have supported or joined the Antichrist in his assault on Jerusalem.[159] Satan will be bound and imprisoned for a thousand years to prevent him from deceiving the nations.

---

[156] On Jesus Christ' victory over Antichrist and allies, see Revelation 19:11-21.

[157] Ibid., 19:19-20

[158] Ibid., 20-21

[159] Jeremiah 25:29-33

After the defeat of Satan, Jesus will judge over the survivors of the tribulation. He will separate the righteous from the wicked. He will send the unrighteous to eternal punishment and the righteous to eternal life.[160]

Jesus Christ Begins His Rule

In the thousand years[161] after the End of the Age, a whole new world emerges. The battle smoke and dust would have settled, the rotting bodies consumed by vultures, the stench blown by the wind, and the noise of the final battle had come to a complete silence. Based on Mt. Zion, Jesus Christ begins His rule over the remnants of humanity.

The era begins in a planet where the wicked and the unrighteous are already taken out in the cataclysmic disasters and the final war. Although doubters will be born in the future, no unsaved person will enter into the new millennium kingdom.[162] Some nations that we now know in the present Church Age will survive, but the people remaining in the land will basically be a righteous society—sans rebellious spirit, sans hatred, sans immorality, and sans arrogance.

In the new millennium, the environmental, spiritual, and societal realities will become much more spectacular than the beauty of the world we now know. Nature will soon be restored to its original order as in the Garden of Eden, in perfection and beauty, as *the*

---

[160] Matthew 25:31-46

[161] Revelation 20:4-7. Jesus will rule the earth for a thousand years, a period referred to by some writers as "the millennium," or "New Millennium."

[162] Ibid., 22:14-15 says: *Blessed are those who wash their robes, that they may have the right to the tree of life and may go through the gates into the city. Outside are the dogs, those who practice magic arts, the sexually immoral, the murderers, the idolaters and everyone who loves and practices falsehood.*

creation itself will be liberated from the bondage of decay.[163] Trees will bear luscious fruits while flowers blossom in exciting colors and flagrance, and the grass unfolds its freshness with all shades of green. Animals will be tame and friendly to man as the lion lies down with the lamb, and the earth no longer release destructive natural disasters, and any geological movement will only be for the replenishment of earth's life.

In that future age, restoration of mankind can then proceed to recover what man lost after Adam and Eve disobeyed. The three areas of man's being – his spirit, body, and soul – will be further nurtured to fulfill their intended use as the Creator designed man to be. Man's intellectual potential will receive challenging stimuli under the direction of the author of creation Himself, Jesus Christ, the Word by which the universe came into being. Under Jesus' rule, a new and vast horizon of science will open and pave the way for mankind's higher reach toward greater technological sophistication. Many more secrets and mysteries of creation, human potential, and man's relationship with the Triune God will be revealed in the New Millennium. After man's exile from Eden, his spiritual potential suffered; but in the coming age, man can expect Jesus to reveal more of man's deeper spiritual links with the Father Almighty. As promised in Romans 8:18, all the sufferings in this present age *are not worth comparing with the glory that will be revealed in us* when we, as children of God, live our freedom from sin's bondage.

Rule with Jesus Over the Nations

When Jesus returns to earth and begins His rule for a thousand years, believers are given authority to sit by Jesus and rule with Him. Jesus promised, *To him who overcomes, I will give the right to sit with me on my throne, just as I overcame and sat down with my Father on his throne* (Revelation 3:21).[164]

---

[163] Romans 8:21

[164] See also Revelation 2:26-27; 5:9-10; 11:15-18; 20:4-6

At present, believers are already given weapons of divine power—such as the full armor of God—against the strongholds of the devil.[165] But in the age to come, having the authority to serve under Jesus will be more than an honor and privilege, for the believers will be equipped with abilities beyond our present human capacities in order to fulfill our new tasks and to fully live His gift of eternal life.

The age beyond the end time will begin in a world where righteousness defines all human affairs. Family lifestyle will be centered on love. Relations between men and nations shall resume without greed, envy, hatred, and violence. Our personal relationship with Jesus will grow with greater intimacy and affection. In the age to come, Jesus will reveal more answers to the quest of humankind:

> *When I consider your heavens,*
>
> *The work of your fingers,*
>
> *The moon and the stars,*
>
> *Which you have set in place,*
>
> *What is man that you are mindful of him,*
>
> *The son of man that you care for him?*
>
> *You made him a little lower than the heavenly beings*
>
> *And crowned him with glory and honor.*
>
> (Psalm 8:3-4)

---

[165] 2 Corinthians 10:4-5; Mark 16:17-18, for example, says, ...*In my name they will drive out demons...* See also John 14:12-14; Acts 2:1-11; 43;3:1-10; 5:12-16

A Glorious Future

Beyond the End of the Age, with greater assurance than human diplomacy can vouch, the promised abundant eternal life of man begins.

When I consider the masterful engineering work that is man, the high price of Jesus' crucifixion by which mankind is redeemed, and the precision of the whole creation in which life exists, I am filled with the thought that God's grace must be for something more than what we now know. The Creator has plans and designs for mankind and the world beyond our imagination, toward the greater glory of the sovereign author of the majestic cosmos.

Thus, I eagerly look forward to the millennium following Jesus' return. If I have to live my life again, I would still choose to place my trust, hope, and confidence in the Triune God of the Bible.

Having *more* knowledge *now* than before about Almighty God, I would choose to *believe* and *receive* Jesus Christ as Lord and Savior and begin the spiritual journey much earlier in my life.

How about you?

Bibliography

Chuck Bagby, Ph.D., *Born To Die: The Jesus Story: What I Wish I Had Known (Book I)*, Burning Heart Bible Studies: San Antonio, TX, 2014.

Reinhard Bonnke, *Even Greater: 12 Real-Life Stories that Inspire You to Do Great Things for God*, Full Flame: Orlando, 2004.

Gracia Burnham with Dean Merrill, *In the Presence of my Enemies*, Tyndale House Publisher: Wheaton, 2003.

Dr. William Campbell, *The Quran and the Bible in the Light of History and Science*, copyright 1986, 2002 by Arab World Ministries.

Susan Crimp and Joel Richardson (editors), *Why We Left Islam: Former Muslims Speak Out*, WND Books: Los Angeles, 2008.

John Hagee, *The Beginning of the End: The Assassination of Yitzhak Rabin and the Coming Antichrist*, Thomas Nelson, Inc.: Nashville, 1996.

_____, *Jerusalem Countdown: A Prelude to War*, Frontline: Lake Mary, 2006, 2007.

_____, *Earth's Final Moments: Powerful Insight and Understanding of the Prophetic Signs that Surround Us*, Charisma House: Lake Mary, 2011.

Paul Hattaway, *The Heavenly Man: The Remarkable True Story of Chinese Christian Brother Yun*, Monarch Books: London, 2002.

Norvel Hayes, *The Winds of God Bring Revival*, Harrison House: Tulsa, 1985.

Patrick Johnstone, *Operation World: The Day-by-Day Guide to Praying for the World,* Zondervan: Grand Rapids, 1993.

Jo Kadlecek, *A Desperate Faith: Lessons of Hope from the Resurrection,* Baker Books: Grand Rapids, 2010.

Lim Kou, *Understanding Job: Reflections on the Meaning and Purpose of Job's Suffering,* ISBN: 981-04-8131-4, also available in www.godandtruth.com, AR005 to AR012: 2003.

Tim Lahaye, *Rapture (Under Attack): Will You Escape the Tribulation?* Multnomah Publishers: Sisters, 1998.

Hal Lindsey, *Apocalypse Code,* Western Front Ltd.: Palos Verdes, 1997.

_____, *Everlasting Hatred: The Roots of Jihad,* WND Books: Washington DC, 2011.

Max Lucado, *Experiencing the Heart of Jesus: Knowng His Heart, Feeling His Love,* Thomas Nelson,Inc.: Nashville, Tenn., 2003

Josh McDowell and Dave Sterrett, *"O" God: A Dialogue on Truth and Oprah's Spirituality,* WND Books: Washington DC, 2009.

Brad O'Leary, *America's War on Christianity,* WND Books: Washington DC, 2010.

Luis Pantoja, Sadiri Joy Tira, Enoch Wan (editors), *Scattered: The Filipino Global Presence,* Lifechange Publishing, Inc: Manila, 2004.

Michael Rice, *False Inheritance: Israel in Palestine and the Search for a Solution,* Kegan Paul International: London, 1994.

Joel Richardson, *The Islamic Antichrist: The Shocking Truth About the Real Nature of the Beast,* WND Books: Los Angeles, 2009.

Joel C. Rosenberg, *Epicenter: Why the Current Rumblings in the Middle East will Change Your Future,* Tyndale House Publishing: Carol Stream, 2006, 2008.

Hugh Ross, *The Creator and the Cosmos: How the Greatest Scientific Discoveries of the Century Reveal God,* Navpress: Colorado Springs, 1984.

_____, *Fingerprint of God,* 2nd Ed. Revised, Promise Publishing: Orange, 1991.

James Rutz, *Mega Shift: The Best News Since Year One,* WND Books: Washington DC, 2011.

Paul Smith, *Jesus: Meet Him Again for the First Time,* Vision House Publishing: Gresham, 1994.

Perry Stone, *Unleashing the Beast: The Coming Fanatical Dictator and His Ten-Nation Coalition,* Frontline: Lake Mary, 2009, 2011.

Brian Sussman, *Climategate: A Veteran Meteorologist Exposes the Global Warming Scam,* WND Books: Washington D.C., 2010.

Dr. Jack Van Impi, *Coming Soon: Earth's Golden Age,* copyright 1999, revised 2008.

Warren W. Wiersbe, *On Being a Servant of God,* Christian Growth Ministries: Quezon City, Philippines, 2004.

Dallas Willard, *The Divine Conspiracy: Rediscovering Our Hidden Life in God,* Harper Collins: San Francisco, 1997.

Philip Yancey and Dr. Paul Brand, *Fearfully and Wonderfully Made*, OMF:Manila, 2000.

Dr. Fenggang Yang, *Religion in China: Survival and Revival Under Communist Rule,* Oxford University Press: New York, 2012.

ADDENDUM

The following discussion is not intended to influence the opinion of the reader on the subject issue. Rather, it is meant to stimulate interest on a development that may have been noticed superficially or passed over, if not ignored totally, by most people. The issue, nonetheless, may be directly relevant to the nature of our time. It can even be central to the fulfillment of the prophecies on the End of the Age.

IRAN'S NUCLEAR PROGRAM
An Omen?

My interest on the technical aspect of the nuclear bomb was deepened during my graduate studies at USC when I wrote my thesis on India's nuclear weapons policy. Although techniques and technology have changed since then, the principles behind nuclear fission and isotope separation remain the same. With such a background, I believe my reading between the lines of news reports on the issue is fairly accurate as the technical aspect of the bomb is an exact science.

The Joint Comprehensive Plan of Action

On July 14, 2015, the foreign ministers of the P5+1 (US, Great Britain, France, Russia, China, and Germany) and of the Islamic Republic of Iran shared the stage at the conclusion of their negotiations in Lausanne, Switzerland. Although the Joint Comprehensive Plan of Action was a result of multilateral efforts, many observers viewed it as mainly reflective of Washington DC-Teheran bilateral affairs.

Other countries in the Middle East, particularly the Gulf Cooperation Council members, fear the agreement confirms US President Barak Obama's suspected effort to nurture Iran as a major regional power. While Obama apologists justify his "wisdom" in raising Shiite-based Iran as a counter-check to Sunni-based Saudi Arabia, his critics warn the so-called "Obama doctrine" may be producing the very threat he wanted to avoid. Arab states initially hoped the US could pry out some political concessions to curb Iran's geopolitical interventions (Teheran's alleged involvement in Yemen, Iraq, Syria, Lebanon, Gaza, and territorial disputes against Bahrain, etc.) in the region. The nuclear deal, however, causes capitals like Riyadh to doubt American protection and serves to justify pursuit of nuclear defense capability of their own.

The JCPOA requires the conversion of the Fordow site from a covert host of uranium enrichment centrifuges to an international research center. The nuclear site at Natanz, which was also enriching uranium surreptitiously until it was discovered, will only use 6,104 units of Iran's first generation enrichment machines; the newer centrifuge versions will be mothballed. In addition, the International Atomic Energy Agency (IAEA) shall also be permitted to monitor the mining, processing, and use of uranium oxide as well as the manufacture and storage of centrifuges. To further assure a longer period of "breakout" (a shift from a non-military to nuclear bomb production program) to one year, Iran's existing stockpile of 430 lbs of 20%-enriched uranium shall be diluted or sold, and its 19,211 lbs (10,000 kg) of low-enriched uranium reduced to 660 lbs (300 kg). Parallel to, but separate from, the JCPOA are two confidential agreements on inspection of the military site at Parchin to assure there is no nuclear research or development project with possible military dimension (PMD).*

Despite the provisions for transparency in the deal, some basic questions remain. Will Iran really live up to the ultimate non-proliferation requirement of complete transparency even to the extent of exposing and compromising its national security? If in the past it succeeded to hide some nuclear facilities, what is the guarantee that it will not do it again? Also, will it not avail of Pyongyang's friendship and co-produce the weapons in North Korea, which is not a signatory to the Non-Proliferation Treaty? Equally important is the question of sanctions: at what point of the deal will the US and the other powers of P5+1 agree to lift the UN economic sanctions and European Union and US oil sanctions? Immediately after Pres. Obama overrides the objection of the US Congress? Or will sanctions be lifted after certification by IAEA of Iran's compliance with inspection requirements? Will the lifting of the sanctions be total with immediate effect, or will it be piecemeal, corresponding to a schedule conditional to total compliance of transparency by Iran? Some observers concluded that while much attention was directed to curtailing breakout, there was not enough thinking given to defining sanctions.

"If he can do it, he will do it."

While the process leading to the lifting of sanctions will be open and observable, any violation of the non-proliferation requirements will be covert. A breakout can start even months before it is detected, so by the time it is discovered, bomb-production may already be accomplished or at least half-way done. Actual breakout may be quicker than the one-year delay time President Barack Obama had promised the public. Such a *fait accompli* cannot be undone (once out, can the toothpaste be pushed back into the tube, or the genie into the bottle?) short of military operation. Besides, "snap back" of sanctions in case of violation is undefined if not impractical: does Iran need to return the assets released, financial aid received, and trade benefits gained during the period the sanctions were lifted? While sanctions can be re-introduced with negative effects mainly on Iran, the impact of Teheran's violation, on the other hand, would be widespread and irreversible. It would encourage regional nuclear arms race and possibly ignite a Middle East war or even Third World War.

In the history of nuclear weapons proliferation, a pattern remained consistent and predictable. Despite their initial claim of "peaceful purposes," additional members of the nuclear weapons club slid ultimately into atomic explosive production even as they continued with their civilian nuclear programs. The old saying, "If he can do it, he will do it," proved true.

A Peaceful Program?

The Teheran government insists that its nuclear program is for peaceful purposes only. Iran's credibility, however, may be viewed from two perspectives: its motive and capability. For now, this paper will not delve into Teheran's motive which is a political question. A glimpse through the technical prism, however, may reveal the country's capability with regard to the issue of nuclear bomb manufacture. Through the technical looking glass, one can determine whether or not the option to produce the bomb is within Iran's grasp. If Iran gains technical capability and independent control of materials for bomb production, will it make a breakout?

Technical Constants

Only a thin line separates the "peaceful" program from the "nuclear bomb" option. First, the technology and hardware used for peace (medical research, electrical power production, etc.) can also be used to produce weapons of war. The same resources that produce low grade fissionable material for research, for example, can also produce high grade material usable for high-power explosive. The amount, grade of purity, and time-length of producing fissionable material will depend mainly on the efficiency of the machine and the state of the uranium metal powder that is fed for processing. Before the JCPOA deal, Iran operated 9,400 gas centrifuges using its early isotope separation IR-1 machines. Although the nominal output is up to 3 SWU (separative work unit), the machines already produced a stockpile of low-to-medium grade enriched uranium, reportedly up to 20 percent purity, for "peaceful purposes." But Iran developed and produced newer and more efficient versions. IR-4 model, for example, has 24 SWU capacity. However, the JCPOA now prohibits the use of the 9,000 units of IR-4 as well as the IR-2, IR-5, IR-6, and IR-8 which are mothballed under IAEA monitoring.

Second, with uranium enrichment capability, no matter how modest is the output, production of nuclear bomb material is just a matter of time, not "if" but "when." In natural uranium, there are basically two isotopes, uranium-235 and uranium-238. U-235 is what is needed for the bomb, so the goal is to separate it from the heavier U-238 which is 99 percent of the uranium oxide.

Both U-235 and U-238 are "fissionable" since they can "fission," or split by neutrons, and release energy in the process. However, U-235 is also "fissile" since it fissions with neutron of any speed or energy and maintain chain reaction; it is therefore versatile for weapons use. By comparison, U-238 requires high speed (or high energy) neutron in order to initiate chain reaction. Though U-238 is more difficult to detonate, it is nonetheless usable for the third stage of a fission-fusion-fission device.

The isotope-separation process is achieved through high-speed spin (100,000 times earth gravity) of a gas centrifuge machine. The heavier U-238 is thrown further leaving the lighter U-235 closer to the center of the spin. To achieve higher ratio in favor of U-235, the concentrated gas is fed into another centrifuge, and the same spin process is repeated until the desired level of U-235 purity is achieved. Earlier generations of atomic bombs had weapons-grade uranium at 80-90 percent purity, and a critical mass (the volume of material needed for spontaneous chain reaction thereby releasing high energy from the splitting atoms) of about 15 kilograms (with heavy tamper, or material to wrap it closely packed).

The Crucial "If's"

Technically, Iran now has the capability to produce high-grade materials for bomb production. If Iran can achieve 20 percent uranium enrichment using IR-1, it is only a matter of time before it can produce higher purity, weapons-grade fissile uranium by using the same machines it uses for peaceful purposes. If left undetected now especially with the use of newer models of centrifuges, Iran can produce the ingredients for a bomb in about two months. If the country decides to breakout, even if the number of its machines allowed to operate are reduced by the P5+1 countries, Iran will only be delayed but can still produce weapons-grade uranium. If Iran can escape detection of the IAEA, will it not make the bomb?

The Plutonium Option

Third, Iran may also choose the plutonium route as alternative to uranium in producing nuclear explosives. Already, Teheran revealed an intention to pursue this route when it initiated construction of the heavy water nuclear plant using the IR-40 reactor with 40 mw (thermal) capacity at Arak. The JCPOA aimed to frustrate further efforts on this option when it required Iran to redesign and rebuild the plant so that the original reactor core will be inoperable and replaced with a core prescribed by the IAEA. Furthermore, the spent fuel from the revised core will have to be shipped out of the country, and Iran is prohibited to build any additional heavy water plant for 15 years. The original reactor core, however, will remain in the country and can therefore be accessed if and when Iran makes a breakout.

Although the original heavy water plant was for medical and industrial isotope production as well as research development, its reactor core IR-40 could convert its uranium fuel rod into plutonium, a portion of which is fissile and usable for explosive. Basically, an irradiated (exposed or spent) fuel rod has as a by-product the isotope Plutonium-239 (Pu-239), which is an alternative to U-235 as the core of an atomic bomb. In the process of irradiation, however, other isotopes—Pu-240 and Pu-242—are also produced; these isotopes are "contaminants" because they can fission more easily and therefore can weaken the explosive power of the bomb or even cause premature detonation.

In the spent fuel, the percentage of Pu-239 as opposed to the contaminants depends on the grade of the uranium oxide and the duration of exposure of the fuel rod. Basically, a non-enriched uranium produces more Pu-239 than a high-enriched uranium oxide, and a shorter exposure time limits the percentage of contaminants. Thus, in the absence of international inspection in the use of the original reactor IR-40, Iran's technicians can control the operation of the heavy water power plant to maximize the production of the explosive-grade material, Pu-239.

Pu-239 is technically less costly to separate compared to U-235 as it can be recovered from the spent fuel rod through chemical process in a plutonium isotope-separation plant. A nominal atomic bomb with 20 kiloton yield would need only 4 to 6 kg with at least 90 percent Pu-239 purity. IR-40 can produce 10 kg of Pu-239 a year.

Before the Joint Plan of Action was concluded in November 2013, suspicions persisted on Iran's intentions especially with the operation of the heavy water production plant at Arak and Tehran's earlier plans (later aborted) to build plutonium separation plant. But the JPOA put a stop to the construction of the heavy water reactor plant, and the JCPOA signed in July sealed the fate of the Arak facilities.

To Tehran, the P5+1 requirement to redesign the heavy water nuclear plant was an acceptable collateral damage in exchange for the lifting of economic and oil sanctions. After all, the intended fuel bundle for the Arak reactor would have been still experimental as it was reportedly a modified fuel system initially intended for graphite-moderated reactor and not heavy water reactor. Furthermore, even if IR-40 was to be replaced, Iranian scientists and technicians will continue to gain know-how, expertise, and technology on plutonium, qualities which will become handy if and when Tehran makes a breakout.

Triggering, Assembly, and other Requirements

If Iran makes a breakout, the cost, technical requirements for assembly and design of the bomb, as well as the maintenance and set-up of testing facilities are additional hurdles the country must face. But with acquired skills, research, help from other countries, and the availability of existing underground caves, Iran can overcome these hurdles.

Technological advances since the first atomic bomb was tested in Alamogordo actually favor any ambitious "eager-beaver" that wants to join the exclusive nuclear weapons club. For example, US Department of Energy in 1994 estimated that 8 kg of weapons-grade uranium was sufficient for a device, much less than the critical mass of earlier versions. Subsequently, the DOE reduced further from 5 kg plutonium critical mass (used in Nagasaki) to 4 kg of Pu-239 as core for atomic weapons. And the "boosting" triggering technique developed by Dr. Edward Teller is now generally used by nuclear weapons countries; it is an improvement to the old "gun" and "implosion" methods used in the early Cold War era. Today, much information on the technical aspects of the bomb is available in the open sources. In the long run, assembly and design of its first bomb will not be beyond Iran's capability.

In view of the above considerations, one can assume that by allowing Iran to continue operating its gas centrifuges, no matter how small are the number of units allowed to operate, it will gain more know-how and capability to produce nuclear weapons. Iran will likely produce the bomb if Teheran can evade international inspection. If and when it operates the newer versions such as the IR4, and Iran would likely try to hide such operation from IAEA inspection, the country can be expected to one day surprise the world with a nuclear test of its own. Alternatively, Iran may even choose not to test the device but would immediately announce its possession of the weapon to blackmail Israel. The threat would be believable as most if not all first device tests by new members of the nuclear club had been successful.

Delivery System

Iran's continuing development of its missile system reflects its long-range intentions with its nuclear program. It can be observed that while Teheran insists its nuclear program is for civilian pursuits, the country has embarked on producing long-range precision guided missiles, a multi-million dollar option justifiable only if ultimately its payload is an atomic explosive.

Iran's missile arsenal is composed mainly of air-to-surface short-range and medium-range missiles mounted on aircrafts. But on March 8, 2015, Iranian defense minister announced the replacement of the earlier versions as he unveiled the deployment of a new surface-to-surface missile that can reach Israel and Europe. Dubbed

Soumar, the 2,000-mile range cruise missile reflects the continuing technical improvement of Iranian scientists and engineers. Though it resembles the Ukrainian Kh-55, originally a Russian-made missile, Soumar is claimed by Iran to have been designed and produced by its own engineers. Western intelligence reports, however, indicate that in violation of Ukraine-Russia agreement, six of the Kh-55 were secretly sold in 2001 to the Iranians who later did reverse engineering and devised an improvised version. Guided by a GPS/INS navigation system, Soumar's accuracy is estimated at about 50 meters with a Mach 0.7 speed. Using a Doppler-pulse radar, it maintains a 300-ft cruise altitude in the last stage of flight towards its target. Unlike the Ukrainian model which is fired from an aircraft, the Iranian cruise missile is fired from a mobile launcher. It has a smaller payload of 150-179 kg, which makes it incapable of carrying a nuclear bomb.** Soumar, however, may presently serve as a foot-at-the-door to convince the P5+1 that Iran's missile program is defensive, intended to carry only conventional—and not atomic—explosives.

However, as the JCPOA does not impose limit on Iran missile program, research and development for increasing the weight-load capacity of its missiles continue. At present, the country's Sajjil-2, a surface-to-surface medium-range missile, can carry more than 750 kgs payload using solid fuel to a maximum of 2,200 km or 1,375 miles. While non-NPT countries such as North Korea may cooperate with Teheran to develop a compact U-235-based device, Iran may produce light-weight missiles based on titanium, or composite material; for this purpose, it can use part of the $56 billion it recovers after sanctions are lifted. An unconfirmed report claimed Iran has begun development of Sajjil-3 that reportedly would have solid-propellant, three stages, a maximum range of 4,000 km, and a launch weight of 38,000 kg (compared to Sajjil-2 launch weight of 23,000 kg).***

The aforesaid considerations reveal Iran's desire to acquire the capability to deliver nuclear payload on a cruise missile as well as on an intercontinental ballistic missile.

An Omen to a Prophesied War?

The selling point of President Obama for congressional acceptance of the JCPOA is the extended breakout period to at least one year. Questions, however, continue. While Iran reaps the financial and economic benefits due to the lifting of sanctions, will it curb its political wrangling against some neighbors in the Middle East? Or will it utilize, instead, the expected economic take-off to acquire more military power and pursue its political agenda and ambitions? Even before reaching the 10- and 15-year prohibitions contained in the JCPOA, Iran would have gained more know-how and technology for military option. If Iran could then build the bomb, and could deliver it to intended targets, would it not do it?

The possibility for Middle East nuclear weapons proliferation multiplies. The one-year breakout period estimated by Pres. Obama does not seem to bring comfort to Israel, Saudi Arabia, and Iran's other neighbors. While Abu Dhabi has already purchased nuclear reactors, Saudi Arabia, Egypt, and Jordan are pursuing nuclear programs of their own and have shown interest on uranium enrichment.****

Will Iran's nuclear program lead to unrest and war in the Middle East, perhaps in fulfillment of a prophecy at the End of the Age?

---

*www.economist.com/blogs/graphicdetail/2015/07/daily-chart-iran-graphics, accessed 25 July 2015.
**Alan Ben-David, "Iran Produces First Long-Range Missile," dated March 14, 2015 in aviationweek.com/defense/iran-produces-first-long-range-missile, accessed June 30, 2015.
***Lennox Duncan, "Sejil (Ashoura)," Jane's Strategic Weapon Systems (Offensive Weapons), September 7, 2012, as cited in "Sejil 1/2/3," by editor of Missile Threat: A Project of the George C. Marshall and Claremont Institutes, April 17, 2013, missilethreat.com/missiles/sejil-123/, accessed December 20, 2013.
****Steven N. Miller, "Nuclear Proliferation," in *The Energy and Security Nexus: A Strategic Dilemma*, edited by Carolyn W. Pumphrey, A Strategic Studies Institute Book: 2012, p. 115.

www.ingramcontent.com/pod-product-compliance
Lightning Source LLC
Chambersburg PA
CBHW071308110426
42743CB00042B/1218